RAM SETU

The sliver that connects the southern tip of India to the northern tip of Sri Lanka, Ram Setu—or Rama's Bridge—is part of the childhood imagination of every Hindu. In this scholarly work, writer Arup K. Chatterjee looks at how the legend, local history and geological reality come together on the ground. Digging meticulously through old maps and forgotten stories, he pieces together the extraordinary history of this remarkable geographical feature.

—Sanjeev Sanyal
Best-selling Author and Economist

We all love a good story. Especially when it enthralls multiple audiences in different ways. In *Ram Setu*, now in its Indian edition, gifted raconteur Arup K. Chatterjee guides us through the many representations of this singular formation: at once majestic in its geology and profound in its symbolism. It lies poised gracefully yet precariously between two nations, land and sea, sacred and secular, tranquillity and turbulence. Here is a rare terraqueous ecosystem of 103 reefs and sandbanks, where islets emerge at low tide. Once an unbroken causeway; shattered by a violent tropical storm in 1480; then the site of the thriving port city of Dhanushkodi; abandoned after another catastrophic storm in 1964 claimed some 1,800 lives. It is a sacred space, a divine work of art and science, and a long-neglected link between Tamil Nadu/India and Sri Lanka. Is it not the legendary land bridge built by a monkey army so that their master could rescue his wife from a demon-king? For the countless species that inhabit its waters and shores, it is home. An oceanic marvel, and more! A mesmerizing read awaits

—Godfrey Baldacchino
Author, Political Thinker, and Professor, University of Malta

Ram Setu offers a rich and layered examination of the historiography surrounding this remarkable formation. Drawing together mythic traditions, literary representations, colonial-era accounts, and present-day political debates, Arup K. Chatterjee illuminates how this geographical feature has acquired such a commanding place in the cultural imagination. The study makes clear that much of the debate around Ram Setu is as much about geology as about its symbolism and public spectacle—what Clifford Geertz, the eminent anthropologist, might have described as 'theatre' in the shaping and reshaping of sacred geographies of India and India's historical expanse as far as up to Southeast Asia.

—**Subhash Kak**
Author, Regents Professor of Computer Science, Oklahoma State University-Stillwater, and Member, PM's Science, Technology, and Innovation Advisory Council

In *Ram Setu: The Memoirs of an Enchanted Bridge,* Arup Chatterjee undertakes an exquisite, evocative and entertaining multidisciplinary journey through time, legend and geopolitics to unravel one of India's most storied and contested sites. From Valmiki's verses to colonial cartographies, courtroom proceedings, satellite imagery, and whispered conversations among coastal fishermen, Ram Setu emerges as more than stone or story—it is a geological marvel, a *civilizational Polaris,* a threshold where 'eons of suppressed memories collide with spectacular intensity'. Engrossing and inventive—at times shimmering with the texture of magical realism—Chatterjee offers not just the beguiling tale of a bridge, but a sublime meditation on belief, belonging, and the haunted architectures of Indian modernity.

—**Ashwani Kumar**
Professor, Tata Institute of Social Sciences, Mumbai, and Author of
Banaras and the Other

Blending the sacred traditions surrounding Ram Setu with its geoscientific understanding, Arup K. Chatterjee presents a compelling narrative of the tombolo that links India and Sri Lanka. Interweaving stories of origins, politics, diplomacy, ecology, and the urgent dilemmas of the Anthropocene, the book speaks directly to current debates over dredging the area. What are the potential risks and rewards for both people and the planet? How do age-old beliefs intersect with the forces of modern commerce? Marked by scrupulous scholarship and cultural insight, *Ram Setu* stands out as a work of lasting relevance and engaging storytelling.

—**Malashri Lal**
Author, Convener, English Advisory Board, Sahitya Akademi, Professor and former Head, Department of English, and Dean of Colleges, University of Delhi

An aerial view of Ram Setu (or Adam's Bridge) reveals a stunningly beautiful strip of shallow limestone shoals in an emerald-blue sea with wispy clouds hanging low in the sky. It is, as this book's author calls it, indeed an enchanting bridge, just 30 miles long, connecting India and Sri Lanka. Richly redolent in epic lore, centuries of cultural memory, it presents a fascinating, if contentious, legacy, from colonial times through India's independence to the present. Professor Arup K. Chatterjee's richly textured account of Ram Setu, as story and symbol, legend and history, politics and commerce, is indeed a treat. His fascinating narrative is, however, tantalizingly restrained, if not deliberately diplomatic, when it comes to any definitive interpretation as regards its meaning or significance. That is how it should be. For with its meticulous, even unparalleled, research, this readerly exegesis invites us to draw our own conclusions. An absorbing and compelling chronicle; highly recommended.

—**Makarand R. Paranjape**
Author and former Professor, Indian Institute of Technology, Delhi, and Jawaharlal Nehru University, Delhi

In *Ram Setu*, Arup K. Chatterjee offers a deeply researched sociocultural exploration of one of the Indian Ocean's most intriguing geological formations—a chain of coralline ridges stretching between Pamban Island on India's southeastern coast and Mannar Island on the northern coast of Sri Lanka. Revered in Hindu legends as the bridge built by Ram's army, this formation has long been a focus of both spiritual devotion and scientific curiosity. Chatterjee's study navigates the intertwined realms of ethnography, historiography and environmental justice, offering novel perspectives on how this remarkable structure might be safeguarded as part of India's shared heritage with Indian Ocean territories, through meaningful cross-cultural collaborations. This is a richly insightful and compelling work—an essential read for anyone interested in the confluence of nature, nurture, culture and belief.

—**C.P. Rajendran**
Earth Scientist, Scholar, Professor, Indian Institute of Science, Bangalore, and National Geoscience Awardee

'*Prabhu mudrika meli much maahin/ jaladhi lnaaghi gaye acharaj naahin*' ('With the Lord's ring pressed to your lips, you charted your sway/ To cross the vast ocean in a sweep—no marvel, as they say!')

(Circa Sixteenth-century Indian Poet Tulsidas in *Hanuman Chalisa*; **Author's Translation)**

'The Mohammedans, who have named this Adam's Bridge, will tell you that on one of these islands are buried Cain and Abel. The Brahmins, however, will tell you the bridge was built by one of their gods, assisted by the sacred monkeys—all in a single night. At any rate, whichever way you take it, you see the little chain of islands...is a spot sacred to the people of the country.'

(Nineteenth-century American Author Mara L. Pratt, in *People and Places*, **1892, p. 131)**

'You must have heard about the tremendous power of faith. It is said in the purana that Rama, who was God Himself—the embodiment of Absolute Brahman—had to build a bridge to cross the sea to Ceylon. But Hanuman, trusting in Rama's name, cleared the sea in one jump and reached the other side. He had no need of a bridge [All laugh].'

(Nineteenth-century Indian Mystic Ramakrishna Paramhansa quoted in *The Gospel of Sri Ramakrishna*, **1902 [1977], p. 87)**

'Who knows for certain, who shall here declare it? Whence was it born, whence came creation? Who then can know the origins of the world? None knows when creation arose, or whether he has or has not made it. He who surveys it from the lofty skies—only he knows, or, perhaps, he knows not.'

(Twentieth-century American Astronomer Carl Sagan quoting 'Nasadiya Sukta', from the *Rig Ved* **in 'The Edge of Forever', 1980)**

RAM SETU
The Memoirs of an Enchanted Bridge

Arup K. Chatterjee

RUPA

Published by
Rupa Publications India Pvt. Ltd 2025
161-B/4, Gulmohar House,
Yusuf Sarai Community Centre,
New Delhi 110049

Sales centres:
Bengaluru Chennai
Hyderabad Kolkata Mumbai

P-ISBN: 978-93-7003-119-7
E-ISBN: 978-93-7003-523-2

First impression 2025

10 9 8 7 6 5 4 3 2 1

The moral right of the author has been asserted.

Disclaimer: *Cover map adapted with the assistance of ChatGPT from James Rennell's Map of
Hindoostan (1782); not to scale.*

*To the memories of Alo Rani (my paternal grandmother, whom
I haven't seen in person), Mrinal Kanti
(maternal grandfather), and Kanai Lal
(my paternal grandfather, whom I haven't seen in person).
Also, in remembrance of the great scholar,
the late Bibek Debroy.*

CONTENTS

List of Illustrations   *xiii*

Note to the Reader   *xvii*

I Believe in Ram Setu   1

The Last Sigh of Adam   37

Building the Second Ram Setu   66

A Suez-Complex in Sethusamudram   96

In the Shadow of Divinity   116

Angling in the Time Conflict   131

Performing Puja in Mid-Sea!   146

A Trojan Horse for Lord Ram?   162

Katchatheevu—The 'Barren' Boon   183

Epilogue   205

Acknowledgements   217

Bibliography   219

Index   248

LIST OF ILLUSTRATIONS

Fig. 1: Map of the 'Paumben Pass' by Henry Beveridge, from *A Comprehensive History of India Div. VII*

Fig. 2: Map of Ram Setu ('Adam's Bridge') and Ceylon by James Steuart, from *Notes on Ceylon* (1862)

Fig. 3: Section of James Rennell's *Map of Hindoostan* (1782) showing 'Adam's Bridge'

Fig. 4: Hanuman and his army 'Building a Bridge to Sri Lanka', from Bhuvanrao Shrinivasrao alias Balasaheb Pandit Pant Pratinidhi's *The Picture Ramayana* (1916)

Fig. 5: A.P.J. Abdul Kalam International Foundation (Photograph by Daniel Stein)

Fig. 6: Rameswaram Temple Corridor (Photograph by Daniel Stein)

Fig. 7: 'The Monkeys and Bears Build a Bridge to Lanka', Anonymous (1850)

Fig. 8: 'Hanuman Assisted by His Associates, Building Rama's Bridge', in Edward Moor's *The Hindu Pantheon* (1864), Plate 30

Fig. 9: Tourists and jeeps at Arichal Munai, the terminating point of Dhanushkodi, marking the beginnings of the legendary Adam's Bridge (Ram Setu) (Photograph by Daniel Stein)

Fig. 10: Map of the pearl fisheries from W.M.G. Colebrooke's 'Account of the Pearl Fisheries of the North-West Coast of the Island' (1833)

Fig. 11: Portrait of Shunmuga Rajeswara Naganatha Sethupathi, from N.V. Pillai's *Setu and Rameswaram* (1929), Plate I

Fig. 12: Arichal Munai, the terminating point of Dhanushkodi, marking the beginnings of the legendary Ram Setu (Adam's Bridge) (Photograph by Daniel Stein)

Fig. 13: James Rennell's *Map of Hindoostan* (1782)

Fig. 14: Cartouche from James Rennell's *Map of Hindoostan* (1782): 'In return for the ... "Shaster" that the Indians give to Britannia, she gifts them 'her' latest achievement, Rennell's map of their land...'

Fig. 15: Emanuel Bowen's *A Map of India* (circa 1747)

Fig. 16: Map of Adam's Bridge named as 'Bridge of Adam or Rama', in Elisée Reclus's *The Earth, a Descriptive History of the Phenomena of the Life of the Globe* (1886)

Fig. 17: Map of Adam's Bridge named as 'Bridge of Rama', in Elisée Reclus's *The Universal Geography: Earth and Its Inhabitants* (1876–94), *Vol. 8: India and Indo-China*

Fig. 18: The approach to Rameswaram Temple as depicted in T.W. Knox's *The Boy Travellers in the Far East* (1880)

Fig. 19: Model of 'Scherzer Double Leaf Rolling Lift Bridge Across Pamban Channel, India', in the *Railway Age Gazette*, 20 March 1913

Fig. 20: A flurry of reports on the Pamban Bridge. Clockwise: 'A Gigantic Bridge Project', *New Oxford Item*, 14 August 1896; 'Lord Morley has Sanctioned...', *The China Mail*, 14 July 1909; 'A Bridge to Ceylon', *Pearson's Weekly*, 11 July 1896; 'Build Island to Construct Bridge', *The Newton Graphic*, 17 July 1914

Fig. 21: Images of the Scherzer Rolling Lift Bridge over the Pamban Channel in *The Engineer*, 7 August 1914

Fig. 22: Map of the proposed route of the Indo-Ceylon Railway, in *The Engineer*, 7 August 1914

Fig. 23: Advertisement by Head, Wrighton & Co. in the Christmas issue of *The Engineer*, 1914

Fig. 24: Distribution of chank fisheries by James Hornell, from Edgar Thurston's *Notes on Pearl and Chank Fisheries* (1890), Plate XII

Fig. 25: Boat Mail crossing the Pamban Bridge, from N.V. Pillai's *Setu and Rameswaram* (1929), Plate VII

Fig. 26: Left to Right: 'Opening of Indo-Ceylon Railway', *The Bombay Chronicle*, 26 February 1914; 'The Indo-Ceylon Connection', *The Bombay Chronicle*, 27 February 1914; 'The Indo-Ceylon Railway', *The Bombay Gazette*, 27 February 1914

Fig. 27: 'The Pamban Railway Bridge', in *The Illustrated London News*, 16 November 1935

Fig. 28: 'Frontispiece to South India and her Muhammadan Invaders' (1921) by S.K Aiyangar, where the author left the region around Ram Setu unnamed

Fig. 29: Gazette notification for the formation of the Mudaliar Committee, 1 November 1955, published in the *Gazette of India*, 12 November

Fig. 30: Painting at Wat Phra Kaew or the Temple of the Emerald Buddha, Bangkok, depicting characters or scenes from *Ramakien*, possibly Hanuman (or Nala) whose back is shown in the form of a living animistic conduit (Photograph by Iudexvivorum)

NOTE TO THE READER

Notwithstanding the implications of this book's title, subject, their attendant sensitivities and semiotics, and whatever the social grapevine may appear to hastily suggest, the reader is requested to consider the following note.

This book was published after six years of rigorous archival and scholarly research, processing a vast body of works, exceeding 2,000 primary sources. When this author's book *Adam's Bridge* (Routledge, United Kingdom, 2024) was published, the need was felt for a new version that could be accessed by non-academic readers, without losing the sincerity and integrity of the work. Owing to an array of factors—like publishing conventions and practical utility—about 24,000 words of sources cited in the original bibliography was reduced to less than half in *Ram Setu*. However, abundant caution was observed that this did not adversely affect the essence of the findings. Also, the deepest care and discretion was exercised to ensure that every word in this book attempted to convey sensitive and conscious articulations of the truth—as experienced by its author after numerous iterations and deliberations.

Ram Setu is not intended to hurt, instigate, provoke, challenge, or appease the religious or cultural sentiments of any community or group. Concurrently, the book in no way undermines constitutional and rational efforts of any religious or scholarly discourse to determine the sacredness of the geological wonder referred to in the title. Given the book's historicist, archival, scientific underpinnings, a large body of authors and commentators has been cited herein. But the book does not morally endorse or renounce all those voices, unless explicitly confirmed by the concluding paragraphs of each chapter or the epilogue. Any unintended interpretation suggesting religious, cultural, caste-based, gendered, or any other form of injury to readerly sentiments is deeply regrettable.

Ram Setu particularly avoids calling the subject of its study a *myth*. In fact, the use of the word 'myth' has been abjured throughout the book, in favour of the more inclusive 'legend', unless the former word was used within quotes or as a citation. The usage of the latter word, *legend*, is based on its early fourteenth-century French origin, where it signifies narratives 'dealing with a happening or an event', derived from the twelfth-century French word *legende*. These disclaimers are cues for the reader to ascertain that this book is a solemn and nonpartisan effort to reach enthusiasts of history, historiography, geology, spiritual studies, and ecological perspectives, transcending cognitive biases brought about by identities of religion, caste, ethnicity, gender, nationality, and the like. While the author is palpably conscious of his own positionality, his approach attempts to prioritize historical accuracy and overarching ethical concerns to the best of his knowledge.

Ram Setu is not a theological or literary analysis of Ramayan, or the Ramayan legacy ushered in by sage Valmiki. Instead, it is an intellectual, sociocultural and historiographical exploration of attitudes towards a captivating geological phenomenon that recognizably surpasses the narrow confines of identity politics. It is hoped that the book will be read in this spirit—as a morally and spiritually motivated inquiry into how the cultural, geological, ecological and historical characters of the titular 'Setu' have been perceived, experienced and represented since about the late seventeenth century. If there is one question that this book seeks to answer—among the many complex and nuanced conundrums that the history charts—it is as follows. Is it enough to ask whether Ram Setu was indeed built by Lord Ram and his hominid allies, or by other humans, or whether it remains among the mysterious works of nature; or are there far more valuable moral, ethical and enchanting questions we could ask of this geological genius?

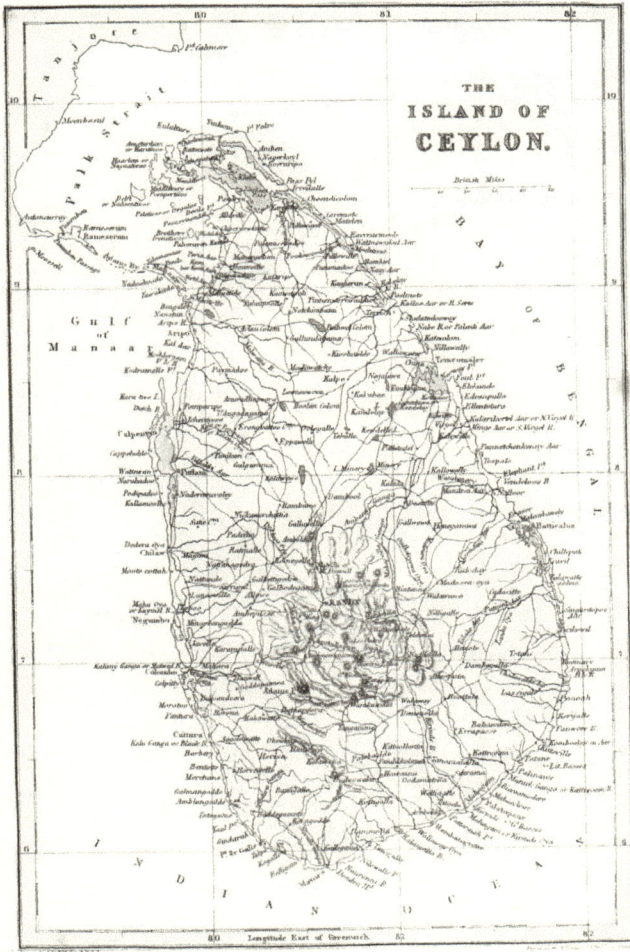

Fig. 1: Map of the 'Paumben Pass' by Henry Beveridge, from *A Comprehensive History of India Div. VII*

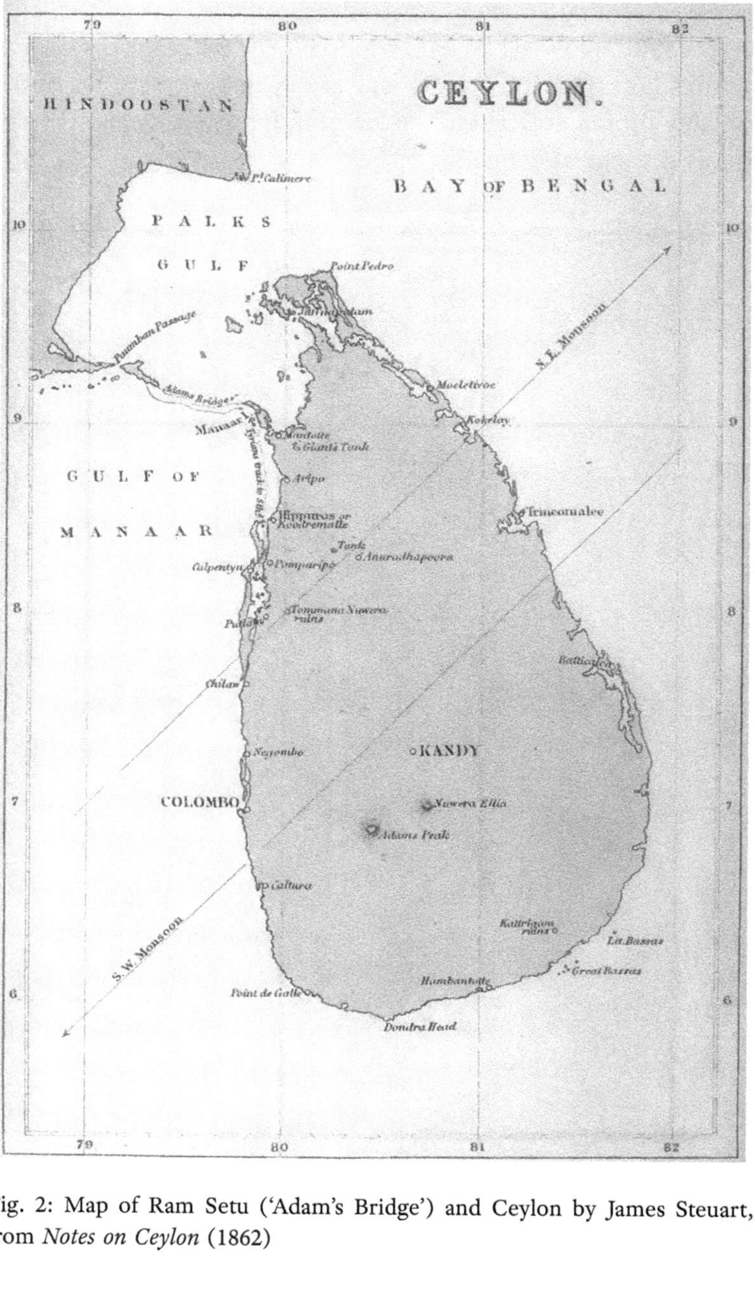

Fig. 2: Map of Ram Setu ('Adam's Bridge') and Ceylon by James Steuart, from *Notes on Ceylon* (1862)

Fig. 3: Section of James Rennell's *Map of Hindoostan* (1782) showing 'Adam's Bridge'

Fig. 4: Hanuman and his army 'Building a Bridge to Sri Lanka', from Bhuvanrao Shrinivasrao alias Balasaheb Pandit Pant Pratinidhi's *The Picture Ramayana* (1916)

I BELIEVE IN RAM SETU

No one who saw it is alive, but a divined bridge was known to have stood for thousands of years, until, one day in the autumn of 1478, the Sea God's whims broke the sacred thing asunder. It was not obliged to make sense to humanity before the landmass was cleaved. It did not make sense afterwards either. Across seven centuries, the chronicle was handed down from generation to generation like a secretly murmured chant. Then, in the spring of 2008, grave doubts were cast by the honourable Supreme Court of India. And there seemed to be but only one truly serious historical question at hand: 'Who worships in the middle of the sea?'

Answering it could entail that reports of the bridge's destruction were greatly exaggerated.

Seeking the precise instant of the origins of the bridge obscured its spiritual legitimacy, while bids to render visible its formless yet palpable sacredness obscured questions of its historicity. But how did it come to be there? Did it exist and possess meaning—as far as a *bridge* has meaning—only when observed? Or did it lose all meaning if no one saw it? Did the wave function of its meanings ever collapse or never collapse at all? Above all, were these the right questions to ask of this stupendous genius of creation?

Nuzzling in a marine churn, that terrain of earth is known to hundreds of millions of Indians as Ram Setu or 'Nala Setu', as a sage called Valmiki named it. In international cartography, it is known as Adam's Bridge. The structure looks like a bland sea log if reduced to its coordinates. Notwithstanding how vague these numbers look to those who are not professional geographers, geologists, or Indiana Jones—Latitude: 9° 04' 08" N/ Longitude: 79° 39' 20" E to Latitude: 9° 08' 59" N/ Longitude: 79° 26' 57" E—they are overladen with inscrutable history and enchantment. At Arichal Munai in Dhanushkodi, the far end of Pamban Island in Tamil Nadu where the Aan Kadal (Indian Ocean or the 'masculine sea') meets Penn Kadal (Bay of Bengal or the 'feminine sea'), eons of suppressed memories collide with spectacular intensity.

Every year, in the islandic hamlets of Pamban, the villagers celebrate Kadal Perunan, the annual sea festival. It blurs communal lines like footprints on wet sand, as everyone attires in their finest, and the whole community of fisherfolks feast on modest victuals in leaf-plates, at the stroke of the dusk that smells of hibiscuses. For as long as one can remember, fisherfolks—from Hindu, Christian and Muslim families—have sworn in harmony: 'Ram Setu is real.' Like their lores, Ram's name has seeped into the fibre of their diurnal maritime existence and their kinship with the ocean. In whispering tones, they warn that anyone who tries to harm the fragile ecosystem in and around Ram Setu will annihilate 'the history of this ancient coastline forever', invoking the wrath of the Sea God's minions—the cyclones, the tsunamis and other such unforeseen catastrophes that they are no strangers to.[1] Back in 2007, when that juridical question was first framed, if the fisherfolks were summoned to court, they would have said: I believe in Ram Setu; Ram Setu has created my fortune; and I intend to bring up my children on that belief.

---

[1]George, *Mother Earth, Sister Seed*, pp. 3–5.

OF LIMESTONE AND STARDUST

Born and reborn of arcane legends, scientific enigmas, cinders of geopolitical flashpoints, stealthily wriggling under the vigilant gaze of satellites and scholars, Ram Setu is a geological miracle; a cultural conundrum; a civilizational Polaris. It is the emblem of the immanence of the supernatural in the existential, for it—to quote Rabindranath Tagore—may free the 'spiritual being from the tyranny of matter.'[2] Ram Setu is often snubbed as an ancient limestone isthmus made of insentient atolls or a patch of shallow reefs emerging from the ocean in an aqueous thoroughfare intersecting the Palk Strait that connects or—as some might argue—bisects India and Sri Lanka. Early colonial geologists unromantically styled it as a series of calcareous sandstones and sand spits. Its creation was attributed to the unsentimental industry of marine Polyzoa and Nullipores; to littoral detritus coagulated since Miocene times; to layers stacked on layers during the ocean's silent uninterrupted artistry. But something beguiling lies beneath these sterile descriptions.

As the British colonial regime itself well knew, and even openly publicized, a pre-Christian Indian sage, Valmiki, had immortalized the structure in his verses, in *Valmiki Ramayan*'s 'Yuddha Kanda', Sarga 22. The canto chronicles the creation of Ram Setu as overseen by Sugriv, the monkey chieftain; Hanuman, the relentless warrior; and Nala, the master architect. Transpired from Valmiki's literary milestone, the legend of Ram Setu is a magical wand to conjure with. Indeed, it is a phenomenon that fogs the line betwixt belief and scepticism. A battalion of hominoids and bears laboured eight days to create the Setu, a causeway to defy time, tide and colonization. And this became, for centuries of Indian memories, a history of sorts—*itihasa*, as

---

[2]Tagore, *Nationalism*, p. 131.

they called it—etched in the cultural mnemonics of the land like a *dhvani* from the lower mantle.

However, very few care to add that in Valmiki's description of the episode of the construction of the said bridge, the poet sage designated the section of the sea as *makaralaya* or the abode of crocodiles that posed a violent resistance to Ram and his allies, but whom the avatar was able to tame with relative ease. It is a conveniently forgotten detail in most credulous citations to the legend of Ram Setu that the shallow straits between Mannar and Dhanushkodi were never known to shelter crocodiles. Nevertheless, what makes the legend of Ram Setu itself a wonder is the wide range of unlikely commentators who have reinforced its legitimacy from time to time.

Way back in the winter of 1792, the eminent philologist and jurist Sir William Jones remarked in a dissertation now fallen to disuse that the 'ferries of rocks' connecting India with Ceylon, 'to which the Muselmans or the Portuguese have given the foolish name of Adam's,' should have been instead 'called Rama's bridge.'[3] Jones' endorsement of the 'bridge' in Valmiki's itihasa might appear egregious to serious scholars. But they might feel a greater shock to note that, even further back, around AD 1028, the Iranian scholar and traveller Al Beruni also corroborated the existence of the 'dyke of Rama' in a historical depiction of *India* (circa 1030). Al Beruni was occasionally deeply cynical towards Indic traditions. Fascinatingly, however, he showed no reservations in underscoring the legend of the avatar of God across the Sethusamudram Sea upon a bridge 'of 100 *yojana* [1 *yojana*=13–15 km] which he had constructed from a mountain in a place called Setubandha.'[4]

Al Beruni's passage was probably well known to colonial historians. As one Victorian antiquarian noted, the appellation

---

[3]Jones, 'Dissertation on the Gods of Greece, Italy and India', p. 324.
[4]Alberuni, *Alberuni's India*, pp. 209, 307.

'Adam's Bridge' was virtually unknown to the Arab world at least 'until the time of Albyrouni (*sic*)'. Remarkably, Khordadbeh's *Book of Routes* (circa AD 850) called it 'Set Bandhai'.[5] It has also been surmised that the Adamic legacy got entangled with the structure in the mid-fourteenth century, when the Moroccan traveller Ibn Battuta visited Ceylon and attempted to advance Adamic (Abrahamic) legends to denote the creationist genesis of Ceylon and Sri Pada (or Adam's Peak) in its central highlands.

These specimens of historical nuance lie forgotten. Nevertheless, in December 2006, the Indian President A.P.J. Abdul Kalam, who was once an aerospace scientist, evoked the legend of the ancient causeway in his identity as the son of a Tamil ferryman who transported pilgrims between Mandapam and Rameswaram. President Kalam's interpretation of the National Aeronautics and Space Administration's satellite imagery as validation of 'the remnants of a bridge'[6] underneath the Sethusamudram Sea is still remembered by observers of all stripes.

But there also loom examples of scepticism to the geography suggested by the legend, from no less than Vedic scholars. One such, T. Paramasiva Iyer, boldly declared, in 1940, that the 'faking' of the shoals beginning from Dhanushkodi as Ram Setu or Nala Setu (the structure's earliest sobriquet noted in *Valmiki Ramayan*) was first executed around AD 1000, sometime before Al Beruni's arrival in India. This was, arguably, done to shift the supposed threshold of Ram's martial mission from Thoothukudi's Korkai Harbour to Pamban's Dhanushkodi. If so, this probably happened during the 'consecration of the Ramesvara Lingam and the erection of the great Ramesvara temple in the Ramesvaram island' in the eleventh century, a phase of undisputed Chola dominance in southern India.[7]

---

[5] Suckling, *Ceylon*, Vol. 1, p. 259.
[6] Kalam, 'Bridging the Hearts', 2006.
[7] Iyer, *Ramayana and Lanka*, pp. xvii–xviii.

While Ram Setu's history and geography—as we shall
soon see—are deeply contested, *Ramayan*'s political contours
have also faced tumult. From time to time, political factions in
India have claimed that sections of *Ramayan* are biased against
vulnerable groups of citizens.

Fig. 5: A.P.J. Abdul Kalam International Foundation (Photograph by Daniel
Stein)

Fig. 6: Rameswaram Temple Corridor (Photograph by Daniel Stein)

A recent example of this happened in 2023, revolving around saint Tulsidas's sixteenth-century epic poem, *Ramcharitmanas*. Originally written in Awadhi, the work is 'akin to the Bible for many Hindus.'[8] However, it triggered an avoidable controversy as some people alleged that a few of its passages were derogatory towards Dalits and women. But the text's significance could not be so easily undermined as during the anticolonial struggle

---

[8]Varma, Pavan, 'Ramcharitmanas: Mantri's remark reeks of ignorance', Deccan Chronicle, 22 January 2023, https://tinyurl.com/55y5m94x.

against the British regime, *Ramayan* performances, folklore
and diverse adaptations joined the league of a popular drama of
pan-Indian consequence, with Jain, Buddhist and other regional
inflections.[9]

The *Ramayan*'s symbolism—from colonial to independent
India—played out in various sociopolitical walks, as also
exemplified in the reception of the incredibly successful national
television broadcast of Ramanand Sagar's *Ramayan* adaptation
(1987–1988). Broadcast again, severally, its 'representation of
Hinduism as a vehicle of modernity allowed its supporters to
suggest that the *Ramayan* was basically a secular epic.'[10] Besides,
Ramayan's televisual and cinematic versions constitute a very
long list of examples with subtle to marked variations in the
text's treatment. And Tamil Nadu—where Ram Setu is generally
located—has had a complex history of *Ramayan*'s reception.

Fig. 7: 'The Monkeys and Bears Build a Bridge to Lanka', Anonymous (1850)

---

[9]Gould, *Hindu Nationalism*, p. 52.
[10]Gould, 'The U.P. Congress and "Hindu Unity"', p. 853.

On the one hand lies *Iramayana Pathirankal* (*'Characters in the Ramayan'*) (1930) authored by Periyar, that criticized the epic as a brazen normalization of a conflict between Dravidians and Aryans. On the other hand, there is the Madras Presidency chief minister C. Rajagolapachari's popular Tamil version of *Ramayan* that was published in the *Kalki* magazine in the 1950s. The renowned Indian English author—of Tamil descent—R.K. Narayan admired the *Ramayan* of Kamban, a twelfth-century Tamil bhakti poet, for disseminating the *Ramayan* legacy in the south.[11] Other similar well-accepted eulogies to the *Ramayan's* legacy from Tamil Nadu include V.V.S. Aiyar's patriotic study *Kamba Ramayana* (1965) and Puthumaipithan's short story 'Saba Vimochanam' ('Deliverance from a Curse') (1976).

HANUMĀN ASSISTED BY HIS ASSOCIATES, BUILDING RĀMA'S BRIDGE.

Fig. 8: 'Hanuman Assisted by His Associates, Building Rama's Bridge', in Edward Moor's *The Hindu Pantheon* (1864), Plate 30

---

[11]Ramanujan, 'Three Hundred *Ramayanas*', p. 32; Shankar, *Flesh and Fish Blood*, p. 41.

Besides, *Ramayan* is also esteemed by Dalits as a pious compendium, not merely since sage Valmiki is often seen as a forebear of sects or castes of Indian citizens administratively categorized as backward castes and scheduled tribes in many regions.[12] Also, the Setu's fabled engineer, Nala, a 'skillful mechanic', was an offspring of 'Tashtri [Vishwakarma], the divine artificer of the Universe.'[13] Accordingly, Nala nominally belonged to what is now seen as the Vishwakarma caste—classified in some Indian regions as part of backward castes or scheduled tribes. Since such and similar intricacies of *Ramayan*'s sociopolitical subtexts surround the epic's reception in modern India, its devotees and critics are rendered susceptible to ideological schisms and manipulations. And *Ramayan*'s contested history leads us to its equally contested geography.

---

[12]Valmiki, generally regarded as a Brahmin, was born as Agni Sharma to Pracheta (alias Sumali), of Bhrgu gotra (Mittal, *History of Ancient India*, p. 270; 'Valmiki's Divine Vision', 2017). In early 2019, the Uttar Pradesh CM referred to Lord Hanuman as a Dalit, followed by India's home minister claiming that Valmiki and Vyas were both Dalits, linking their epic poetry, the Indian Constitution authored by Dr Babasaheb Ambedkar, and sanitation workers and the avatar of Prime Minister Modi carrying a broom (Roy, 'Authors of Hindu epics', 2019). In October 2022, the Karnataka CM offered rich tributes to sage Valmiki during 'Valmiki Jayanti', reaffirming the stance of the state government 'to provide opportunity for the oppressed classes like the Scheduled Castes and Scheduled Tribes to live with dignity, equality, self-reliance and self-respect,' in the same vein as he spoke of Valmiki's Ramayan as 'one of the best 10 great works in the world' and the essence of 'a pious life' (PTI, 'Karnataka Government Committed', 2022). It has been argued that the continued association of the Valmiki caste with the author of the *Ramayan* is an example of Dalit Sanskritization (Jaoul, 'Casting the "Sweepers"', 2020), that began with the encouragement given by Arya Samaj reformers to Dalits in the 1930s, and the impact of the RSS-led and Gandhian 'Harijan' movements of the following decade that promoted an 'older Adi Hindu ideology' fostering the notion that Dalits were 'ancient India's original inhabitants' (Gould, *Hindu Nationalism*, 2005; Gould, *Religion and Conflict*, p. 290).

[13]Roy and Ganguli, *The Mahabharata*, p. 607.

Ramayan's odysseys begin with Ram, the prince of Kosala, being awarded fourteen years of exile by his father Dasarath, thanks to the insistence of Ram's foster mother, Kaikeyi, who wants her son Bharat to be enthroned on the seat of Ayodhya in his stead. Ram's devoted wife, Sita, and his faithful brother, Lakshman, accompany him by choice. According to Valmiki's cultural geography—generally known to devotees of *Ramayan*—with some help from professional geographers, the journeys of Ram, Sita and Lakshman can be vaguely traced on the map of modern India.[14]

After crossing the Tamasa (Tons) River in the southern part of Ayodhya, Ram, Sita and Lakshman traversed several rivers, including the Vedasruti, Gomati, Ganga and Yamuna, before reaching Madhya Pradesh and entering the Dandakaranya forest. This vast forest spanned present-day Madhya Pradesh, Chhattisgarh, Odisha, Andhra Pradesh and Maharashtra. According to *Ramcharitmanas* by Tulsidas (circa 1633), Ravan abducted Sita from this region. However, *Valmiki Ramayan* places Sita's abduction in the Vindhya range, covering parts of Madhya Pradesh, Chhattisgarh and Bihar. Following the abduction, Ram and Lakshman are believed to have travelled through the Kraunch forest and Hampi before meeting Hanuman and the *vanara*s at the foothills of Rishyamukha, near Malayagiri and Kishkindha. Their journey continued towards Prasravana Hill or Malayavana, located near Daroji Sloth Bear Sanctuary in Bellary, Karnataka. They then scaled the Sahyadri range in the northern Western Ghats, proceeded through Malayagiri in the southern Western Ghats, and finally ascended Mahendragiri Mountain in southern Tamil Nadu. From here, they descended to reach the shallow straits in the Indian Ocean, from where the *vanar sena* began constructing Setubandha, or Ram Setu, that helped them reach Ravan's kingdom and liberate Sita.

---

[14]Singh, 'Rama's Route After Banishment', pp. 39–42.

One could have easily believed in this geography. But one obstacle that comes in between is that India's geography and geology have altered significantly over the last ten thousand years. Yet, this was not a good enough deterrent to faith.

GOD IN THE COURTROOM

30 September 2007 was the day of the Lord. The Supreme Court seemed to be busy in deliberating whether—after sixty years of independence from British colonial rule—Indians could legitimately 'believe' in the legacy of Lord Ram. But the decision would extend to the fate of the wriggling strip of sandbars peopling the choppy waters of the Indian Ocean flowing from Pamban to Mannar.

The modern judicial system is an outcome of the years of European Enlightenment that occurred thanks to scientific and empirical rationality in the seventeenth and eighteenth centuries. Almost no modern judiciary in any democratic jurisdiction is wholly equipped to adjudicate what religious principles people are allowed to believe in or not, especially if the jurisdiction constitutes a nation whose Constitution guarantees religious freedom to its citizens. One of the revolutionary voices born of the European Enlightenment—of Karl Marx— also acknowledged that faith was 'the sigh of the oppressed creature, the heart of a heartless world, and the soul of soulless conditions.' [15, 16] Nevertheless, Marx would go down in history as a deeply contradictory observer of Indic religions, as manifest in his 'The British Rule in India', that was carried by the *New York Daily Tribune* on 25 June 1853.

---

[15]Generally, the following Marxist aphorism is shortened as the famous phrase, 'Religion is the opium of the masses', whose preceding sentences have been quoted above. See, Blau, 'What is the Opium of the People?', 2015.
[16]Marx, *Contribution to the Critique of Hegel's Philosophy*, p. 175.

Therein, Marx reprimanded Indians for their 'brutalizing worship of nature, exhibiting its degradation in the fact that man, the sovereign of nature, fell down on his knees in adoration of Kanuman [*sic*; Hanuman], the monkey, and Sabbala, the cow.'[17] Marx's view of South Asian faiths was hurriedly born of speculations disseminated by Georg W.F. Hegel's fragmentary notions of Indian *history* (or its alleged absence). For Hegel, India was timeless and thrived on despotic regimes and 'violent emotion without any goal of advancement or development.'[18] This was, probably, Hegel's interpretation of European modernity's own 'primitive' psyche.[19] Though these European commentators were not wholly wrong about India, they were demonstrably insincere in seeing India's colonization as enacted by a singular entity. India was not ruled by a unitary Western dominance since the early 1600s but a multicolonial regime.[20] Naturally, this would only complicate the various traditions, epistemes, rituals and austerities through which one wished to pursue—or choose not to pursue—God-realization or self-realization in postcolonial India. Hence, people's scepticism or belief in Ram Setu was not at the mercy of the Supreme Court decision. Rather, what the apex court was really deliberating on was whether it was legally kosher to dredge the shallow stretch of aqueous terrain between Pamban and Mannar—across the marine territory known as the Sethusamudram Sea—for enabling large vessels to easily navigate between the two nations.

Known as the Sethusamudram Shipping Canal Project in modern India, the passage was envisaged as far back as the 1770s by the British East India Company's principal geographer and oceanographer James Rennell, for whom no religion was

---

17Marx, 'The British Rule in India', 1853; for Marx's ambivalence, see Boer, 'Toward a Materialist Theology', 2010.
18Hegel, *Philosophy of History*, pp. 113–114.
19Banerjee, *Politics of Time*, pp. 10; 26.
20Bhaduri, *Polycoloniality*, 2021.

so dense that cartography could not explain and inscribe on ordnance sheets. Very few seemed bothered by—if indeed aware of—the fact that for nearly 400 years, the Portuguese, the Dutch and the British had merely hoped to find a navigable passage between Dhanushkodi and Thalaimannar, even at the risk of dredging or blasting Ram Setu. Everyone had failed.

Hindutvavadi activists demanded in their petitions for a meticulous archaeological survey of Ram Setu to disclose to the public whether the structure could be memorialized in keeping with the Ancient Monuments and Archaeological Sites and Remains Act of 1958. Archaeology, a discipline of studying material remains of human civilizations, can only reveal aspects of tangible human-made structures and their relics. Since archaeology deals with the human—not the religious, metaphysical, spiritual, or divine—an archaeological survey of Ram Setu, as if it were a monument like the Babri Masjid, Qutb Minar, or Gyanvapi Mosque, would mean legitimizing the humanness of the sacred. In other words, it could reduce the divinity of Lord Ram to a historical personage. So, subjugating *his* bridge to an archaeological study was tantamount to eroding the divinity of Ram Setu. If, on the other hand, it was acknowledged that the sacred 'bridge' could not be explored archaeologically because it was metaphysical, its divine stature could be upheld. However, that would probably leave no prospect of empirical grounds for the courts to adjudicate the matter.

As if to augur which way the scales of justice were tilting, pilgrims began flocking to the ghost town of Dhanushkodi to witness the spectacle that they instantly recognized as the prehistoric bridge built by Lord Ram's vanar sena. Not all Indians who made that pilgrimage on that Sunday, and in the weeks and months to come, knew this legend by heart. But they believed Ram Setu to be mystical. So, they made a beeline on ramshackle tourist jeeps and buses towards what they thought of as a 17,000-year-old monument from the *Ramayan* era. Jeep

fares doubled overnight from ₹700 to over ₹1,000, resulting
in ad hoc fortunes for tour conductors. The scattered shoals
in the sea transformed into a canvas for a Bollywood thriller,
featuring ambitious politicians, reckless tycoons, idealistic—
though silenced—scientists and environmentalists, woebegone
fishermen and frantic masses. What could the next twist in this
plot entail? Would the judiciary summon God to bear witness
for his own bridge? There is delay in the court of God but not
darkness—as they say.

Flashforward 10 years.

Fig. 9: Tourists and jeeps at Arichal Munai, the terminating point of
Dhanushkodi, marking the beginnings of the legendary Adam's Bridge (Ram
Setu) (Photograph by Daniel Stein)

In January 2018, a clip from a short film by 'Science Channel'
(c/o Warner Bros. Discovery) was distributed on *YouTube*. The
film's narrator alluded to satellite pictures of the semi-submerged
structure caught in the aspic of the Palk Strait. In fact, these
images were first released in the 1990s (when they did not
really affect public imagination) and then in 2002 (when they
created an uproar among Hindutvavadi activists, thanks to the
spread of the internet). Instantaneously, the activists had taken
to publicizing the pictures as key evidence of the existence
of the divine bridge. What did the pictures contain? Several
thousands of words, one might say. Or as another might put it,
they were a representation of a geological structure as a dotted

line that seemed to connect the Indian peninsula with northern Sri Lanka, merely reflecting the magnificent luminescence of the intermingling waves of the Indian Ocean and the Bay of Bengal.

The raconteur's voice was strategically punctuated by erudite though dramatic reflections by American geologists and scientists. 'On closer analysis of the satellite image,' remarked the invisible narrator, 'investigators calculate the line of rocks is over 30-miles-long. What makes the image especially intriguing is that the rocks are in an area of sea mentioned in an ancient Hindu poem that also refers to a magic bridge.'[21] The American researchers argued in unison that the baffling sandbars of Ram Setu comprised a row of shoals approximately 4,000 years old, flanked by rocks 7,000 years old. Seemingly, the latter were brought by human effort from somewhere else. The oceanic formations were autochthonous or indigenous; the rocks were allochthonous or extrinsic to the foundation.

On the last day of that January, another stunning scientific report was published by researchers from Madras University and Anna University. It was a day following the seventieth martyrdom anniversary of Mahatma Gandhi, for whom Ram Setu was particularly sacred. The report detailed a carbon-dating analysis conducted on *Cibicides margaritiferus* microfossils discovered near Ram Setu. Findings from the study suggested that the structure dated back approximately 18,400 years.[22] By then, the 'Science Channel' clip had reached more than eight million watchers. The most replayed part of the teaser was the one recalling the 'ancient Hindu poem' authored by Valmiki.

On the Diwali of 2022, a much-awaited Hindi film, *Ram Setu*, would be released. Set against the background of archaeological and geological surveys into Ram Setu, Puranic lore, and the Sethusamudram Shipping Canal Project. By the end of the film,

---

[21]'Could This Be the Legendary "Magic Bridge"', 2018.
[22]Raman, 'Ram Setu 18,400 years old', 2018.

its hero, an archaeologist and a 'sworn atheist and champion of "scientific method"', comes to acknowledge the veridicality of Lord Ram 'through his encounter with the hard "facts" "proving" that the geological formation Ram Setu...was in fact a bridge built by Ram and his army to reach Sri Lanka from India.' [23] The film's lack of commercial success amidst a citizenry that was believed to be turning Hindu-centric was itself a mystery. What did the 'Science Channel' documentary succeed in that the film failed to offer?

In December 2022, when India's minister of state in the Ministry of Personnel, Public Grievances & Pensions was questioned in the Rajya Sabha about India's official stance on whether Ram Setu could 'be scientifically proved by images taken by our remote sensing orbiting in space,' he replied that the structure was yet to throw up incontestable signs of the 'remnants of a "bridge"'. This was a metaphor President A.P.J. Abdul Kalam had introduced about 20 years ago to describe Ram Setu while rebaptizing it in public consciousness as a prehistoric bridge.[24] Could Kalam, the aerospace scientist, be doubted about his claims on a bridge of Indic antiquity?

GEOLOGY GONE ROGUE

Dhanushkodi—a name that doubly implies the 'tip of the bow' or the end of the Setu—had already been a hub of religious and cultural pilgrimage for many centuries, owing to its proximity to Rameswaram. Home to one of India's 12 jotirlingas of Lord Shiva (where Shiva is believed to embody his universal energy), Rameswaram is a sacred landmark on the Hindu pilgrimage circuit. Rameswaram is where Ram is supposed to have worshipped Lord Shiva, before his siege on Lanka and the

---

[23]Varghese, 'Archaeology for the Courtroom', p. 2.
[24]'Scientific Evidence to India's History', 2022.

assassination of the *asura* king, Ravan. The complexity of Hindu
Puranic epistemology is such that Ravan—widely seen as Ram's
archenemy, hence the object of effigy burnings during annual
Dussehra ceremonies—was himself the priest appointed by Ram
for the sanctification of the idol that the latter worshipped before
waging war on Lanka.

Ravan—sometimes rhetorically denoted as a wronged
Dravidian or a Dalit crusader—is one of the greatest scholars
known in the Hindu pantheon. Ironically, he was a Brahmin.[25]
He was also the greatest devotee of Lord Shiva, and is credited
with the authorship of *Shiva Tandav Stotram*, a fiercely
synesthetic verse believed to be endowed with the essence of
Shiva himself. Ravan is said to have recited it on an impulse
while in the throes of an ecstatic pain that seized him as he
tried to transplant Shiva's abode, Mount Kailasa, and Shiva—
propelled by the consternation of his consort, Durga—squeezed
the thumb of his foot onto the mountain, that then squashed
Ravan's hand. Impressed by Ravan's scholarship and poetical

---

[25]Ravan's initial obscurity, compared to his later mightiness as seen in the
'Uttara Kanda' of *Valmiki Ramayan*, possibly resulted due to interpolations
in the latter that sought to create him as a formidable adversary to Lord
Ram. See Goldman and Masson, 'Who Knows Ravaṇa?', 1969; Nagar, *Sri
Ranganatha Ramayaṇa*, p. x; Borde, 'Did the Subaltern Speak?', p. 281;
Flueckiger, 'Standing in Cement', 2017. Ravan's Brahminical avatar has been
a cultural hero of the Sinhala people, especially after the Lankan civil war,
even though the identification of Ravan's legendary 'Lankapuri' as Ceylon
or Sri Lanka was arguably 'a late first millennium South Indian innovation,
sustained by the Arya Chakravarti kings of Jaffna' (Henry, 'Ravana's Kingdom',
pp. 27–28). In several parts of India, too, especially throughout the Chhota
Nagpur Plateau, Jharkhand, Chhattisgarh, Uttar Pradesh and Madhya Pradesh,
indigenous tribes and Brahmin clans revere Ravan, the Brahmin or the wronged
asura, and oppose burning his effigies during Dussehra—which is seen by
some Brahmin sub-castes as an anti-Brahmin ritual. See, Santoshi, 'In MP's
Ravan Village', 2013; Agnihotri, 'Madhya Pradesh Towns Where Ravana is
Worshipped', 2016; Qureshi, 'A Dussehra Without Burning Ravana', 2016; 'In
Sasural Mandsaur, Demon King Gives "Permission" To Be Slain', 2019.

prodigy, Shiva blessed him with miscellaneous boons, including that of putative immortality. The Puranic epistemology looks even more absurdly complex as one encounters the fact that Ravan was merely the human personification of one of Vishnu's most beloved celestial janitors. He had been transferred onto earth as part of a punishment posting, as it were, on account of a petty misdemeanour. Ravan's pre-earthly form well knew—but Ravan himself had forgotten—that he was supposed to be sent back to heaven after the completion of a Puranic mission. This was to be his elimination at the hands of Vishnu's avatar, Ram. Therefore, Ravan's abduction of Ram's faithful wife, Sita, and his villainy in the Indian imagination, as a consequence, were nothing but ruses for him to return to his coveted post of being the gatekeeper of Vishnu's abode in Vaikuntha.

Compared to the unfathomable complexity of these Puranic legends, the Adamic associations of Ram Setu are outstandingly simple, though fabulous still. After being ostracized from Paradise, Adam descended on the central Sri Lankan highlands, around Nuwara Eliya, and crossed over to India across the narrow strip of shoals that supposedly pre-existed his entry into Palk Strait. From there, he went ahead in search of Eve, who, following her expulsion, had descended somewhere in Arabia. The origin of the Abrahamic name, Adam's Bridge, is said to date back to the ninth-century Persian geographer Ibn Khordadbeh. However, it is also conjectured that Adam's association with Ram Setu reclaimed currency following the fourteenth-century Moroccan traveller Ibn Battuta's visit to Ceylon in the mid-1340s.

As far as recorded history can empirically testify, the name 'Adam's Bridge' gained prominence most likely between AD 1500 and 1600. Ceylon was occupied by the Portuguese in 1505. The Dutch colonized it in 1668. Thus emerged the Abrahamic lore of Adam, the first man, crossing the shallow straits between India and Ceylon after his descent from Paradise. Abrahamic legends hold that Adam's descent landed him in Serendip—present-day

Sri Lanka's central highlands—and he entered India via the Palk Strait, over a pre-existent primeval 'bridge' across the seabed. The hilltop where he supposedly landed is known as Sri Pada, after Buddhist legends. Shaivite Hindus, in their turn, came to recognize it as Sivanoli Padam. Thus, the footprint is variously believed to be the impression of Adam, the Buddha, and Lord Shiva. However, as the nineteenth century matured, the Adamic monopoly remarkably declined. As the vision of Valmiki regained prominence, voices like Percival's became rarer.

Depending on where one sees from and what one chooses to see, Valmiki could well be the name of a man or a tradition. He is said to have lived around 500–100 BC. One wonders how Valmiki, a sage born and based around present-day Bihar, captured the incident of building a bridge between Lanka and India in the Indian Ocean, at a distance of over 1,600 miles from his *karmabhoomi*. Be that as it may, his conception of the episode of the building of the bridge to 'Lanka' is globally renowned as one of the *Ramayan* legacy's best-known and deeply loved scenes.

In Valmiki's telling, Ram Setu's plan was originally proposed by Sugriv and seconded by Vibhishan (Ravan's brother, and later, Lord Ram's ally). The building of the 'Setu' then proceeded with the Lord attempting to conciliate Sagar, the sea-god. Lord Ram's desire for a boon from Sagar, in the hope that it would pacify the Palk Strait's choppy waters, led him to propitiate the sea-god for three days. Even after that, the latter remained unmoved. This compelled Lord Ram to pierce the ocean with arrows, sending a tempest through habitats of marine species. Finally, Sagar appeared before the Lord, yielding to be bridged by him and his allies. The sea-god reminded the Lord of the presence of Nala, the divinely gifted son of Lord Vishwakarma, the architect of gods. The fortuitous presence of Nala in Lord Ram's army and his illustrious lineage meant that none other was more suited to construct the bridge for the Lord. Hence,

Valmiki Ramayan chose to name the bridge as 'Nala Setu'—a name almost forgotten today.

The question of Ram Setu's divine or man-made origins is not simply a matter of faith versus reason. It was also a question of free will versus predestination. If the 'bridge' were proven to have antecedents that were constructed—by divine or human agency—it could signal the triumph of humanlike free will over the Sethusamudram Sea. However, if Ram Setu was nothing but what British molecular biologist Richard Dawkins might call a brilliant meme—a grandiose fiction told and interpolated over two millennia—then that would signal the triumph of predestination, since it would imply that the scattered shoals in the region were purely a work of unintentional geological evolution with no credit to anthropomorphic gods. To the uninitiated, this may sound as being in tune with what British colonial geologists might have thought about Ram Setu. Presumably, in the century that Charles Darwin dethroned the hallowed place of the Trinity, and religion in general, Victorian geologists would have spared no moment to rubbish the legend of Ram Setu. But history tells a very different tale.

In 1883, the *Memoirs of the Geological Survey of India* made an astounding claim, more so for its phraseology than its scientific findings. Accordingly, the narrow strip of coralline shoals between India and Ceylon so strongly resembled a row of enormous steppingstones, that the reefs indeed seemed to be an ancient causeway built with the agency of mortals. It added that the famed origins of Ram Setu were well within historical possibility. Rather, there seemed to be no reason why the construction or creation of Ram Setu may not have occurred in an age preceding the invasion of Buddhist Lanka by Indians of the north and south. For a preeminent journal of geology to interpret landforms in an idiom anchored in ancient religious legends is not only counter-intuitive but also bewildering. Where was the imperial hostility that most observers would expect in British scientific pronouncements on Hindu culture? And how come even geological evidence seemed to validate indigenous folklores and legends of India? More strangely, the *Memoirs* was neither alone nor idiosyncratic in its description of Ram Setu.

In the early twentieth century, Oxford Indologist A.A. Macdonell famously wrote in the *Encyclopaedia of Religion and Ethics* (published between 1908 and 1921) that 'perhaps no work of world literature, secular in origin, has ever produced so profound an influence on the life and thought of a people as the *Ramayan*.' By then, not only had Europe outlived Hellenic legacies in the continent's daily rituals, but also that the colonial establishment in India had developed a theory around Ram Setu that would make even the most nationalistic Hindu thinkers of today feel staggered. Even back in 1890, German geologist Johannes Walther's report in the *Records of the Geological Survey of India* (1890) had already described Ram Setu as an organic structure, though likely reconstructed by humans across millennia. Walther's findings claim that the bridge existed in ancient times, before being destroyed by unknown causes, only to be rebuilt, and then again destroyed by a fourteenth- or fifteenth-century cyclone. Until then, India and Ceylon were connected by this causeway as suggested by evidence of several faunal migrations from one territory to the other.

Reading such accounts, it is hard to overcome the surprise one feels while reconciling this semi-creationist theory with Charles Darwin's heretical *On the Origin of Species* (1859), published in the same century. Even by the end of the eighteenth century, Europeans had acquired phenomenal knowledge regarding Ram Setu. They were not after religious knowledge. They were drawn to the nearby pearl fisheries and—as may be clear by now—the economic prospects of having an uninterrupted marine stretch between Dhanushkodi and Thalaimannar.

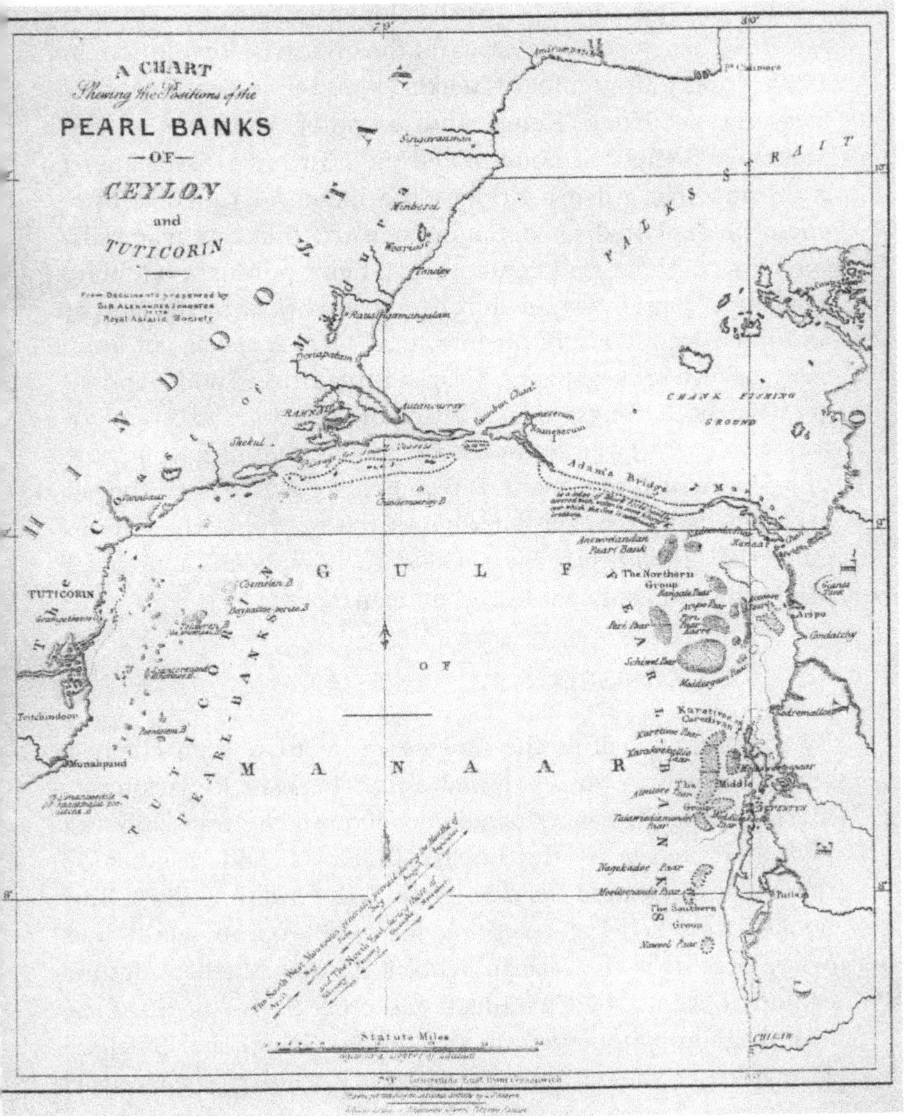

Fig. 10: Map of the pearl fisheries from W.M.G. Colebrooke's 'Account of the Pearl Fisheries of the North-West Coast of the Island' (1833)

A substantial part of early British colonial writings on Ram Setu saw it as a heap of raw materials for the Industrial Revolution. In 1837, Robert Montgomery Martin (a mid-nineteenth-century treasurer of Hong Kong, and founding member of the Statistical Society of London and the East India Association) suggested that Adam's Bridge—the name he called it by— could be exploited for obtaining construction raw materials, since its coralline sediments were 'a light, porous, crumbling substance, sometimes cut and shaped into bricks by the Dutch; and more frequently burnt into lime. Of this species of lime, the late fort of Negapatam [Nagapattinam] was built; and so great is the hardness which it acquires by long exposure to the weather.'[26] Twentieth-century geologists did not outgrow this commercial sentiment. But some, like A.R. Lomas, began acknowledging that the building of the bridge in the 'Hindu epic, the "*Ramayana*"' was likely to have been 'a poetical rendering of events witnessed by man.'[27]

EUROPEANS CHANTED 'RAM'?

By the second half of the nineteenth century, even colonial voices seemed to possess a new cultural sensitivity lacking in Martin's time. This new paradigm followed the translation of *Valmiki Ramayan* by the English Indologist and member of the Indian Education Service Ralph T.H. Griffith in 1870. The book's overwhelming reception in the European world was a key precursor to German scholar F. Max Mueller's future explorations into the Upanishads and other *Sacred Books of the East*, beginning in the late 1870s. Besides Griffith and Mueller, several lesser-known nineteenth-century scholars vociferously legitimized the episode of the construction of a sea-bridge in

---

[26]Martin, *The British Colonial Library*, p. 31.
[27]Lomas, 'On the Origin of Adam's Bridge', pp. 203–204.

Valmiki Ramayan as a quasi-historical tale. One such account published in *The Calcutta Review* of 1854 by Italian Indologist Gaspare Gorresio waxed eloquent about the episode of the building of the bridge by Hanuman's simian compatriots. This possibly wielded great influence on future minds, both European and Indian, writing on Ram Setu.

> The active monkeys at once started in every direction to bring materials, and tear up rocks, and dash them into the flood. Some of the blocks, in the hurry of the transit from the Northern Himalaya to the ocean, were dropped, and still remain as monuments of the feat: to this we owe the rock of Goverdhone, near Muttra: to this the whole of the Kymur range in Central India: so the Hindus will have it. Everywhere in India are scattered erratic blocks, the monuments of the great Diluvium, and attributed by the geologists to the action of ice, but by a people zealous of their traditions, to the bridge-builders of Rama. Rama is said to have exclaimed proudly, that so long as the sea remained, and the mountains did not move from their foundation, so long would the bridge bear his name; and his prophecy promises to come true. There it stands a natural barrier of rocks, extending from shore to shore, known in the European maps as 'Adam's Bridge'—known in India as 'Ram Setu'.[28]

By the turn of the century, accounts like Gorresio's ceased to be exceptional. The influence of early nineteenth-century utilitarians like James Mill and Thomas Babington Macaulay—widely known for suppressing native and colonial sympathy with Indian antiquity—did not disappear. However, since Griffith's translation, if not sooner, the British regime began altering its tenor as to the literary and geological genius of the

[28]Gorresio, '*Ramayana*', p. 209.

legend of Ram Setu. Many geologists even acknowledged the
Hindu legend as a loosely spun chronicle of possible eyewitness
accounts of an enchanting geology. Even to deny Ram Setu's
divinity, commentators referred to its legend. Although the
structure retained its Abrahamic name on maps and official
parlance, it became increasingly less fashionable to dwell on
the Adamic legend.

For instance, the late nineteenth-century British Sanskritist
Charles Henry Tawney was sceptical towards Adam's association
with Ram Setu. Accordingly, the moniker of 'Adam's Bridge' was
retrospectively 'adopted from the Arabs, who regard Ceylon as
the place of Adam's exile after he had been driven from Eden,'[29]
while the Indic belief seemed remarkably older. Tawney's
contemporary F.E. Pargiter, of the Bengal Civil Services, saw
Valmiki Ramayan as a minefield of pristine truths. To him, it
showed 'a picture of ancient India' that was 'in many respects
unique' and endowed with 'perplexing questions of history,
mythology, social life, topography, etc.' Pargiter concluded
that Valmiki 'had a real knowledge of Central and Southern
India' and that Ram Setu was indeed situated to the southeast
of Tamil Nadu.[30]

Then there was the *living* link between the legend of Ram Setu
and the Ramanathapuram district in the clan of the Sethupathis
or Ramnad chiefs. Having ruled the Ramnad kingdom since the
1100s (in alliance with the Madurai Nayaks in the seventeenth
century), the Sethupathis were seen as the hereditary guardians
of Ram Setu since antiquity. Interestingly, Jaffna's Aryacakravarti
kings also styled themselves as *Sethukavalar*s or 'guardians of
Setu' in parallel with the Sethupathis. One of the most striking
colonial descriptions of the Sethupathis' association with
Ram Setu came not in the work of some historian but the

---

[29]Tawney, Somadeva's *Katha Sarit Sagara*, pp. 84–85.
[30]Pargiter, 'The Geography of Rama's Exile', pp. 263–264.

Madras government biologist James Hornell. In 1922, Hornell acknowledged the religious, economic, military and political influence of the Sethupathis over the Ramnad region.

> The present Zamindar of Ramnad is styled Raja, a distinction conferred by Government in recognition of his public spirit; in former days Setupati (or Sethupathi) and Tevar were titles more particularly distinctive and peculiar to these chieftains. The Raja of Ramnad is the hereditary head of the warrior Maravar caste, of which the honorific and generic caste name is Tevar (or Thevar); from this was derived the title Tevar, by which the Dutch referred to the Sovereign of Ramnad in all their documents, usually under the form Theuver or Teuver. The Rajas of Ramnad have always been identified with the great Hindu shrine of Rameswaram; they are its hereditary guardians. Their ancient title of Sethupathi is connected directly with this honourable distinction, for in its meaning of 'Lord of the Causeway' it connotes the guardianship of the sea between Ceylon and India, and of Adam's Bridge, the line of islets and sandbanks connecting the islands of Rameswaram and Mannar.[31]

Hornell's knack for the uncanny unravelled what even Ram's devotees might have missed. His strange and unique findings, circulated in the *Memoirs of the Zoological Survey* (1916), reimagined Ram Setu as a prehistoric passage made of chank shells—a species of calcareous life with special significance in the Indic tradition.

---

[31]Hornell, 'Historical Survey', p. 27.

Fig. 11: Portrait of Shunmuga Rajeswara Naganatha Sethupathi, from
N.V. Pillai's *Setu and Rameswaram* (1929), Plate I

Fig. 12: Arichal Munai, the terminating point of Dhanushkodi, marking the
beginnings of the legendary Ram Setu (Adam's Bridge) (Photograph by Daniel
Stein)

Surely, the eerie significance of his inference was not lost on
Hornell himself.

> We have incontestable evidence ... that the geological
> phase existing in the Gulf of Mannar and Palk Bay region
> antecedent to the present condition was that of a land
> barrier stretching continuously from India to Ceylon in
> the region now known as Adam's Bridge. Further we have
> geological evidence that this phase was preceded by one
> where the level was even lower than it is now and when
> no land whatever existed between what is now the Gulf of
> Mannar and Palk Bay. During this phase ... a single form
> of *Turbinella pirum* [chank] peopled the whole stretch of
> these coastal waters ... Such uniform conditions disappeared
> immediately upon the formation of a continuous land
> barrier between India and Ceylon on the line Pamban—
> Rameswaram—Adam's Bridge—Mannar.[32]

Put simply, Rameswaram, Ram Setu and Ceylon stayed underwater
in the Miocene epoch. Since about 8000 BC, the vegetational
complexity on both sides of Ram Setu began interchanging traits
due to links between Ceylon and the Indian mainland.[33] What,
in the future, would be known as Ram Setu was, according to
Hornell, an unbroken marine passage guarded by conch shells—
the instrument with which millions of Indian households are
known to observe their morning and evening prayers.

AN ENTANGLED SACREDNESS

Suppose the legend of Ram Setu was not fiction, but fact.
And suppose it still existed. But what if it existed elsewhere,
altogether. The colonial historian Jonathan Forbes, for instance,

---

[32]Hornell, 'Indian Varieties and Races of *Turbinella*', p. 120.
[33]Hornell, 'Historical Survey', p. 56; Wait, 'The Distribution of Birds in Ceylon',
1919.

held that 'Lanka' was not the island of Ceylon, but a name signifying the word 'Laka' (million or multitude) denoting an archipelago or a submerged civilization. Thusly, the land of the demon-king Ravan, Lankapura, could well be located around Maldives or to the southwest of Kerala—as recent interpreters have also suggested. This paved the possibility of Lanka being speculated to have been in or around Lemuria, the drowned civilization of Lemurs.

At the time when the honourable Supreme Court was in adjournment over the Ram Setu decision, two of India's eminent historians, Ram Sharan Sharma and Romila Thapar, reminded that the 'Lanka' of *Ramayan* was not a name that ancient texts, like Lankan epic *Mahavamsa* (circa AD 50), used for Ceylon. Instead, they called it Ojadipa, Varadipa, or Mandadipa. Ancient Greek and Latin sources, earlier than the time of the Mauryan Empire (321–185 BC), knew Sri Lanka as Tamraparni, Tambapanni or Taprobane. Interestingly, a third-century Ashokan edict did, after all, refer to Tamraparni as being on the southernmost part of India. But the name might have meant the Indian river, not Sri Lanka. Moreover, 'Sinhala' or 'Sinhaladveep' was often referred to as Silam or Sieledib in Greco-Latin writings, until about AD 1000. Given the absence of historical mentions of 'Lanka', critics suggested that Valmiki should have chosen names like Tamraparni or Sinhala if he had ancient Sri Lanka in mind.

Confronted with this question, Valmiki's Lanka seemed to be a fluid idea that shapeshifted over time, signifying one place in one iteration of the epic and a wholly different place in another. The disputes against the veridical historicity and cartography of Ram Setu resounded opinions of a well-known body of scholarship. Joseph E. Schwartzberg, editor of *A Historical Atlas of South Asia* (1978), held that *Ramayan*'s Lanka was not in Sri Lanka but in the Vindhyas, some 20 miles north of Jabalpur in Madhya Pradesh. This echoed the views of H.D. Sankalia, an eminent Indian historian, who thought that Lanka was not Ceylon but somewhere in central India. He believed that interpreters had confused *Ramayan*'s links to the Godavari River and Dandakaranya region; thus, instead of Dhanushkodi, Ram Setu should have been in Amarkantak, or the Chhota Nagpur region, or Odisha's lower Mahanadi Valley. Sankalia's book *Ramayana: Myth or Reality* (1973) even cited the mystic Sri Aurobindo, who, purportedly, saw 'no ground' to consider Ram 'a historical figure' (though Sri Aurobindo was a Vaishnavite devotee during his spiritual awakening and upheld the centrality of Ram's salvific legacy in Indic life).[34] Inspired by similar views, others located Ram Setu as far as Linga Island, on the eastern coast of Sumatra's Riau province.

Something else besides these alternative geographies obscured Ram Setu's location. That was *Ramayan* itself. So powerful was the *Ramayan* legacy that it unleashed a global tradition of adaptations, translations and transcreations. The lack of consensus on the geography of Ram Setu was largely because of this: that this was a battle over how history would be woven. It was not about rediscovering a mystical bridge or a holy land. The contours of Ram Setu could redetermine the contours of India's past and who possessed the keys to a national identity. For *Ramayan*'s varied interpretations and narratives, one did not have to go to Southeast Asia or Pakistan (an Islamic state with its own versions of *Ramayan*). The Indian context was sufficient to befuddle theologians and historians.

The Buddhist version of *Ramayan*, called *Dasarat Jataka*, took a very different line from *Valmiki Ramayan*. Therein, Ram hailed not from Ayodhya but Varanasi. Sita was not abducted in this tale, and she and Ram left for the Himalayas, instead of the Vindhyas and Deccan, during their exile. More glaringly, this Buddhist version had no mention of the building of Ram Setu.

---

[34]Sankalia, *Ramayana: Myth or Reality*, p. 32.

Then there was the Jain retelling, *Paumachariya* (circa AD 678), where Ram marries thrice during exile, and Ravan is presented as an anti-hero, not a demon. In Hemachandra's Jain text, *Trishashti Shalaka Purusha Charita* (circa 1100–1200), the bridge is more metaphysical than real, as Ravan's two loyal Vidyadhar kings are overcome by Nala and Nila to protect Ram's glory. While *Valmiki Ramayan* is believed to contain interpolations from between 400 BCE and AD 400, the Buddhist, Jain and other adaptations go on to contain scenarios where Ram and Sita are even shown as siblings and Ravan is represented as a distinguished Meghavahana noble. This diversity made the debate on the *Ramayan* legacy more profound and hotly contested.[35]

Hindutvavadi activists, in turn, cited other kinds of evidence that traced the idea of Ram Setu southwards of the Vindhyas and Deccan. To begin with, Ram Setu was the titular reference in the Vakataka dynasty king, Pravarasena's *Setubandha* (circa AD 400–500). Notably, the Vakataka kingdom revolved around central India, while covering parts of coastal Odisha and Andhra—if not Tamil Nadu. But Kulavanikan Seethalai Satanar's Tamil Buddhist epic *Manimekalai* (AD 500–600) traced Ram Setu in the Tamil temple town of Kanyakumari in the deep south, closer to Dhanushkodi. Subsequently, Thevaram (Devaram) chants written by seventh–eighth-century Tamil Shaiva poets reimagined Ram Setu as being at Rameswaram.[36] Further, *Thirumalai* (circa AD 700–800), a compilation of 45 Vaishnav hymns by Tamil poet-saint Thondaradipodi Alvar, though not reflective of Ram Setu's geography, is rich in references to the *Ramayan* legacy. Thondaradipodi's affiliation to the Ranganathaswamy Temple in Srirangam, in Tiruchirappalli, not very far from Dhanushkodi, made this piece of evidence important in the public eye.

---

[35]Thapar, 'Fallacies of Hindutva Historiography', p. 69.
[36]Rajarajan, 'Reflections on Rama Setu', pp. 2–4.

Then there was Nammalvar, besides other seventh–eighth-century Tamil Vaishnavite Alvar poet-saints, who fostered devotion to Lord Ram as a Vaishnavite avatar in Tamil Nadu's temple towns, including Rameswaram. Around AD 740, Adi Shankaracharya and his follower Padmapadacharya are said to have had ablutions in Dhanushkodi. Padmapadacharya narrated to his disciples the lores of the land which he defined as: '"He who is the Lord of Ram (i.e., Siva)," if it is taken as Ram's statement; "He to whom Ram is the Lord (i.e., Siva)," if taken as Siva's speech.'[37] Once again, these did not constitute evidence of a causeway across the Palk Strait, but certainly signified a very long tradition of the *Ramayan* legacy's immanence in Tamil Nadu.

By about AD 1000, *Ramayan* iconography thrived in Tamil Nadu under the 'genius of the Cholas'. Bronze artefacts from the age of Rajaraja Chola I (AD 985–1010) characterize a regime that saw the 'rise in the stature of Rama as an iconic figure in Chola art.'[38] In 1905, archaeologists discovered copper plates of Rajaraja I memorializing his grants to the Tiruvalangadu Temple. The king modelled himself after Ram's imperial image. He evidently looked upon the legend of Ram Setu as a significant regal trope.[39] Thus, it is not surprising to see allusions to the Setu in the thirteenth–fourteenth-century Tamil Vaishnavite scholar Vedanta Desika's *Raghuveera Gadyam*, a verse transcreation of *Ramayan*. As it was written in the Tamil temple-town of Tiruvandipuram, its propinquity to Rameswaram reinforced the notion that Dhanushkodi was a key threshold for the sacred bridge.

The fourteenth-century Sanskrit epic from Kerala, *Suka Sandesa*, by Laksmidasa, also traced the Setu near Rameswaram.[40]

---

[37]Vidyaranya, *Sankara-Dig-Vijaya*, pp. 162; 166.
[38]Srinivas, 'Ramayana Bronzes', pp. 105–106.
[39]Sanford, 'Ramayana Portraits', p. 54.
[40]Henry, *Ravana's Kingdom*, p. 44.

Besides Sangam literature, believers could always turn to the *Linga Purana* (one of the eighteen Mahapuranas of the Hindu tradition), which depicts Ram halting at Rameswaram, after his triumph in Lanka, to construct a *lingam* near the coastline and repent the assassination of Ravan, a Brahmin. The tale of Ram's atonement near Rameswaram was also widely prevalent in Jaffna, as reported by Portuguese occupants of early sixteenth-century Ceylon.[41] Passionate Hindutvavadi activists also added that Ram Setu was illustrated in a narrative bas-relief—starring the hominid army commandeered by Sugriv—at Java's Prambanan. Not too far from there were the murals in the gallery of Bangkok's Temple of the Emerald Buddha, representing the eighteenth-century Thai epic, *Ramakien*. Though unclear how this constituted evidence for supporting Ram Setu's Tamil geography, it kept the intellectual embers alive.

While this was roughly the extent of the range of ideas on both sides of the spectrum, no one seemed to question whether history of these various ideas of Ram Setu concealed more sinister themes.

The region around Ram Setu has been a geopolitical hotspot for nearly a century and a half, if not longer. A barren island—lying less than 20 miles northeast of Dhanushkodi, where the Indian part of the bridge begins—known as Katchatheevu still reminds one of the horrors of the Lankan civil war. This marooned plot of earth has been the source of simmering tensions between Indian fishers and the Lankan navy since at least 1974, when the island was strategically awarded to the Lankan administration by the then Indian prime minister, albeit without parliamentary consent. Home to a solitary church, bereft of drinking water, and profusely stocked with cacti, the name 'Katchatheevu' is a misnomer. Though it literally means a 'barren island', its symbolic worth is enormous. It continues to

---

[41]De Queyroz, *The Temporal and Spiritual Conquest*, p. 58.

be the nucleus of disputes around fishing rights between Indian and Lankan fishers, making it a fertile ground for violence, leading to property damage and loss of livelihoods, sometimes of lives too.

Then there is something else that makes the Sethusamudram region a beleaguered ground for the two nations. In the Anthropocene—the epoch when Mother Earth finds itself under the irreversible influence of the race of homo sapiens—Ram Setu has become the epicentre of a submarine civilization of over 4,200 species of plants and animals, many of which are endangered, thanks to an interspecies battle that has besieged the region since the arrival of Norwegian trawlers in the 1960s.

Back at Dhanushkodi, the fishing community of Hindus, Muslims and Christians have been scarred by a bilateral maritime conflict and a moody landscape. Their survival depends on propitiating the capricious sea, whose tectonic shifts, *Acropora* species, and raised reefs have summoned the ground beneath their feet into existence. Some seniors of the community, who either experienced the cyclone of 1964 or heard reports of it, still experience nightmares. The storm wiped out a complete township, engulfed an entire train from the British-built Pamban Bridge, and along with it, nearly 120 passengers aboard. The community of fishers have their own legends about cyclones. Accordingly, these were no meteorological events but quarrels between the 'feminine' and 'masculine' seas—a folkloric catharsis to an event that was too painful to heal from. The Anthropocene has united these races of people who live the mundane as the mystical.

In the cobalt depths of the Gulf of Mannar, about 5,000 women divers—living in 25 villages—are known to comb the seabed for algal seaweeds, holding their breath with a precision born of dire necessity. The women scratch the ocean's scars, which prick their skins, leaving occasional wounds. These are also legends, not accomplished for personal glory but for their daughters to be able to study and continue the tradition their mothers have upheld for more than three decades. But the ocean exacts a heavy price. The Gulf of Mannar Marine National Park, protected by law, places these women on the edge of legal righteousness.

Despite the adversities, the lives of Pamban's fishing community reflect a rare truth also felt in this author's experiences of communal coexistence and shared traditions that he saw decades ago, growing up near a slum in Calcutta. Saraswati Puja, the festival of the deity of learning, was celebrated by Muslims and Christians, while Hindus waited with bated breath for Eid sweets and Christmas plum cakes. Somewhere down the line, these mundane ecstasies that defied the rigid boundaries of maps and ordinances had eroded. The author grew up hearing the legend that when Ram Setu was being built, Ram's battalion included a nondescript squirrel, swivelling in the seashore, and then drying itself onto the sandbars being laid down by the vanar sena. When Ram asked the squirrel what it was up to, the latter, without recognizing the future king of Ayodhya, responded by saying that it was helping build the bridge of Dharma. When Ram asked if the squirrel knew who the bridge was meant for, the squirrel answered that it could not care less if history remembered the insignificant non-human as having performed its spiritual calling.

Ram Setu is the embodiment of a solitary teardrop shed by the Indian Ocean in the hope that one form becomes indiscriminately dissolved in another, like the ageless Vedantic metaphor of the wave in the sea—each in each, indistinct from another. It embodies the hope of peace, reason, harmony, solidarity, truth, and above all, trust in the infinite capacity of humankind to rise above its earthly digressions in the spirit of enormously large-hearted sacrifices and unprejudiced loyalties. The saga that follows is hoped to be of such a creed. *Satyameva jayate!*

THE LAST SIGH OF ADAM

To James Rennell—pioneer of modern oceanography and British geography—ordnance maps and charts were more than navigational tools. They were instruments to erase and reclaim in the guise of mapping and naming. Having arrived in India 15 years ago, Rennell finished his famous *Map of Hindoostan* in 1782—an extraordinary feat of precision and ambition, the first modern scientific survey of India. That, along with his previous work, *Bengal Atlas* (1779), and the one to be published the following year, the *Memoir of a Map of Hindoostan* (1783), warranted his pre-eminence as a cartographer. These also become the leitmotifs for the inglorious maps undergirding the future British Indian Empire. However, lurking in their fine prints, so to speak, were more than territories to be taken. They embodied the hubris of an imperial imagination that sought to subsume ancient landscapes and their placemaking legends into an outwardly rational order of cartographical science.

Rennell's road to glory was not without powerful benefactors. Among the most prominent of these, Sir William Jones, the polymath—philologist, judge at the Supreme Court of Judicature at Fort William, and passionate Indologist, who rechristened Kalidas as the 'Shakespeare of India'—delivered a speech, in 1785, to the lately inaugurated Asiatic Society in Calcutta. These were the principles he laid down, which his colleague, Rennell, had already ardently disrupted in his map:

[...] [Y]ou will investigate whatever is rare in the stupendous fabric of nature, will correct the geography of Asia by new observations and discoveries; will trace the annals, and even traditions of those nations, who from time to time have peopled or desolated it; and will bring to light their various forms of Government, with their institutions civil and religious; you will examine their improvements and methods in arithmetic and geometry, in trigonometry, mensuration, mechanics, optics, astronomy, and general physics; their systems of morality, grammar, rhetoric, and dialectic; their skill in surgery and medicine, and there advancement, whatever it may be, in anatomy and chemistry. To this you will add researches into their agriculture, manufactures, trade; and, whilst you inquire with pleasure into their music, architecture, painting, and poetry, will not neglect those inferior arts, by which the comforts and even elegances of social life are supplied or improved.[42]

For Jones, Indian differences were the fodder for drawing kinships instead of imposing the alienness of British technology onto the colonized landscape.[43] If one turned to the later viceroys of India, one might find a far greater overlay in their sentiments with Rennel's ideology than with Jones' somewhat romanticized ideals of British honourableness. Take for instance the speech of Viceroy Lord Curzon, delivered on 20 May 1912, at the Royal Geographical Society. To Curzon, geography was 'the most cosmopolitan of all sciences' that had aided 'in the illumination of the dark places of the earth and in the diffusion of truth, scientific and divine.'[44] What Curzon's words crystallized in the year of the annulment of the horrid partition of Bengal that he

---

[42]Jones, 'A Discourse', p. 4.

[43]Pande, 'Medicine, Race and Liberalism in British Bengal', p. 29.

[44]Curzon, *Subjects of the Day*, pp. 155–159.

had effectuated seven years earlier, Rennel's *Map of Hindoostan* signified for the late eighteenth century. That is, geography was 'an active writing of the earth by an expanding, centralizing imperial state' that epitomized 'an almost mythical power of geographic authority inscribing lines of antagonism and identity across the face of the earth.'[45] Colonial mapmaking was not just 'mythically about the god-trick of seeing everything from nowhere, but to have put the myth into practice,'[46] precisely at the moment when the myths of indigenes and aboriginals were deemed to be unfit for colonial scientific rationality.

Fig. 13: James Rennell's *Map of Hindoostan* (1782)

---

[45]Neocleous, *Imagining the State*, p. 121.
[46]Haraway, 'Situated Knowledges', p. 459.

DITCHING A 'DUTCH' COINAGE

True to its decree, Rennell's *Map* was a declaration of dominion. Britannia herself was depicted therein, seated regally, receiving the sacred texts of India—the 'Shasters'—as in the form of oblations offered by Brahmin priests. Behind her, a lion rested a paw on a globe. At her feet lay the tools of survey. In her shadow were the untold stories of those that had been silenced, their voices drowned out by the roar of empire. As one historian poignantly described the politics of the event:

> Rennell's *Map of Hindoostan*, the first map of India based on scientific survey and measurement, published in 1782 soon after the territorial conquest of the subcontinent by the British had begun. The cartouche, according to Rennell himself, shows Britannia 'receiving into her Protection, the sacred Books of the Hindoos, presented by the Pundits, or Learned Bramins [sic].' At her feet lie what look like the tools of the surveyor, and behind her on a pedestal stands a lion with its foot resting on a sphere. The cartouche has been variously interpreted by other scholars, but for the purposes of my argument, what it confirms is the circulation of power/knowledge that we have learned to associate with modern empires. In return for the sacred textual knowledges of the East, symbolized by the 'Shaster' (sacred books) that the Indians give to Britannia, she gifts them 'her' latest achievement, Rennell's map of their land, the cartographic embodiment of the new rational, scientific ordering of ('Indian') space.[47]

The East—that would be henceforth defined as having been once *barbaric*—was all set to look more transformable and civilizable in the eyes of the colonizer. To the latter, its people as much

---

[47]Ramaswamy, 'Catastrophic Cartographies', p. 121.

as its landscapes could now be rationed into orderly grids of empirical cognition for utilitarian control. But Rennell's dessert could not be seized from him, regardless of his ideology.

Fig. 14: Cartouche from James Rennell's *Map of Hindoostan* (1782): 'In return for the ... "Shaster" that the Indians give to Britannia, she gifts them 'her' latest achievement, Rennell's map of their land...'

A founding member of the Royal Geographical Society, Rennell is the first known Briton to propose the 'practicability of widening the [Ram Setu] for ships.' Whilst almost 'no notice was taken at the time of the suggestions put forward by so young and unknown an officer, the idea was revived some sixty years later.[48] Besides, Rennell had little interest in the legend of the sacred causeway. So, he called the tombolo as 'Adam's Bridge', becoming the first English mapmaker of widespread renown to do so. But although his nomenclature entered official parlance, it was not here to stay. Rennell would be confirmed to be wrong twice—first, by his own illustrious colleague and benefactor; second, by the unfathomable queerness of the structure that he, so cavalierly, saw as being subservient to the power of British gunpowder and steam navigation.

History has its ways of being remembered and unremembered. And so, Rennell seems to have been accorded a disproportionate degree of credit or notoriety for renaming Ram Setu. Prototypes or variants of the name 'Adam's Bridge' had been in currency among Europeans since at least about the sixteenth century. The first known map to feature one such variant was the Dutch traveller Johan Nieuhof's *Map of Southern India* (1682), that named it 'Adam's Brug'. François Valentyn's Dutch *Map of Southern India* (1724–26) echoed Nieuhof's nomenclature. Then there were Homann Heirs' German *Map of India* (1733), Guillaume de L'Isle's French *Carte des Côtes de Malabar et de Coromandel* (1745), and Giovanni Maria Cassini's Italian *Map of India* (1797), that called the structure 'Pons Adam', 'Pont d'Adam', and 'Ponte d'Adam'.

Taking from Nieuhof's name, Philip Baldaeus and Adrian Reland's eighteenth-century Dutch *Map of Ceylon* also termed it 'Adams brugk'. Valentyn, a Dutch Calvinist minister, who arrived in India in 1685 as a Dutch East India Company hydrographer, acquired fame as the author of *Oud en Nieuw Oost-Indiën* (*Old and New East-India*) (1724–26). There, he wrote that the Adamic

---

[48]'Rennell, James, *The Penny Cyclopaedia*, p. 389; Rennell, R., 'Major James Rennell', *The Geographical Journal*, p. 291.

association with Ram Setu was of Portuguese origins.[49] And it was probably this work of history that set the ball rolling for Adam's Bridge as the official cartographical signifier in the European imagination of southern India.

Nonetheless, the above rule was not without decisive exceptions. The Welsh engraver, Emanuel Bowen's *Map of India* (circa 1747), the mid-eighteenth-century English map, *A New and Accurate Map of Coromandel, Malabar, Bengal, & c.*, and Thomas Kitchin's 'Map of India' in *A New General and Universal Atlas* (1761) by Andrew Dury, curiously kept the sandbars nameless though nominally identifying the temple town of Rameswaram. These omissions were by no means trivial. And they begin to acquire meaning as we dive deeper into the intellectual history of Ram Setu in the eighteenth century, especially with regards to how Europeans saw and spoke about it. Much of that vision was drawn from not only professional Dutch historians but also amateur—even armchair—geographers and cartographers. A major source for a lot of these was Valentyn's history, which, in turn, drew most of its intelligence from the Dutch Calvinist minister and traveller, Baldaeus's *A True and Exact Description of the Most Celebrated East-India coasts of Malabar and Coromandel* (1671).

Robert Knox—an English sea captain of the East India Company, and author of *An Historical Relation of the Island Ceylon* (1681)—arguably scrounged the bulk of his information from Baldaeus's memoirs, including mapwork.

---

[49]Suckling, *Ceylon*, p. 58.

Fig. 15: Emanuel Bowen's *A Map of India* (circa 1747)

Curiously, although the publisher of Baldaeus's book, Johannes Janssonius van Waasberge, agreed for the plates from the book to be syndicated by Moses Pitt for the *English Atlas* project (1680–81),[50] the latter chose to leave the sandbars between India and Ceylon unidentified. These cartographic exclusions of Ram Setu—or 'Adam's Bridge', as contemporary European navigators seemingly called it—in English maps has perhaps no rational explanation other than the notion that British cartographers were careful to eliminate a name of Portuguese and Dutch jargon. If this explanation is indeed admissible, it would imply that the British were palpably aware of the fraught nature of the name of the structure.

However, the antithesis to this appears in the fact that several British accounts written on the Pamban region during this period seemed to have no qualms about recognizing their debt to Baldaeus—and to call the sandbars 'Adam's Bridge'. For instance, Herman Moll's *Atlas Geographus* (1712) confirmed the synchronicity of the Abrahamic and Hindu legends in coastal Tamil Nadu. Even so, Moll acknowledged that Adam's Bridge was a name preferred by 'those of Ceylon',[51] not otherwise. Moll's particulars of Ram Setu are made more significant with the fact that it is the oldest recognizable reference to the structure in a book published in English. To Moll, Ram Setu was a 'sand bank' seized from the Portuguese by the Dutch in 1658 'after a flout Resistance, by 1000 chosen Men and 12 Frigats,' in what became 'one of the greatest Actions betwixt those People and the Dutch, and that the latter were only 800 strong.'[52] If 'Ram Setu' was an instant signifier of the legendary and symbolic battle between Ram and Ravan, the Dutch had created their own battle legend out of 'Adam's Bridge'. It recalled the Luso-Dutch contest for Nagapattinam and the celebrated Pearl Fishery—whose

[50]Winterbottom, 'Producing and Using the "Historical Relation of Ceylon"', pp. 522–523.
[51]Moll, *Atlas Geographus*, p. 602.
[52]Ibid., p. 644.

degradation set in during 1666–69 after Dutch colonization. But such mythmaking was short-lived.

British observers of the Ram Setu, who followed Moll, did not seem entirely welcoming towards the Luso-Dutch name. Alexander Hamilton, a Scottish East India Company captain, and future commander of the Bombay Marine, also referred to Ram Setu in *A New Account of the East Indies* (1727). Hamilton, who lived in India between 1688 and 1723, and travelled as far as Ayutthaya, in Siam, was sceptical towards the Adamic legends of 'Zeloan' (Ceylon) and Nagapattinam. Although he documented the existence of the Ceylonese lore 'that *Adam* was created on the spot' named as Adam's Peak (Sri Pada), he clearly called 'Adam's Bridge' the European substitute for what was originally known to the indigenous populace as '*Ramena Coil*' or Ramancoil—the bridge or temple dedicated to Ram. Hamilton underscored that Adamic legend was an invention of the Luso-Dutch occupations of Nagapattinam, Tuticorin and Mannar.[53] Thanks to Moll and Hamilton, eighteenth-century Britain was rendered practically immune to a purely Europeanized imagination of Ram Setu. Thus, in 1743, when the industrious British author John Lockman paid a tribute to the structure in the *Travels of the Jesuits*, he clarified that the 'Chain or Rocks called by some Adam's Bridge' was indeed a bridge 'built anciently' by apes or non-humans who, 'being more brave and industrious than those of the present Age, built a Passage for themselves from the Continent to the Island of Ceylon: That they then seized upon it, and delivered the Wife of one of their Gods who had been forced away thither.'[54]

Lockman's primary aim was to discuss Ram Setu not as a *bridge* but as a barrier to maritime traffic between India and Ceylon. Yet, he left a laudable legacy in terms of influencing

---

[53]Hamilton, *A New Account of the East Indies*, pp. 336; 334–335; 345.
[54]Lockman, *Travels of the Jesuits*, p. 375.

succeeding representations of Ram Setu, such as in Joh Dunn's English translation of *A Collection of Curious Observations* (1749), a widely read book written by the French author Claude-Francois Lambert. Either Lambert or Dunn had made an intimate study of Lockman's passage that is unmistakably echoed in the words of the *Collection*. Accordingly, Ramancoil's locals held 'that this bridge was built by the apes of former times,' and 'that these animals being more brave and industrious than the modern apes, made a passage from the main-land into the island of Ceylan, that they rendered themselves masters of this island, and rescued the wife of one of their gods, who had been carried off.'[55] Despite this uneasy resemblance to Lockman's words, Lambert has to be thanked for bringing the legend of Ram Setu to literally the first page of his book and in a tradition of subsequent connoisseurly histories of India. The English translation of the *Collection* ran into several editions, reprints, even getting reprinted under the pseudonym of Edward Howard, being then retitled as *Travels Through Asia, Africa, and America* (1755), published by M. Cooper, besides being rehashed in other versions with other titles. Crucially, each of these retained the introductory chapter containing the all-important passages on Ram Setu.

A DISENCHANTED BARRIER?

By mid-eighteenth century, the growing British literati of writers, journalists, editors, East India Company spokespeople, and a clique of mercantile informants became desirous of more on the Pamban region, alongside those from Tuticorin, Mannar and Jaffna. An outcome of this was Cooper's publication of Captain Cope's *A New History of the East Indies* (1754), which was rather hawkish in its view of Ram Setu. For Cope, the battle of Indic and European legends was only a minor philological scuffle.

---

[55]Lambert, *A Collection of Curious Observations*, pp. 1–2.

Simply put, what the Ceylonese called 'Hamalet' (Sri Pada) had
been rechristened by the Portuguese as 'Adam's Peak', 'Adam's
Foot' and 'Pico de Adam'.[56] It was to be imagined, therefore,
that the Portuguese and Dutch had subjected Ram Setu to a
similar fate. But more importantly, for Cope, Ram Setu was 'a
Reef of Rocks to the Island of *Zeloan*,' and a key landmark near
the Pearl Fishery, to its north, that made the Dutch company
richer by £20,000, annually.[57] Cope's account of Ram Setu—or
the lack of an account, as it were—ushered a new paradigm in
which to see, or rather, unsee the semiotics of the structure.
His was not a vision that prioritized a European legend or
religiosity over an Indic variant. Rather, his unsentimental and
entrepreneurial view of the sandbars meant that the structure
could be, henceforward, shrunk as a cartographic footnote in
the map of European commerce between southern India and
Ceylon.

This trend was replicated in the English translation of
French geographer Jean Baptiste Bourguignon D'Anville's *A
Geographical Illustration of the Map of India* (1759), William
MacKay's *Dictionary of Religious Ceremonies* (1787), Jedidiah
Morse's *The American Universal Geography* (1793), John Malham's
The Naval Gazetteer (1795), and the Scottish covenanter William
Guthrie's *An Improved System of Modern Geography* (1789).
Instructively, the last title explicitly saw Ram Setu as nothing
but a blockade to lucrative sea route between Pamban and
Ceylon—'the only place which produces the true Cinnamon.'[58]

As late as 1830, *The London Literary Gazette* would parrot
Guthrie's view of Ram Setu's 'great importance to the maritime
interests' of Alexandrine Greece. 'The island was separated from
the continent by shoals, through which there were passages,

---

[56]Cope, *A New History*, p. 36.
[57]Ibid., p. 317.
[58]Guthrie, *An Improved System of Modern Geography*, pp. 792–793.

narrow, but very deep, sufficient to allow ships of 3000 amphoras to pass.' Apparently, according to Pliny, ancient vessels were known to use Ram Setu as a pass 'during four months, according to the change of the monsoons.' For Nearchus (Alexander's naval commander), Ram Setu was 'the emporium of the cinnamon and other Indian wares, which were conveyed from thence to Babylon,' a status it held on to in the Roman period.[59]

Gradually, it seemed that British citations to Ram Setu sought to eradicate all mystical or supernatural semiotic associations, spotlighting commercial realism instead. So, when Andrew Brice's *A Universal Geographical Dictionary* (1759) dismissed the structure's legends, he did so first in relation to the Adamic myths in dismissing the faith of 'ignorant Natives that Adam was here created and buried' at Adam's Peak or Sri Pada.[60] Views such as Brice's were attuned to the new materialist reality of the 1750s, that panned out as a prelude to a global conflagration, with the Seven Years' War between Britain and France carving into India's soil. Their surrogate battlegrounds arose in Bengal—Calcutta, Chandernagore and Plassey—and the Carnatic, and the inevitability of the Battles of Plassey (1757) and Buxar (1764) would shatter the fragile equilibrium, before the granting of the diwani of Bengal to the British in 1765. This cracked open a vault of ambitious prospects for the British East India Company, as Bengal's gunpowder reserves became the key to unlocking dominance over southern India and extending its dominion to Ceylon. But underneath this geopolitical chessboard lay a subtler conquest. The Company's ambitions crystallized in the creation of British colonial cartography, officially helmed by Rennell in the late 1770s. Yet even the age of fierce cartographical reason could not drain the mystique from Ram Setu or reduce it to bland and sterile coordinates. That is because a rebellion was

---

[59]'Steam Navigation to India', p. 434.
[60]Brice, *A Universal Geographical Dictionary*, p. 304.

brewing from within as allegory became a new aesthetic to counter cartography.

A streak of such defiance showed, for example, in *The Modern Part of an Universal History* (1759) that amplified Ram Setu's elements as 'great stones, which rise two or three feet above the surface of the sea ... of an enormous size,' some reaching up to 'eighteen feet diameter, and others more. They leave spaces between them from three to ten feet wide: and the gaps, or intervals, through which barks pass, are still wider.' The passage reflected the still prevalent desire in eighteenth-century British readers for enchantment, whether of a sacred or a scientific dimension. 'It is not easy to imagine,' the passage went on, 'that this is a work of art; for one cannot conceive from whence such enormous masses could be taken, and still less how they could be brought hither. But, supposing it to be a work of nature, it is one of the most surprising our author ever beheld.'[61] Like Lockman's influence in the previous decade, *The Modern Part of an Universal History* too became the model for many armchair commentators to derive their imagination of Ram Setu—without having to set foot in India. A thinly camouflaged mimesis of the previous passage could be seen, for instance, in the English lens-maker-turned-author Benjamin Martin's *Physico-geology* (1769). Martin, who tried to preserve Ram Setu's ambiguity as something-in-between a human-made bridge and natural formation, wrote that historians lacked consensus as to whether it was 'a work of Nature or of Art'; if it was the latter, it was surely 'one of the most surprising.'[62] Like Martin, his contemporary, the physician and amateur-geographer-historian Richard Brookes also emphasized that 'Adam's Bridge' was a name conferred by Europeans, since neither Indians nor the Ceylonese saw Adam

---

[61] *The Modern Part*, 572.
[62] Martin, *Physico-geology*, 458.

as 'the first man'.[63] In the eighteenth century, anyone talking of nomenclatural politics or revisiting the debate of whether Ram Setu was natural or ceramic posed a de facto challenge to the commercial aesthetic of denuding the structure of its historical, cultural, political and spiritual values. Martin and Brookes were by no means marginal voices in that scheme, given the popularity of their treatises, albeit repurposed from secondary sources.

So, towards the end of the century, clearly two camps emerged in the British intelligentsia. The first comprised the likes of Scottish cartographer John Hamilton Moore, for whom authors of Ram Setu were summarily dismissed as 'gross idolaters' and residents of a 'savage nation', whose shrines were stupendous, but houses were backward.[64] The second boasted of voices like *The Modern Part of an Universal History*, that went into meticulous details about not only Ram Setu but also the Maravar territory, and Ramnad's Sethupathis. The latter even attempted to offer explanations as to the symbolic truths of Ram Setu by recalling the historical episode when a 'prince of *Marava*, when pursued by the kings of Madurey [Nayaks of Madurai], used to retire into the isle, by means, of great beams laid upon those rocks, which are so many platforms; over which he passed his army, with all his train of cannon and elephants.'[65] A third kind of impression of Ram Setu happened to be those instances when expeditions to the sandbars returned from midway owing to the sheer resistance put forth by the structure's environment—or the powers that be.

An example of the third type could be seen in *A Collection of Plans of Ports in the East Indies* (1787), edited by the Scottish geographer Alexander Dalrymple, chief hydrographer of the East India Company and the British Admiralty. Dalrymple was a forerunner of avant-garde knowledge, including being the

[63]Brookes, *The General Gazetteer*, p. 6.
[64]Moore, *A New and Complete Collection*, p. 673.
[65]Ibid.

proponent of the theory of the existence of the hypothetical continent, *Terra Australis Incognita*. However, Dalrymple was not known to harbour any romantic ideas about Ram Setu. It was natural, then, for his *Collection* to include a report by William Stevens—an East India Company surveyor based in Madras—named 'An Account of a Voyage to Examine the Arches of Adam's Bridge' (1765). Stevens was determined to censor all sacred or enchanting values of the structure from his 'voyage'. He set sail from Fort St. George on 13 February 1765, in the evening. Ten days later, he 'went with two Toney Boats,' which he had brought from Cuddalore, 'to examine the Passage between Point Ramen and Paumancotan (Pamban); a small Fort on the Island of Ramisseram which the Dutch formerly took from the Great Marawar [Sethupathis] but abandoned it 9 months later.'[66] Despite his confidence, Stevens made no progress beyond Rameswaram. His expedition was cut short by strong currents and lack of practical vessels. His voyage, or the absence of it, was substituted by an implicit invitation to his higher-ups to take stock of the real-estate business and commerce of cloths and dyes between India and Ceylon monopolized by the Dutch. The irony did not end there, in that he could not complete his survey of Ram Setu, but extended to the fact that he relied on hearsay and gossip furnished by Rameswaram's natives for his commercial intelligence—at a time when the so-called gossip of the legend of Ram Setu would have been anathema to his ears.

THE ORIENTALIST CRUSADE

Besides these three kinds of narrative stereotypes that Ram Setu's descriptions had acquired in eighteenth-century Britain, there was another kind that was unapologetically Indologist, even

---

[66]Stevens, 'An Account of a Voyage to Examine the Arches of Adam's Bridge', p. 65.

going as far as seeing the events of *Ramayan* and the building of the Setu by Ram's vanar sena as a historical episode. Take for instance the English Orientalist Charles Wilkins, who translated the *Bhagavat Geeta* (1785), and also a curious archaeological discovery, 'A Royal Grant of Land: Engraved on a Copper Plate Bearing the Date Twenty-Three Years Before Christ', that was found at Monghyr in 1781. According to Wilkins, Ram Setu had supposedly been mentioned in the said copper plate—that dated back to as early as 23 BC—bearing the allusion to the legend of the bridge that was built for Lord Ram 'in his wars with Raabon [Ravan].'[67] Wilkins' entry—which most modern professional historians would find extravagant and unserious, to put it euphemistically—was no flash in the pan. In fact, the Orientalist aesthetic was so strong that even prestigious periodicals of the late eighteenth century may have practised literary gatekeeping as to the appropriate proper noun to be used for the sandbars.

When *The View of Hindoostan* (1798) by Thomas Pennant was reviewed in *The British Critic*, the reviewer found the author's reference to 'Adam's Bridge'[68] highly objectionable. The former went on to add that it 'should have been noticed as a mistake, for it ought to be Rama's Bridge.'[69] This intervention was owed—in no small measure—to a crusade of sorts that had been spearheaded by Wilkins, and the lodestar of the Orientalist movement, William Jones. And while Jones held the fort in India—quite literally, too, since he was posted at Calcutta's Fort William—his Oxonian colleague, Thomas Maurice, supplied lethal intellectual ammunitions from Britain.

Back in 1793, excerpts of Maurice's magnum opus, *Indian Antiquities*, were carried by *The Monthly Review* (1793). Along

---

[67]Wilkins, 'A Royal Grant of Land', p. 260.
[68]Pennant, *The View of Hindoostan*, pp. 15; 213; 284.
[69]*The British Critic*, p. 148.

with that, it also carried an extraordinary footnote: 'Sir Will. Jones contends, [Adam's Bridge] should be entitled Rama's bridge: and the present name of this promontory and island strengthens his remark.' The editors reinforced this view by adding: 'Of this we have little doubt. In all the oriental dialects, the D & R have been frequently confounded; especially in proper names.'[70] That *The Monthly Review* and its editorial staff were incredibly keen to establish the premise that phonemes in the word 'Adam'— whether containing any value for Christian and Islamic faiths or not—was most probably a spin on the monosyllable in 'Ram'. By that logic, revising the Abrahamic coinage 'Adam's Bridge' *back* to 'Ram's Bridge' was ethically, philologically, semiotically and historically accurate, in the Orientalist school of thought. It was a school based in Jones' less-known testimony regarding the sandbars between Ceylon and India, 'which the Muselmans or the Portuguese have given the foolish name of Adam's (it should be called Rama's) bridge.' Was it not likely, asked Jones rhetorically, that Ram's 'army of satyrs' comprised 'a race of mountaineers' whom the avatar had 'civilized'?[71] Maurice was prompt to leap to his defence in corroborating the historical reasoning behind calling the structure 'Rama's Bridge'.[72] But Maurice's response was not without political motives.

Maurice took a romantic and liberal view of *Valmiki Ramayan*, being desperate to cling on to an old-world epistemological structure that had not been overturned by the French Revolution. Jones's Orientalism came to his rescue to re-enchant his world. The campaign led by Jones in India inspired Maurice to write—in no manner of mockery or satire—that 'innumerable battalions of apes, or mountaineers' had indeed 'constructed a bridge of rocks one hundred leagues in length'; that the 'miraculous bridge' was

---

[70]Maurice, *Indian Antiquities*, p. 131.
[71]Jones, 'Dissertation on the Gods', p. 324.
[72]Maurice, *Dissertation I*, p. 25.

eventually crossed by Ram 'at the head of no less formidable a body than 360,000 apes, commanded by eighteen kings, each having under him 20,000.'[73]

The allegorical reason of Jones, Maurice, Wilkins did not necessarily overthrow Rennell's cartographic reason or even marginalize it. But it paved the way for a parallel world where it was permissible to hold the somewhat pantheistic view that *Ramayan*'s apes were foresters from Deccan whom Ram liberated from a 'savage state' by enlisting them in his crusade against the king of Lanka. The latter was, in Maurice's view, a prototype of Napoleon, a 'tyrant' and 'a monster of injustice, cruelty and lewdness'. Unlike the more complex nonbinary view that Indian attitudes take of Puranic traditions and fables, Maurice highlighted an ineffable binary betwixt Ravan (a Brahmin and emperor-scholar possessing 10 metaphorical heads), who had 'spent ten thousand [lunar] years, on the mountain of Kylass, in worshipping God', and his adversary, Ram (the saviour of India's multitudes through his 'divine vengeance'). Maurice did acknowledge that Ram Setu's creation could very well also be attributed to 'some stupendous convulsion of nature.'[74] However, he saw greater value in equating the ancient Greek notion of metempsychosis to the powers of Ram, who, in *Valmiki Ramayan*, had revived the dead warriors of Hanuman's army after Ravan's defeat.

No matter how unbelievable, the theory of a semi-human and semi-divine bridge promulgated by the Orientalists had a broad church of acceptance. Reverend John Robinson, the principal of Ravenstonedale school in Cumbria, had no hesitation to call Ram Setu a creation of 'the almighty Rama' in the *Modern History, for the Use of Schools* (1807).[75] Likewise, Maria Graham (the

---

[73]Maurice, *The History of Hindostan*, pp. 241–242.
[74]Ibid., pp. 242; 235; 249.
[75]Robinson, *Modern History*, p. 118.

daughter of the British East India Company's naval chief George Dundas, and wife of Thomas Graham, a Scottish naval officer), in her *Letters on India* (1814), boldly avowed that 'Rama's Bridge' constructed by 'the indefatigable Hanuman' was altered by 'Mussulmans' and 'Christians' as 'the Bridge of Adam'.[76] More affirmations of the Orientalist stance came in William Ward's *History, Literature, and Religion of the Hindoos* (1817) and Robert W. Pogson's *A History of the Boondelas* (1828). For Ward and Pogson, Hanuman's army 'tore up the neighbouring mountains, and cast them into sea,' as he 'brought three mountains on his head at once, each 64 miles in circumference, and one on each shoulder, equally large, together with one under each arm, one in each paw, and one on his tail.'[77] Similar histories of India written during this period regularized the *Ramayan* legacy in ordinary registers of British connoisseurly attraction to the Orient. But the Orientalist imagination of Ram Setu had to grapple with vociferous and, sometimes vituperative challengers.

INDOPHOBES IN DENIAL

Unlike Wilkins and Jones, Robert Percival, who was based in Ceylon, wrote his *Account of the Island of Ceylon* (1803) to carve a sovereign identity for British Ceylon. And so, he prioritized its Abrahamic legends. In Percival's reading of the Adamic association with Ram Setu, 'Ceylon, at a distant period, formed a part of the continent, and was separated from it by some great convulsion of nature.' He reasoned so after having pondered on 'the narrowness of the intervening space, and the numberless shallows with which it abounds,' which made him reckon 'that some violent earthquake or, what is still more

---

[76]Graham, *Letters on India*, pp. 141–142.
[77]Ward, *History, Literature, and Religion*, 215; Pogson, *A History of the Boondelas*, p. 3.

likely, some extraordinary irruption of the ocean, might have placed Ceylon at its present distance from the continent.'[78] This explanation for calling the structure Adam's Bridge was equally valid for naming it after Ram. But Percival might have been more prepared to accept the British artist Captain Charles Gold's vision of *Ramayan* than that of Jones.

Gold's *Oriental Drawings* (1806) mimed sections of Maurice's *history* of Ram Setu in the description to his depiction of Hanuman. However, Gold surreptitiously affixed to it an excerpt from Robert Orme's *History of Military Transactions of the British Nation in Hindostan* (1745), which called the Hindu pantheon 'a heap of the greatest absurdities', whose fables were 'extravagant and incoherent', except dashes of 'moral or metaphysical allegory'.[79] In a similar vein, William Vincent, the dean of Westminster and author of an eminent translation of the Greco-Roman history, *The Periplus of the Erythræan Sea* (circa 100–300 AD), dubbed Ram's march 'to Ceylon and his victory over Rhavan' as 'one of the wildest fables of Hindoo mythology'.[80] Such disparaging views would also go on to have their minor legacies as Vincent's words were reproduced verbatim by J.W. Jones, the translator of the Italian diarist Ludovico Varthema's *Travels* (1510; trans. 1863).[81]

The bulk of the early nineteenth-century cynicism against the legend of Ram Setu characterized an early period of what has come to be classified as British Indophobia, whose 'single most important source' was James Mill's *History of British India* (1817).[82] Mill saw Indian historians as more competent in 'exaggeration' over 'exactness' and 'poetry' over 'history'.

---

[78]Percival, *An Account of the Island of Ceylon*, pp. 51–52.
[79]Gold, *Oriental Drawings*, p. 152; Orme, *A History of Military Transactions*, pp. 2–3.
[80]Vincent, *The Commerce and Navigation*, p. 502.
[81]Varthema, *The Travels*, p. 185.
[82]Trautman, *Aryans and British India*, p. 99.

Wanting in 'intellectual maturity' and any methodology of
'ancient civil history', Hindus were—in Mill's theory—greatly
indebted to the 'Mahomedan conquests' and 'Mahomedan
pens' for knowledges of their past. Thus, according to Mill,
considering 'the poems *Mahabharat* and *Ramayan*, as a sort of
historical records' would drill irresoluble gorges between the
truth of 'human affairs' and 'grotesque productions' of untruth.[83]
As for Orientalism itself, 'Mill roundly dismissed it as savagely
barbaric, thereby pointing the way to Macaulay's Minute and
the Anglicizing educational policies of the 1830s,'[84] whose
'secularizing genius' and 'evangelical ambition was to convert the
subcontinent through education—Indophobia minus God and
the Bible.' This was to be interlocked with the utilitarian strategy
of 'transforming India through legal reform.'[85] Mill also triggered
the view of occasional cynics, like Monier Monier-Williams, who
found India's otherwise epistemologically rich Puranic traditions
to be trivial.

> Its policy being to check the development of intellect,
> and keep the inferior castes in perpetual childhood, it
> encouraged an appetite for exaggeration more monstrous
> and absurd than would be tolerated in the most extravagant
> European fairy-tale. The more improbable the statement,
> the more childish delight it was calculated to awaken. This

---

[83]Mill, *The History of British India*, pp. 374–375.

[84]Scott, *Spiritual Despots*, p. 31. Those that continued to refer to Ram Setu's
Hindu sacred geography included Hamilton's *The East-India Gazetteer*, p.
453; and Fullarton, *A Gazetteer of the World*, p. 87. Others, like Arrowsmith,
A Compendium of Ancient and Modern Geography, pp. 623–24, exclusively
mentioned the Abrahamic legend instead. For early nineteenth-century
secular geological and nautical studies of Adam's Bridge, see Horsburgh, *India
Directory*, p. 398; Martin, *History of the British Colonies*, pp. 345–46; *Report
from the Select Committee on Steam Communication with India*, pp. 105–106;
and Steuart, 'A letter on steam navigation', p. 4.

[85]Sullivan, *Macaulay*, p. 141.

is more true of the *Ramayana* than of the *Mahabharata*; but even in the later epic, full as it is of geographical, chronological, and historical details, few assertions can be trusted. Time is measured by millions of years, space by millions of miles; and if a battle has to be described, nothing is thought of it unless millions of soldiers, elephants, and horses are brought into the field.[86]

REVIVING RENNELL'S DREAM

It may be tempting for both colonial apologists and nationalists to exhaust the complete spectrum of verbal assaults that the Orientalists and utilitarians heaped against each other in the guise of glorifying or denigrating an Indian civilizational character. But Ram Setu was no longer just a historical curiosity. If the eighteenth century had taught Europe anything about the tombolo, it was that much of the commercial futures of the three East India Companies that had struggled for supremacy in southern India depended on the destiny of this illusory oceanic wonder.

In 1824, the Dutch Company's commerce in Ceylon and southern India came to an end as all European businesses in the region were overtaken by the British—even though the French stayed in Pondicherry. The year also marked a turning point in the intellectual history of Ram Setu as colonial geologists from India and Ceylon started exploring the Pamban Channel more rigorously to realize Rennell's dream of a quicker sea-route between Pamban and Mannar.

What might bewilder Hindutvavadis of the twenty-first century is that even around 1830, dredging Ram Setu was not an emotional religious matter for Hindu merchants of southern India and Ceylon. Alexander Johnston's dispatch in the *Transactions of the Royal Asiatic Society* (1827) used this as

---

[86]Monier-Williams, *Indian Epic Poetry*, p. 53.

the ground to recommend 'restoring the northern, eastern, and western provinces of Ceylon to their ancient state of agricultural improvement, by affording to the Hindu capitalists of Jaffna, and the opposite peninsula of India, such privileges and immunities' to aid the resurgence of 'their ancient state of commercial prosperity, by establishing free ports in the most convenient parts of the island.' This could re-envisage 'the chank and pearl fisheries on the coasts of Ceylon and Madura' as what was seen by pre-medieval Indian entrepreneurs—'the great emporium of all the trade which was carried on by them with Egypt, Arabia, Persia, and the coast of Malabar, on one side; and the coast of Coromandel, the eastern shores of the Bay of Bengal, Malacca, Sumatra, Java, the Moluccas, and China, on the other side.'[87]

Throughout the 1820s, the Mannar and Pamban channels were surveyed by the British Indian and Ceylonese governments. Successive expeditions were headed by Sir Arthur Cotton of the Madras Engineers, Captain Dawson of the Royal Engineers, and Captain James Steuart, a master attendant at Colombo. A report dated 5 December 1822, by H. Fullerton, civil engineer of the Southern Division, Trichinopoly District, to the Inspector of Civil Estimates, hastily recommended that Ram Setu was 'well adapted to blasting' since the structure was anyhow 'undermined by the action of the water' and abraded into 'natural arches'.[88]

Fullerton's naiveté was, at least partially, influenced by the Cornish doctor, chemist and inventor John Davy, who represented the Benthamite camp of the newly emerged utilitarian ideology; his view of Ram Setu was warped by lenses of that colour. In 1821, Fullerton had argued that:

> It is natural to enquire, do the same animals occur in Ceylon as on the adjoining continent of India?—In respect to the mammalia, I am not aware that any species unknown on the

[87]Johnston, 'A Letter to the Secretary', pp. 537–538.
[88]Fullerton, 'Report dated 5 December 1822'.

continent is to be found in Ceylon, though there are several unknown in the latter, that are common on the continent; for instance, the royal tiger, the wolf, and different species of antelope. From the absence of these animals, it has been argued by some, that Ceylon was never an integral part of India. But the circumstance of the majority of the mammalia of the continent and of the island being the same, is a better reason to suppose, that they were once united and that the narrow and shallow strait which now separates them, was formed at a period not very remote in the history of our globe. Indeed, no one who looks at a map, and sees the little distance between the nearest points of the island and continent, and how, by the chain of rocks and sand-banks, commonly called Adam's Bridge, they are still imperfectly connected, can entertain much doubt, that the connection was once perfect. This enquiry is rather curious than useful. It would be much more useful, to endeavour to complete that which nature has begun, and make the channel, which is now so obstructed and dangerous, clear and safe, and fit for the purposes of coast-navigation. The accomplishment of this is said to be impossible. It may be so; yet I cannot help thinking, that the decision has been rather hasty and premature, and made from imperfect information. An object surely of such importance should not be relinquished, till its impracticability is demonstrated; and I believe no very minute survey has been made of the channel to warrant any decided opinion on the subject.[89]

Even this flawed exegesis was not original. It recapitulated Colonel Colin Mackenzie, a Scottish army officer in the British East India Company, and the first surveyor general of India.

---

[89]Davy, *An Account of the Interior of Ceylon*, pp. 78–79.

Mackenzie, respectfully saw 'Ramiserum' as 'the land of demi-
gods and *Dewatas*.' However, he was also the pioneer of the
notion that Ram Setu needed to be 'rendered useful' to a 'means
of deepening the channels, or preventing their being filled up
when deepened, by the sand thrown in by the S.W. and N.W.
monsoon.'[90] Inspired by Mackenzie's confidence, Davy considered
any thought of abandoning plans of dredging Ram Setu to be
'rather hasty and premature.' Ironically, even as late as 1835, Ram
Setu's mysterious 'chain of rocks and sand-banks' would remain
inaccessible to dredging operations due to heavy surf.[91]

In 1829, Major Sim, inspector general of Madras Engineers,
authored the 'Report on the Straits Which Separate the Ramnad
Province in the Peninsula of India from the Island of Ceylon'.
Sim believed that although dredging operations could 'obtain
anywhere through the straits a channel sufficiently deep for
all classes of ships,' it would not secure 'the practicability of
opening such a channel, and of keeping it open.' Even a 'strong
double bulwark of stones across the bank, extending into deep
water on both sides, with a narrow opening of 100 or 200 feet'
would be disarmed by the action of coralline and sedimentary
masses.[92] Sim saw Ram Setu as 'a very extraordinary formation'
made up 'entirely of sand, partly above and below the water',
guileful enough to be able to magically reconstruct the 'bridge'
if dredging was ever carried out.

Wise as he was, Sim advised against dredging Ram Setu
and, instead, canalizing the 'strait between Ramisseram and
the Ramnad coast', because the former alignment would pose
such a great economic drain that 'could only be justified by its
being considered an object of high national importance to have a

[90]Mackenzie, 'Remarks on Some Antiquities', 429; Davy, *An Account of the
Interior of Ceylon*, pp. 78–79.
[91]'Survey of the Gulf of Mannar', p. 379.
[92]Sim, 'Report on the Straits', p. 9.

passage sufficiently deep in time of war for the largest vessels.'[93] Sim's report reaffirmed Dawson's opinion that 'any opening through' Ram Setu would be 'brought back to its present state, by the storms which usually prevail at the commencement of the monsoons.'[94] Despite the forewarnings, the administrations of both territories remained inexplicably determined to find a marine passage across Ram Setu, only to be disillusioned in expedition after expedition.

Ram Setu may not have been conducive for a navigable passage. But that did not stop the surveys from yielding stunning fortuitous discoveries. One of these was the uninterrupted diggings of deadened chanks in the Jaffna Peninsula after 1820.[95] Being so prevalent as an icon in Indic ritualistic uses of conch, these added a mystical authority to cultural memories harking back to the times of *Ramayan* and *Mahabharat* that Mill seemed to have so forcefully slammed. Another astonishing finding was that of a gigantic antique anchor discovered in the Jaffna Peninsula, in 1845, that was interpreted to constitute evidence of the Palk Strait being passable, as once alleged by Baldaeus. While the British surveys chose to keep both Indic folklore and Dutch secular legends at arm's length, both seemed to resurface with each new discovery.

The Madras administration, meanwhile, tasted minor successes in its plan to obtain a quicker maritime passage between Ceylon and India. Some aspects of the Pamban Pass were blasted in the 1830s with an English dredger, Calcutta steamers, and a 'gang of convicts at Ramisseram', under the supervision of Colonel William Monteith of the Madras Engineers.[96] Remarking

---

[93]Ibid., p. 7.

[94]Campbell, *Excursions, Adventures, and Field sports*, p. 87.

[95]Suckling, *Ceylon*, p. 60.

[96]Pridham, *An Historical, Political, and Statistical Account of Ceylon*, pp. 507–508. Also see De Butts, *Rambles in Ceylon*, pp. 102–104. For an account of the blasting operations at the Pamban Passage, see chief engineer Colonel

on the blasting, a British chronicler noted that where destiny had 'in a sportive or capricious mood, barred or endangered the progress of man, it is to be observed, she has ever summoned forth increased energy and resolution in her children for the encounter.'[97] Yet, Ram Setu was to be unconquered by the British. Hence, the chronicler did not shy away from calling it 'Rama's Bridge', besides citing the 'Hindoo' reasons for revering the structure and the numinous names bestowed by 'natives'— '"Tiroowanai" or the sacred embankment' and '"Seetpandanam" or the structure of Seeta.'[98]

Meanwhile, Colonel Monteith's manoeuvres had laid open the Pamban Passage to colonial ships. By 1840, over 50,000 tonnes of commodities were being trafficked between the Indian mainland, Dhanushkodi and Ceylon.[99] On 15 January 1843, the Indian magnate, Prince Dwarkanath Tagore, registered himself as one of the first passengers to cross the Pamban Passage— only deep 'with nine feet water'—in a British steamer without orbiting Ceylon.[100] But even as late as 1870, a year after the inauguration of the Suez Canal, Rennell's dream was nowhere close to fruition. The Madras and Ceylon authorities were still mulling over the next survey in line to crack the mysteries of Ram Setu that could permit a rapider traffic of coolies and goods.[101] An ancient, immutable waterscape—that would continue to serve as the crossroads of myth, memory and ambition for numerous decades to come—had so far halted the British

---

W. Monteith's 'Account of the Operations for Widening the Channel of the Pamban Passage', pp. 111–142.

[97]Pridham, *An Historical, Political, and Statistical Account of Ceylon*, p. 507.

[98]Ibid., pp. 503–505.

[99]Capper, 'Outline of the Commercial Statistics,' p. 432.

[100]*The Asiatic Journal*, April 1843, p. 436.

[101]According to one estimate, about 27,000 coolies were crossing the Pamban Channel, annually, by the 1890s. See, Taylor, 'The West Coast of Hindustan Pilot', p. 106.

Empire's juggernaut from transplanting the Suez experience on to the Sethusamudram Sea. What was in store now for the maritime monument of Sage Valmiki's epic?

Perhaps 'The Bridge-builders' of Rudyard Kipling knew the answer. Or, perhaps, they did not...

BUILDING THE SECOND
RAM SETU

The London and China Telegraph of 3 June 1873 went full throttle at deconstructing the century-old ambition of a navigable sea route between Dhanushkodi and Thalaimannar. Its publication of two successive reports on the slackening proposals to deepen the Pamban Passage meant that shareholders, company directors and lawmakers at Westminster were keenly observing the developments in and around the Madras Presidency. The goal had become too elusive.

Back in 1860—the report began—Commander A.D. Taylor of the Indian Marine had mooted fresh plans of dredging Ram Setu. What the report skipped mentioning was that when he was summoned by a Select Committee at the House of Commons, on 22 May 1862, to be asked his opinion on dredging Ram Setu, his views were ambiguous: on the one hand, he endorsed it, but on the other, he added that the Sethusamudram Sea was especially prone to 'fearful' hurricanes and cyclones.[102] However, the report alluded to Major Sim's report (cited in Taylor's proposal) and a proposal by Major Townsend (1861) for dredging the channel—both Sim and Townsend had strongly advised against it. Nevertheless, following Taylor's deposition before the Select Committee, the governor of Madras, William Dennison, commissioned another study of the feasibility of

---

[102]*Report from the Select Committee*, p. 31.

dredging Ram Setu. It revealed that there were other suitable sites in the Palk Strait to dredge the channel. Townsend, who had already prepared a budget, estimated the cost of dredging to be about £1.4 million sterling.

GEOLOGY TURNS MYSTICAL

A year before the reports were published in *The London and China Telegraph*, a new government survey assigned by harbor engineer George Robertson, and executed by Messrs. Stoddart and Robertson, also advised against channelling Ram Setu. They recommended dredging the Pamban Pass, near Rameswaram, more for reasons of economy. The revised budget was reduced to less than £700,000 sterling, first, and less than £500,000, later, for dredging approximately 2 million cubic yards.[103] The administrations of Ceylon and Madras seemed desperate to operationalize the 'Paumben Channel' to 'save 700 miles of distance' and profit 'handsomely from the first month' of its inauguration.[104] But this was simply not acceptable to the powers that be.

Ask engineers, geologists, economists and economic historians, and you will find a *rational* answer. Turn to the cultural zeitgeist instead, and you might hear what probably defies logic. It was no longer possible to censor the association of Valmiki's Vaishnavite avatar with the allegedly lifeless shoals of Sethusamudram. It is no coincidence that three years before the above reports declared a state of urgency, the celebrated Indologist Ralph Thomas Hotchkin Griffith's translation of *The Ramayan of Valmiki* (1870) was published. The son of an English chaplain, Griffith was a Boden Professor of Sanskrit at the University of Oxford, and later, principal of the Benares College.

---

[103]'The Paumben Channel', 3 June, p. 357
[104]'The Paumben Channel', 9 June, p. 376.

Griffith's task as a professor was to aid in the conversion of Indians to Christianity. But he understood his mission somewhat tangentially. He became one of the first Europeans to seriously translate Vedic texts and Sanskrit literature, including Kalidas's *Kumara Sambhava*. In his later life, Griffith was to retire to the hill station of Kotagiri, in the Nilgiris, and is believed to have lived here till the end of his life with his brother, Frank Griffith. The latter, an engineer in Bombay's public works department, was unlikely to have been unaware of the developments in the Pamban region. Nor was Ralph Griffith.

It would be an understatement to claim that Griffith's translation stirred the public imagination. Among other episodes that reverberated in the minds of his readers was Valmiki's narrative of Ram Setu's construction by Nala and his troop of hominids. Two scientific essays of paramount importance, published in the decade following Griffith's translation—Edward Balfour's *Cyclopædia of India* (1873) and the *Memoirs of the Geological Survey of India* (1883)—not only avoided challenging Pamban's sacred Indic geography but also actively interpreted scientific facts as if tailored for a religious renaissance. Until about the 1840s, it was nearly impossible to convince British geologists even to agree that India and Ceylon were once connected by the will of nature. But now scientific logic went as far as acknowledging that Ram Setu might indeed have been a hybrid between natural and human engineering.

Griffith was not the only one to popularize the Sanskritic tradition in the 1870s. There was also his fellow Oxonian, the German scholar Max Mueller, whose *Sacred Books of the East* (containing the Upanishads and other Indic classics) began being published in 1879—the same year that Edwin Arnold published the Buddha's poetical biography, *The Light of Asia*. It was not entirely startling, therefore, to see the Geological Survey of India referring to the 'series of large flat blocks which so strongly resemble a series of gigantic steppingstones,' presumably indicating 'that the rocky ridge was really an old causeway of human construction.'[105] In that perspective, the construction that Valmiki had narrated in his *Ramayan* was 'well within the limits of historical possibility', since there was 'no apparent reason why the proved upheaval of Rama's bridge may not have taken place within the semi-mythical time preceding some invasion of the heretical Buddhist kingdom of Lanka (Ceylon) by the Brahmanical Aryans of the mainland and their Dravidian allies.'[106]

It did not end there.

The eminent German geologist Johannes Walther published his study of Ram Setu in the *Records of the Geological Survey of India* (1890), where he characterized the tombolo as an organic creation, though probably reconstructed a few times by mortal hands across millennia.

> [Ram Setu] existed once, a long time ago; that it was destroyed by unexplained causes, and that the fragments were again recemented only to be broken asunder again in the beginning of the fifteenth century ... a land connection between India and Ceylon existed twice, and has been twice interrupted, and that more than one migration of the fauna from India to Ceylon could have taken place.[107]

Walther's study will not qualify as the evidence to believe in Ram Setu's Puranic origins. However, it did qualify, back then especially, as a strong rejoinder to all theories—geological, economic, or navigational—that made invisible the environmental, geological and historical legacies of Ram Setu. The new idiom of late nineteenth-century geologists paved the way for an unforeseen theory. This was that Ceylon was once a part of the Indian Deccan plateau, and had been laid asunder

---

[105]'The Sub-recent Marine Beds', p. 74.
[106]Ibid.
[107]Walther, 'Report of a Journey', p. 116.

by primitive volcanic activity, and apparently, such convulsions had slung several minor, low-lying islets between Mannar and Rameswaram that could be spanned by Ram's draftsmen with materials obtained from the Deccan and the Western Ghats.[108]

Understandably, the latter part of this theory lies beyond the purview of serious professional geologists. But doubts might be cast even on its former part—the empirical suggestion that Ceylon was amputated from India by forces of nature. Nevertheless, in the early twentieth century, there emerged a transdisciplinary discursive trend of a primordial overland route between Ceylon and India. See, for instance, the famous British ornithologist and civil servant W.E. Wait's article in *Spolia Zeylanica*, that straddled avian history and geology, to conclude that Ram Setu was a 'dry land until the dawn of historical times', before marine 'encroachments by the sea off Mannar and Colombo'. However, as he added, 'within a measurable distance of historic times, re-elevation set in, and continuous communication was again established with India.'[109]

This, too, did not imply that the resumption of the land-route was due to Ram and his vanar sena building a bridge across the Sethusamudram Sea. But what this theory did was to marginalize the Dutch theory that the Palk Strait was permeable by sea in times known to humankind, while subtly paving the way for theories of Indian invasions of Ceylon via a land route in recorded phases of human history. Simultaneously, such theories complemented the more fabulist voices from the nineteenth century, like the popular historian J. Talboys Wheeler, whose *History of India* (1867) recognized Valmiki's 'bridge' as one that was based on 'a contemplation of the physical geography of the locality', or the English feminist and Indophile Mrs Charlotte Manning Speir, who had spryly

---

[108]Das, *Note on the Ancient Geography of India*, pp. 46–48.
[109]Wait, 'The Distribution of Birds in Ceylon', p. 28.

designated the sandbars of Dhanushkodi as the 'vestiges of Rama's bridge'.[110]

For readers—impatiently trying to process the relevance of these new findings, lexicons, and leaps of imagination apropos of the legend of Ram Setu—what might suffice is that while none of these could scientifically prove the supernaturality of the bridge, Rennell's dream of a navigational canal project was now a ghost story, where the British Empire's march into the twentieth century had been dared and forced to retreat by naturalist forces.

A MOST CREDIBLE LEGEND

As dead ends became the norm in each subsequent survey of the Pamban region, the legend of Ram Setu spread across the Anglosphere—it may not be an exaggeration to say—like forest fire. In the wake of Griffith's translation of *Ramayan*, the late Victorian French cartographer Elisée Reclus (1876–94) reproduced Pamban's map, naming the sandbars between Dhanushkodi and Thalaimannar as the 'Bridge of Rama', instead of Adam's Bridge, in *The Earth, a Descriptive History of the Phenomena of the Life of the Globe* (1886) and *The Universal Geography: Earth and its Inhabitants* (1876–1894). This was a major leap, since European cartography of the region, for nearly a century, had avoided the semiotics of Indic traditions. Following Griffith, Reclus's cartographical reform, as it were, banished the inhibitions of an imperial regime that no longer seemed to have any qualms about celebrating the antiquity of the jewel in the crown.

For instance, in 1880, the eminent English antiquarian Thomas Wright's translation of *The Travels of Marco Polo* (first published in 1854) reminded the English-speaking works that 'Rama's bridge', which, though fallen into 'disuse', could

---

[110]Speir, *Life in Ancient India*, p. 117; Wheeler, *History of India*, p. 358.

be found as a subject of discussion 'in the works of all the oriental geographers and historians who have treated this part of India.' Later that year, the *New York Herald* correspondent Thomas Wallace Knox counted Hanuman's construction of Ram Setu—'of ten mountains, each measuring sixty-four miles in circumference'—among the 'miracles in Hindoo mythology'.[111] While this itself was not so remarkable, what stood out was the sheer absence of belittling insinuations and other shades of cynicism that had characterized Western representations of Indic legends in James Mill's heyday.

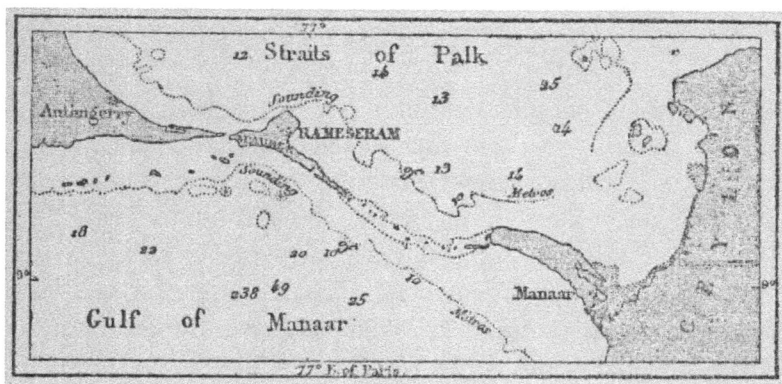

Fig. 16: Map of Adam's Bridge named as 'Bridge of Adam or Rama', in Elisée Reclus's *The Earth, A Descriptive History of the Phenomena of the Life of the Globe* (1886)

In 1881, the *American Library of Universal Knowledge* joined the bandwagon that seemed to prefer the term 'Ramasetu' to the now unfashionable 'Adam's Bridge'. It even went on to add, albeit erroneously, that the bridge was the outcome of Hanuman's feat of transplanting Himalayan pillars onto the Indian Ocean. Published in 1886, the *Hobson-Jobson* made Ram Setu the pretext for occasional glimpses of India's sacred

---

[111]Wright, *Travels of Marco Polo*, pp. 380–381; Knox, *The Boy Travellers*, pp. 56–57.

geography—possibly derived from Thomas Maurice's *Indian Antiquities*—harking back to a eleventh-century copperplate from Kalyana's Chalukya dynasty, bearing the inscription '"from the Himalaya to the Bridge" i.e., the Bridge of Ram.'[112] In 1896, even *The Strand Magazine* reasserted the present-day straits to be the 'remnant of the bridge'.[113] Six years later, no less than the journal *Indian Engineering* hailed 'Rama, the Indian Hercules' as having 'succeeded in doing in a single night what would baffle the modern Engineer on the score of cost.'

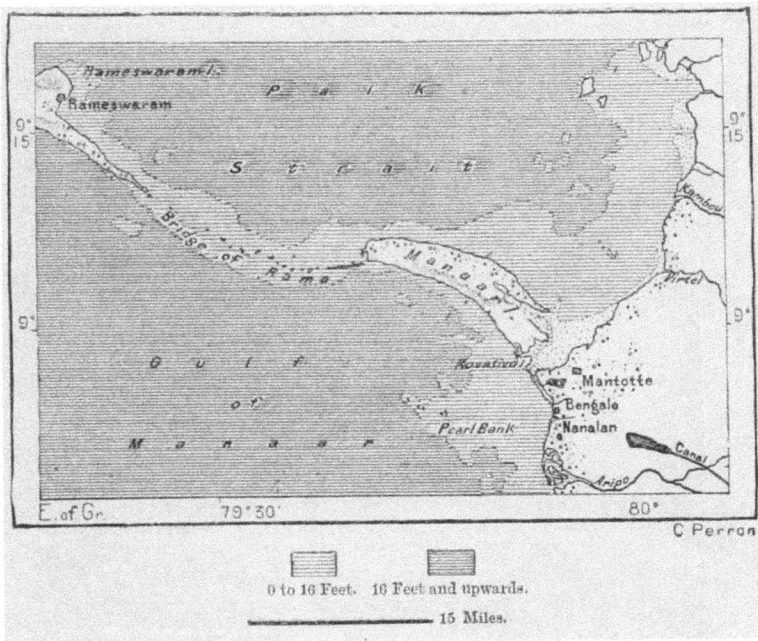

Fig. 17: Map of Adam's Bridge named as 'Bridge of Rama', in Elisée Reclus's *The Universal Geography: Earth and Its Inhabitants* (1876–94), *Vol. 8: India and Indo-China*

---

[112]Yule and Burnell, *Hobson-Jobson*, p. 433.
[113]'Idols', pp. 514–515.

Fig. 18: The approach to Rameswaram Temple as depicted in T.W. Knox's
The Boy Travellers in the Far East (1880)

By the turn of the century, the knowledge of Ram Setu's
impenetrability to colonial technology was no longer confined
to geologists and engineers. Popular voices like the American

author Mara L. Pratt remarked that the colonial government had 'already proposed cutting through this reef to allow large vessels to pass through; but the cost will be so great, that great as would be the convenience to commerce, it will not be done for some time.'[114] Naturally, then, even British engineers became amenable to accept in public that 'the ancient origin of the desire to connect the south of India with the northern part of the island of Ceylon' probably dated back to some Indian avatar.[115] And so, the amateur English archaeologist Henry William Cave virtually wrote the obituary of the utilitarian disinclination to 'accept the theory that Paumben Passage was once blocked by an artificial causeway, over which millions of pilgrims came to visit the sacred Rameswaram.' Cave specifically set his theory in the context of the millennial puzzle left by *Valmiki Ramayan*'s 'Yuddha Kanda'.

As if popular commentaries were not enough, *The Numismatist*'s September 1905 issue reported on a rare '"Setu" bull coin, said to have been issued by the Sethupathi Lords of Ramnad, and hereditary guardians' of Ram Setu,[116] which had been discovered, recapitulating Pamban's links with its antiquity. In a perfectly rational world, devoid of the capacity for hankering after meaning, narratology, poetic imagination, and everyday symbolism, many of these assertions and findings could simply have been left to ripen as disconnected museumized intellectual relics. But being attached to the *Ramayan* legacy, the agglomeration of these bricks of data validated a colossal meme in the public psyche—the scene of the hominid figure of Nala overseeing a bridge dedicated to Lord Ram being built by countless apes and creatures of the wild that had willingly dispensed their freedom for the reestablishment of Dharma.

---

[114]Pratt, *People and Places: India*, p. 130.
[115]'Communication Between India and Ceylon', p. 147.
[116]Pieris, 'Coins of Ceylon', p. 264.

Many strains of this uninterrupted symphony of enthusiasm for the *Ramayan* legacy echoed previous commentators. One such, the indefatigable Orientalist Robert Needham Cust, fashioned Ram as the Indian 'Hercules'. Cust's analogy, in turn, echoed Gaspare Gorresio, the Italian Indologist, whose article in *The Calcutta Review* of 1854 had christened 'Ramesurum' as 'the pillar of Rama', thus being of such 'great repute and renown as the pillars of the Western Hercules.'[117] Between 1880 and the onset of the Great War, an eclectic range of journalists, intellectuals, scientists, geologists, archaeologists, and even zoologists counted Ram Setu as a key itinerary in their studies of the Pamban region—and yes, many of them did make it a point to reflect on the legend of Ram Setu, in perceptibly respectful tones, while manifestly avoiding any discussion of the Adamic mythology.

RETURN OF THE BRIDGE-BUILDERS

Interestingly, Rudyard Kipling, the man who gave coinage to the 'white man's burden', himself made use of Valmiki's landmark, though referring to it in the old Abrahamic style in his *Departmental Ditties* (1890): 'From Adam's Bridge to Peshawur'. But what made Kipling stand out was the surreal link between his work of fiction, the short story 'The Bridge-Builders' (1893), and a real bridge built over the Palk Strait. In Kipling's story, colonial bridge builders are shown to brave the vagaries of Indian climate and perceived superstitions while building a bridge over river Ganga, at Kashi, along with the blessings of the gods of Hindustan. Almost as a case of reality imitating art, the British colonial regime, which had by the beginning of twentieth century virtually given up on its plans of canalizing Ram Setu, now proceeded to build a second historic overland

---

[117]*Library of Universal Knowledge*, p. 127; Cust, *Linguistic and Oriental Essays*, p. 100; Gorresio, *Ramayana*, pp. 209–210.

bridge across the Indian Ocean. The final nail in the coffin of Rennell's dream came on 2 October 1906, when M.M.S. Gubbay, the colonial Indian government's under-secretary, contacted the Ceylon Chamber of Commerce's secretary, to inform him that the idea of dredging the Sethusamudram Sea had been substituted with the plan of extending 'the South Indian Railway to Rameswaram', with the help of a cantilever bridge. The task was projected to cost ₹4,200,000.[118]

By now, both British geology and popular histories seemed amenable to Puranic legends. The time seemed ripe for British engineers to reenact the *Ramayan* legacy. Four years before Gubbay's letter, works had already commenced for constructing a giant cantilever bridge across the Pamban Channel. Railway officials and workhands with prior experience of working on Himalayan railroads were employed on this momentous project. British companies exported assembled parts from Europe 143 erected pillars and a Scherzer rolling bascule—built on the design patented by American engineer William Scherzer—were integrated in the middle to facilitate the navigation of large vessels across the passage.[119]

It may wrongly appear that the Madras administration and the South Indian Railway (which funded the Pamban Bridge) suddenly woke up to the possibility of an overland bridge instead of a marine canal at the dawn of the twentieth century. But a railway link between Ceylon and India had been mulled over since at least the 1880s. Two principal reasons explained the colonial administration's eagerness to build the railway bridge between mainland India and Rameswaram Island—that could be hopefully extended to Ceylon.

The first was that, on 1 January 1880, a new railway route was inaugurated between Madras and Tuticorin

---

[118]'Proposed Canal through the Island of Rameswaram', pp. 50–51.
[119]Baxter, *A History of the World*, p. 95.

(of less than 22 hours)—on the route of the present-day Pearl City Express—with a 24-hour-long steamer connection to Colombo. Naturally, the administration wanted to retain the momentum of this engineering exploit. The second reason was the traffic of labourers from the Madras Presidency to Ceylon. Much of this was recruited for Ceylonese tea plantations owned by Lipton, Mazawattee, and other leading tea companies. Their stakes had only swelled by the end of the 1880s, as the joint exports of Indo-Ceylonese tea varieties to Britain overtook Chinese tea exports in the face of increased Sino-British political unease.

Between 1893 and 1905, the South Indian Railway Company carried out surveys of both Adam's Bridge and Rameswaram Island. These corroborated the profitability of having a railway connection between mainland India and Rameswaram, and further between Dhanushkodi and Colombo, via Thalaimannar, through a ferry service in between. In 1907, the South Indian Railway's chairperson—Sir Henry Kimber—was petitioned by a delegation of British-Ceylonese tea merchants, who encouraged him to plan for better communication between the two territories for seamless traffic of Indian workers to Ceylonese estates. The meeting paved the way for further discussions between secretary of state Lord Morley, colonial secretary Lord Elgin, and officials of the Ceylon Government Railway Company.

As planning and works for the connection of Mandapam with Rameswaram and Dhanushkodi were already underway, the company agreed to undertake the building of a nearly 70-mile branch line from Ceylon's Madawachiya to Thalaimannar. Since Ram Setu could not be canalized, the administrations of India and Ceylon hoped to use a different strategy to tame the oceanic marvel which separated the two territories by 21 miles.

The new consensus that emerged was if a railway bridge could be constructed between Dhanushkodi and Thalaimannar, over a solid embankment, gradually Ram Setu would accrue greater precipitation of sand, limestone and coralline detritus, triggering the formation of an overland terrain connecting the two islands naturally.

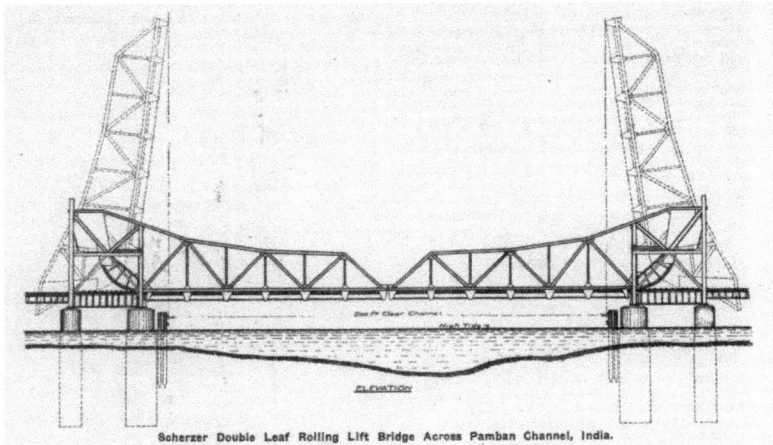

Scherzer Double Leaf Rolling Lift Bridge Across Pamban Channel, India.

Fig. 19: Model of 'Scherzer Double Leaf Rolling Lift Bridge Across Pamban Channel, India', in the *Railway Age Gazette,* **20** March 1913

With this hope, the South Indian Railway conducted another survey, in 1913, to study the feasibility of a bridge between Dhanushkodi and Thalaimannar, spanning a little over 20 miles— about 7.2 miles on the shallow sands of the scattered reefs and the remaining on water. On 17 July 1914, the Massachusetts-based newspaper, *The Newton Graphic,* reported: 'to facilitate the work of sinking the bridge cylinders, an artificial island, made of coral boulders and concrete in sacks, was created, one on each side of the stretch of water.' While the coralline reefs posed no obstruction to the construction, the parts of the bridge over the sea were planned to be aided by a dual row of reinforced concrete pillars joined by light concrete arches, chains and transverse ties, with reinforced concrete slabs attached behind the pillars, and the bottom slabs submerged in the oceanic bed.

A Gigantic Bridge Project.

The great project of bridging over alk's strait, separating the island of eylon from the mainland of India, or which such important advantages re claimed, is said to be again under insideration by the Government of eylon. The strait is some forty-one miles broad at its narrowest point, eing double the width of the English hannel; but it is very shallow, in many places being not more than six feet deep. The island reefs and channels in it have been recently accurately surveyed and mapped, and the cost of he work, extending over sixty-one miles, including the Pamban Channel and the Adam's Bridge reef, is estimated to reach some 28,000 rupees. The plan of work contemplates the connection of the eight miles of railroad with Ceylon's great harbor of Ceylon, and by ninety miles of Modura, the nearest point on the Indian railroad system, on the narrow gauge is used this calculated, for 11,000 or more.

Lord Morley has sanctioned th sed Indo-Ceylon railway in conn th the project for making a ross the Pamban Channel, and i ng a ferry between Daneshkod anaar. The South Indian Rail ancing the scheme. The Pamban l, a shallow piece of water, lies b andadam, on the Indian mainlan o island of Daneshkodi. From D di to Manar the distance to be c y the train-ferry is about thirt iles. Mannar almost adjoins the nd of Ceylon.

Build Island to Construct Bridge.

With the completion of the Pamban channel viaduct connecting Tonitural in India with Pamban on the Island of Rameswaram the first link has been forged in the railway line between the south end of the Indian peninsula and the island of Ceylon. This viaduct is 6,776 feet long. Rail connection is made across the island of Danishkodi and then by steamer t to the island of t the Ceylon rail extended.

wo k of sinking an artificial is boulders and con created, one on etch of water. ade by Indian la tractors. There ometimes by no lry between the rs.

A BRIDGE TO CEYLON.

THE great project of bridging over Palk's Strait, separating the island of Ceylon from the mainland of India, for which such important advantages are claimed, is said to be again under consideration by the Government.

The strait is some forty-one miles broad at its narrowest point, being double the width of the English Channel, but is very shallow, in many places being not more than six feet deep. The islands, reefs and channels in it have been recently accurately surveyed and mapped, and the cost of the work, extending over sixty-one miles, including the Pamban Channel and the Adam's Bridge reef, is estimated to reach some two million pounds.

Fig. 20: A flurry of reports on the Pamban Bridge. Clockwise: 'A Gigantic Bridge Project', *New Oxford Item*, 14 August 1896; 'Lord Morley has Sanctioned...', *The China Mail*, 14 July 1909; 'A Bridge to Ceylon', *Pearson's Weekly*, 11 July 1896; 'Build Island to Construct Bridge', *The Newton Graphic*, 17 July 1914

Fig. 21: Images of the Scherzer Rolling Lift Bridge over the Pamban Channel, in *The Engineer*, 7 August 1914

The height of the proposed Indo-Ceylonese railway bridge was estimated to be six feet above sea level, supposedly encouraging sand and coralline deposits that could eventually amount to a

new, artificial island, connecting the islands of Rameswaram and
Mannar. The projected cost of the bridge was ₹28 million, with
an additional ₹11 million for a railroad connection from Madurai
to Colombo.[120] However, the First World War intervened, and
the plans of this bridge were given up in favour of the Pamban
Bridge. Instead, two piers each were built at Dhanushkodi and
Thalaimannar for a steamer service connecting the railways of
the two territories. One of these was built on the north side, for
the months of the southwest monsoon, and another was built
on the south side, for the months of the northeast monsoon.
Initially, this steamer service was intended to convey the entire
train, but the plan was altered to make it a passenger service.

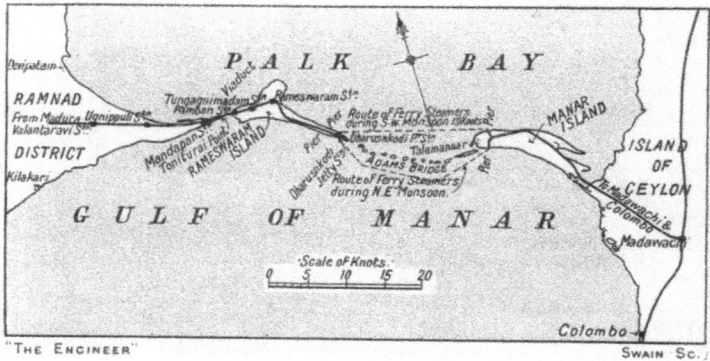

Fig. 22: Map of the proposed route of the Indo-Ceylon Railway, in *The Engineer*,
7 August 1914

A PREHISTORIC MONUMENT?

In February 1914, the Pamban Bridge was finally inaugurated.
The bridge was designed by the Scherzer Rolling Lift Bridge
Company of Chicago and built by Head, Wrightson & Co.
Ltd. of Thornaby-on-Tees, incorporated in Britain. The bridge

---

[120]'Bridges', p. 293.

shortened the space between Colombo and Tuticorin from 270
to about 50 kilometres. The bridge comprised 145 spans with
openings of 40 to 44 feet in width. Building the viaduct, the
Scherzer bridge, the piers, the railroad link from Rameswaram
to Dhanushkodi, and steamship connectivity, was undertaken
at a cost of £466,666 sterling.[121] During the inauguration, the
governor of Madras, the governor of Ceylon, and the managing
director of the South Indian Railway Company paid lavish
tributes to the *Valmiki Ramayan* and its hero, Lord Ram. Given
the kind of speeches that these colonial dignitaries delivered
and given the sort of media coverage that the event garnered in
India, Britain and America, the British imperial administration
seemed to pride itself on having virtually authored a new Indian
epic on the lines of the *Ramayan*.

Fig. 23: Advertisement by Head, Wrighton & Co. in the Christmas issue of
The Engineer, 1914

---

[121]'Railway Connection Between India and Ceylon', p. 525.

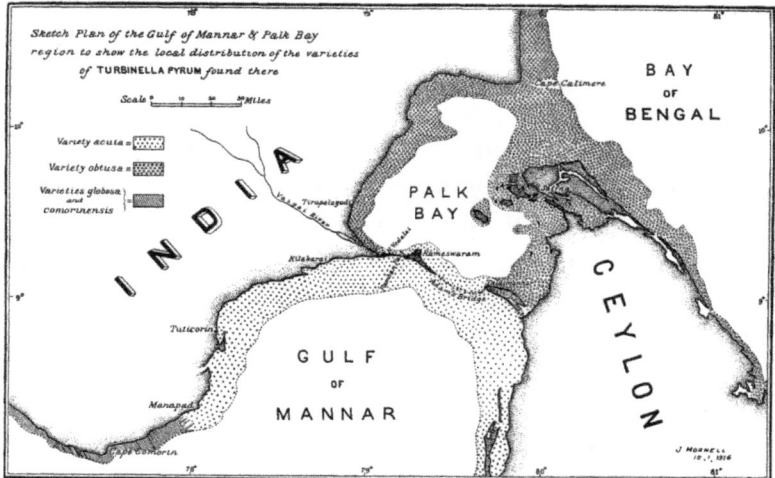

Fig. 24: Distribution of chank fisheries by James Hornell, from Edgar Thurston's *Notes on Pearl and Chank Fisheries* (1890), Plate XII

Fig. 25: Boat Mail crossing the Pamban Bridge, from N.V. Pillai's *Setu and Rameswaram* (1929), Plate VII

OPENING OF INDO-CEYLON RAILWAY.

INTERESTING SPEECHES AT
INAUGURAL CEREMONY.

(ASSOCIATED PRESS.)

MANDAPAM, Feb. 24.

The formal inauguration of the Indo-Ceylon connection took place this morning with considerable ceremony. Their Excellencies the Governors of Madras, Ceylon and Pondicherry, the Rajas of Puddukotta and Ramnad and other notabilities, European and Indian, attended.

In the course of his address Mr. Priestley, Managing Director of the South Indian Railway Company, gave a succint account of the origin of the development and the completion of the huge project. He referred to the mythological fact of the building of Adam's bridge by Rama's army of apes. In conclusion he thanked the Governors of Ceylon and Madras for their presence on this historic occasion and requested the latter to declare the railway open.

The Governor, replying, congratulated the South Indian Railway Company on their splendid achievement and feelingly referred to the absence on this occasion of Sir Henry Kimber, Director of the Company. He referred to the sympathetic support which the project has received from successive Governors of Ceylon.

At 11-30 the S. I. R. Company gave a ceremonial breakfast at which upwards of 200 guests were present. At the conclusion of the breakfast, after a loyal toast, Mr. Priestley proposed the health of the Governors to which Their Excellencies made suitable replies individually. The Governor of Pondicherry also made an impressive speech in French.

Later in the afternoon the opening of the Pamban Viaduct took place in the presence of the three Governors, after which they bade farewell to each other.

THE INDO-CEYLON CONNECTION.

The ceremony of formally declaring open the Indo-Ceylon connection at Dhanushkodi in the presence of the Governors of Madras, Ceylon and Pondicherry, reported in yesterday's telegrams, recalls the old legend in the Ramayana of the invasion of Ceylon by Rama, who commanded Hanuman to build a bridge across the sea. Immediately, so the story goes, Hanuman turned on his army of monkeys to the work, and in the incredibly short period of five days a causeway was constructed which enabled Rama to complete his journey and recover his queen. Whatever influence this legend might have had on the orthodox Hindu mind during the long passage of centuries, there is no doubt that the desire to enter into Ceylon by way of Adam's Bridge has existed from generation to generation. The question of opening the route was definitely raised in 1876. Nothing, however, was done till 1894 when an estimate was prepared by Mr. F. J. Waring, on behalf of the Ceylon Government, which showed that the cost of bridging the twenty-two miles of sea would be not less than 259 lakhs. In the following year another survey was made on behalf of the Indian Government by Mr. E. J. Shadbolt, which brought the cost down by ten lakhs. These estimates were considered a greater outlay than the anticipated traffic would justify, and the idea of bridging the sea between Ramaswaram and Manaar was for the time being abandoned. Next followed, in 1896, a survey for a line of railway from Madura to Rameswaram, and it was then suggested that a harbour should be created at Kundagat Point, which should become the port for all traffic to and from Colombo. Many variations of the scheme were from time to time suggested, and there was a good deal of controversy as to the best methods of giving effect to it, but in 1906 Mr. Neville Priestley, C.I.E., of the Southern Indian Railway, proposed a return to the original idea of a direct connection with Ceylon by the Adam's Bridge route, substituting a floating for

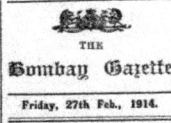

THE

Bombay Gazette

Friday, 27th Feb., 1914.

THE INDO-CEYLON RAILWAY

Of the various constructive professions engineering is probably the most freely endowed with romantic associations. The Indo-Ceylon Railway, which has just been formally opened, is not only a splendid monument to engineering skill, but it is associated with one of the most wonderful stories of ancient Hindu mythology. Rama when he pursued the giant king of Ceylon, who had abducted his wife, found his progress barred by the ocean, but summoning the aid of the monkey-god, Hanuman, he saw a bridge of rocks, earth and trees built by the monkey hosts of the forests rise within five days above the waters. By these means was Rama's army enabled to cross to Ceylon and avenge the insult which had been put upon its leader. Tradition has it that the chain of rocks now known as Adam's Bridge form the remains of the bridge miraculously built by Hanuman's workers, volcanic convulsions and the upheaval of the monsoon having accounted for the portions which have disappeared. These associations freely supplied with imagery the speakers at the opening ceremony, which three Governors attended. At the same time the accomplishment of a project which for many years baffled the ingenuity of the cleverest brains is in itself a romantic event. The desire to bridge the space between India and Ceylon naturally first arose, in modern times, in Ceylon, so much the smaller territory, and it was some thirty-eight years ago that the feasibility of the project began to be discussed there. This discussion was continued for eighteen years before any definite step was taken, and then, in 1894, an estimate was prepared, which represented the cost as 259 lakhs or one and three-quarter million pounds. A second survey in the following year reduced the cost by ten lakhs, and on account of the magnitude of these sums the scheme was given up for some time. In 1899 an alternative scheme was suggested, which with many variations continued to occupy attention until 1910, when Mr. Neville Priestley, now Managing Director of the South Indian Railway, was that Company's Agent in India. He then proposed a return to the original idea of a direct connection with Ceylon by the Adam's Bridge route, but with the important modification that a floating bridge should be substituted in the central stretch of sea for a permanent one until traffic had sufficiently developed to warrant the additional outlay which the latter would involve. The suggestion was thoroughly discussed on both sides of the Straits, and eventually it was decided that with a further modification the scheme could be carried into effect. For the time being it was considered advisable to abandon the idea of building either a permanent or a floating bridge over the

Fig. 26: Left to Right: 'Opening of Indo-Ceylon Railway', *The Bombay Chronicle*, 26 February 1914; 'The Indo-Ceylon Connection', *The Bombay Chronicle*, 27 February 1914; 'The Indo-Ceylon Railway', *The Bombay Gazette*, 27 February 1914

THE PAMBAN RAILWAY BRIDGE: A DRAWBRIDGE ACROSS THE PAMBAN CHANNEL, CONNECTING THE MAINLAND WITH AN ISLAND IN PALK STRAIT, BETWEEN INDIA AND CEYLON.

Fig. 27: 'The Pamban Railway Bridge', in *The Illustrated London News*, 16 November 1935

The South Indian Railway Company's advertising initiatives for the Pamban Bridge actively 'recapitulated the building of the Ram Setu,' making it 'an extended signifier of "India," across the Indian Ocean, into Rameshwaram, *en route* to Ceylon.'[122] Some years ago, Mohandas K. Gandhi had acclaimed Ram Setu or 'Setubandh' as a testimony to India's 'farseeing ancestors'.[123] But dignitaries of the colonial administration— that had in fact banned Gandhi's book *Hind Swaraj*—went a step ahead. When the Pamban Bridge was opened to traffic on 24 February, rich accolades were lavished on the *Ramayan* legacy and the 'mythological fact' of 'the bridge miraculously built by Hanuman.'[124] That was not all. In May 1914, the *Journal of the Royal Society of Arts* connected the Indo-Ceylon railroad's

---

[122]Chatterjee, *The Purveyors of Destiny*, p. 112.

[123]Gandhi, *Hind Swaraj*, p. 48.

[124]'Opening of Indo-Ceylon Railway', 1914; 'The Indo-Ceylon Railway', 1914.

history with 'mythological times' and 'Rama's monkey friends' who had begun the task 'thousands of years ago' and which the British administration finally saw through to its conclusion.[125]

On 1 March Dhanushkodi became a new port, enabling imports like cotton and piece-goods, eggs, vegetables, brass and aluminum goods, and preserved fish and oil from South India, which were then slated to be exported to Ceylon and beyond. A new train service was launched from Madras to Dhanushkodi, which was in turn connected to Thalaimannar by a 22-mile ferry route. The combined train-and-ferry service was named as the Ceylon India Boat Mail Express, which soon rose to eminence. Three carriages of the Boat Mail were named after three British viceroys (Curzon, Elgin and Harding). Inaugurated by the governor of Madras, Lord Petland, in April 1914, the Boat Mail was to be the precursor to the colonial railway bridge across Ram Setu. Even as far back as February 1911, *The New York Times* had informed that the Ceylonese and Indian administrations had agreed on bridging the two territories across the Sethusamudram Sea to foster smoother passage for 'coolies' and goods.[126]

Later, reports published on 17 April 1915, in *The New Statesman*, and on 26 June 1915, in *The Los Angeles Times*, indicated that the ferry service between Dhanushkodi and Thalaimannar was by no means the final end of infrastructural works in the islandic region.[127] In September 1916, the *Scientific American* added more details to the evolving scenario in an article republished in the London-based journal *Concrete and Constructional Engineering*. Accordingly, the 20 miles of 'sandbanks stretching between India and Ceylon' was still under active consideration for a railway bridge between the

---

[125]'Railway Connection Between India and Ceylon', p. 525.
[126]'An Indo-Ceylon Railway', 1911.
[127]'Indian Railways', 1915; 'A Long Bridge', 1915.

two territories given the proposed construction of a 'solid embankment' through the straits at a projected £740,000.[128] Of the 20 miles, seven were to 'be built upon the dry land of the various islands, and thirteen miles in water.'[129] Undoubtedly, negotiations to bridge Thalaimannar and Rameswaram continued relentlessly throughout the years of the Great War. Eventually, however, the plan had to be stalled owing to unforeseen engineering hazards and untamable currents. The British Empire had built the world's second-largest railway system in India. But Ram Setu would remain unconquered.[130]

A BRIDGE TO NATIONALISM

The nationalist Indian psyche—that had by now been mobilized by the last five decades of colonialist attention to Ram Setu—took to reclaiming it as a monument in popular nativist imagination. As if to reinforce the indigeneity of Ram Setu's discourse, in 1921 the Kriya Yogi Panchanan Bhattacharyya, who was also the founder of the Arya Mission, reminded that Ram Setu had been a historic landmark for 'holy temples' and 'religious establishments endowed at the expense of Ahalya Bai [the eighteenth-century regent of the Maratha Empire].'[131] Likewise, K. Rama Aiyangar, a Madras Legislative Council member, delivered a heated speech in the assembly in 1926, wherein he argued that 'long before the Railway was introduced,' Ram Setu attracted 'lakhs of pilgrims coming from all parts of India, and after the introduction of the Railway, it need not be described.' Aiyangar was speaking against the motion of repositioning the Rameswaram railway

---

[128]'By Rail to Ceylon', p. 183.

[129]Ibid.

[130]Waring, 'On the Physical Features of "Adam's Bridge"', 1917; Bristow, Brodie and Carey, 'Correspondence on the Physical Features of Adam's Bridge and the Currents Across it', 1917.

[131]Bhattacharyya, *Ideals of Indian Womanhood*, p. 281.

station, and he reasoned that the temple town attracted yearly proceeds of ₹2 million—besides the tremendous curiosity and excitement the region had garnered in the British imagination of its sacred geography.[132]

Simultaneously, Ram Setu began being reimagined by Indian and even Ceylonese nationalistic imagination as having been, quite literally, a trading outpost and military highway for South Asian kings—even if not necessarily a monument from the *Ramayan* era. 'In remote antiquity,' wrote the Lankan historian Mudaliyar C. Rasanayagam in *Ancient Jaffna* (1926), 'the coasting trade from one half of Asia to the other half must have passed by the deep passages across the Adam's Bridge or by the Straits of Mannar, and consequently, a great port must have risen on the North-west coast of Ceylon.'[133] This was five years after S. Krishnaswami Aiyangar, the well-known Indian historian, Dravidologist, and fellow of the Royal Asiatic Society, had recapped 'that the years A.D. 1340-42 were the years in which the Hoysala Vira Ballala III [the last great emperor of the Hoysala Empire] made a serious effort at hemming' foreign invaders into Madurai, as evident in an inscription from AD 1340, 'that lays claim to his having erected a pillar of victory at "the root" (Setumula) of Adam's Bridge.'[134]

Aiyangar's contemporary, the distinguished historian, P.T. Srinivas Iyengar's *History of Tamils* (1929) took to citing the Ceylonese barrister Donald Obeyesekere's *Outlines of Ceylon*, to narrate the legend of a Chola king's siege on the Sinhala kingdom of Wankanasikatissa (AD 113–116).

---

[132]'Resolution Re Retention in its Present Site of Rameswaram', pp. 82–83.

[133]Rasanayagam, *Ancient Jaffna*, p. 82.

[134]Aiyangar, *South India*, p. 184.

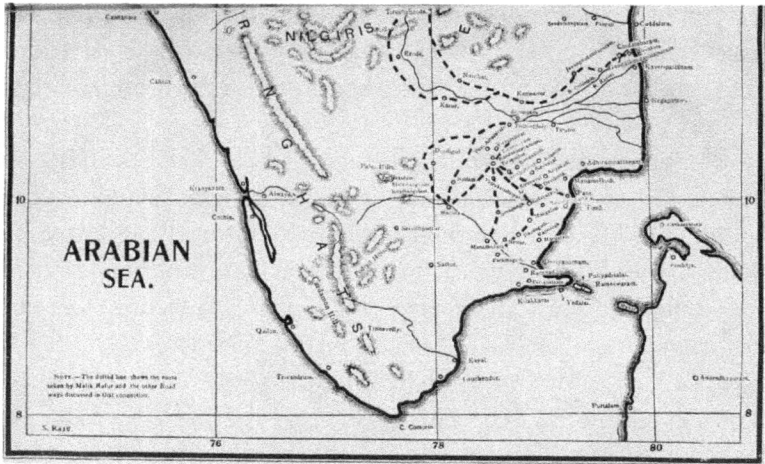

Fig. 28: 'Frontispiece to South India and her Muhammadan Invaders' (1921) by S.K Aiyangar, where the author left the region around Ram Setu unnamed

The king of Tanjore was believed to have 'invaded Ceylon with a large army' around this time, sacking northwestern and central Sri Lanka, up to Anuradhapura (in north-central Sri Lanka). He returned 'with an immense quantity of plunder, and not less than 12,000 prisoners.' Subsequenty, Wankanasika's son and successor, Gaja Bahu, 'avenged the insult' by marching across Ram Setu 'with a large force under the command of Nila-Yodhaya, devasted the country, and threatened to raze the city of Tanjore to the ground, unless the King of Tanjore consented to return the 12,000 Sinhalese,' and 'double that number of Tamils to be taken to Lanka as hostages.' Gaja Bahu was reportedly triumphant. In addition to freeing the Sinhalese hostages, he claimed 'the foot-ornaments of Patiny Devi and the arms of four gods which Gaja Bahu's forces had plundered.' Since Iyengar could not keep his nationalist priorities aside, he gingerly added that the latter part of the tale was mythical since Tanjore was adopted as the Chola capital only in AD 850; therefore, the aforementioned 'untrustworthy legend' was probably conceived after that.[135]

Iyengar's colleague and cultural historian N. Vanamamalai Pillai was more ambitious. His book *The Setu and Rameswaram* (1929)—dedicated to 'The Lord Sree Ramanatha and to his Devoted Servant' Shunmuga Rajeswara Naganatha Sethupathi, and fortified with a foreword by the Madras High Court judge, Sir C.V. Kumaraswamy—nominated Ram Setu as the gateway to 'frequent invasions of Ceylon' since the reign of 'the Aryan prince, Vijaya, from North India in the 6th century BC. The invasions became more frequent as the relations with Pandya and Chola kingdoms increased.' Fixing Iyengar's modest claim of the 'untrustworthy legend' of Gaja Bahu's revenge, Pillai added that Gaja Bahu's visit to India did indeed occur, but merely as a deed of 'peaceful' diplomacy, activating a 'long series of Tamil immigrations' to Ceylon between AD 400 and 700. Pillai was emphatic in his view that 'Adam's name has nothing to do with the ocean bridge, unless one fancies that after the curse, he and his wife crossed over to Ceylon, in the course of their wanderings, by making a bridge or by using an already existing one.' Instead, the structure deserved to be linked only to 'the tradition of Rama's invasion of Lanka.' Somehow, in Pillai's experience, the evidence of this was 'the rapture of a pilgrim on encountering it after his long land-journey from North India' on beholding 'the sight of the grand phenomenon of two oceans making advances to each other, on either side as he nears the Mandapam Station.'[136] Pillai was certain that an unmitigated tradition of pilgrimages to Ram Setu from distant parts of India existed since pre-Christian times. Towards maintaining his belief, he even accepted the Aryan invasion theory that indicated

---

[135]Iyengar, *History of Tamils*, pp. 370–371; also see, Obeyesekere, *Outlines of Ceylon*, pp. 56–58.

[136]Pillai, *The Setu and Rameswaram*, p. 6.

a history of bellicose Brahminical or Aryan emigrations from
the north to the south in ancient India when the Dravidian
country was apparently divided from the north by a hypothetical
Rajputana Sea. What he clearly felt to be sophisticated historical
arguments in favour of Ram Setu were, however, only a veneer
to Pillai's pantheism. Of the joys of witnessing the meeting of
the seas at Dhanushkodi, he wrote:

> The temporary meeting of the Bay and the Ocean at
> Pamban is again interrupted by the pleasant island of
> Rameswaram with its sand-dunes and forests of umbrella
> trees (locally called 'Odai') here and there interrupted by
> small villages and cocoanut and plantain topes; and after
> the train leaves Pamban one feels oneself to be voyaging
> in the midst of angry waters rather than travelling by train.
> After wondering sufficiently at the Pier and the Steamers
> and the influx and efflux of passengers to and from Ceylon,
> one gets down at Dhanushkoti [sic] station and trudges
> along the sands to the point, where the Bay and the Ocean
> seem to clasp each other in an eager embrace, and feels
> that it is one of the grandest and most impressive scenes
> that the earth has to show.[137]

Pillai believed Ram Setu itself to be 'Nature's own temple where
the Gazer's spirit came into direct touch with the Infinite' to
create 'exaltation combined with a chastening of the spirit, a
sublime feeling of humiliation and wonder at the sight of the
Indian Ocean, dark, heaving boundless, endless and sublime—
the image of Eternity, the throne of the Invisible.'[138] His account
was peppered with such phenomenological reflections juggled
with sharp historicist opinions like Ram being a 'historical
person'. On other occasions, he even let his doubts get the

---

[137]Pillai, *The Setu and Rameswaram*, p. 6.
[138]Ibid., p. 7.

better of his devotion. 'Could the Setu have been constructed by monkeys,' he asked, 'though instructed by human beings, considering the fact that the South Indian Railway Company with all its resources of wealth, science, labour and skill has abandoned the project of a huge Ocean-bridge between Ceylon and the Mainland estimated at some hundreds of crores of Rupees?'[139] To the serious reader, it would be evident that Pillai was not able to prove his hypothesis and eventually settled for the self-assured claim that the structure's intellectual provenance should be associated only with the *Ramayan* legacy and no other culture. And any obstacle due to scepticism could very well be resolved if only the reader was 'The genuine pilgrim', who would:

> ... give his due value to such doubts and discussions, but look to the main issue, namely the purification of his body and soul in the places sanctified by the foot-steps of the ancient hero, who toiled for Dharma and who has through his valour, nobleness, and purify, come to be regarded as an incarnation of the supreme spirit of the Universe, that which loveth and maketh for righteousness. [140]

Iyengar was one such pilgrim. Accordingly—and almost echoing the voices of colonial geologists—he argued that Ram Setu 'must have been frequently broken up by the rulers of Ceylon, in order to obstruct the invaders. But the fertility of Ceylon made it too attractive to the adventurers from the mainland to be so easily given up.'[141] One way or another, the *Ramayan* legacy dazzled at the nucleus of these antiquarian speculations. As Pillai determined, with a straight face, 'it is improbable that Rama's pioneer adventure was not imitated by succeeding

---

[139]Ibid., p. 31.
[140]Ibid., p. 19.
[141]Iyengar, *History of Tamils*, pp. 370–371; also see, Obeyesekere, *Outlines of Ceylon*, pp. 56–58.

generations of Aryans. Notable conquests of Ceylon seem to have taken place in the 7th, 10th and 16th centuries.'[142] As if ensuing from this inference, *The Early History of Bengal* (1939) portrayed Samanta Sena (the eleventh-century founder of the Sena dynasty that governed Bengal until about AD 1230) as a warrior who commandeered triumphant militias 'as far as the Adam's bridge and punished the spoilers of the fortunes of the Karnata [Karnataka] country.'[143]

On an obvious level, these writings popularized the name 'Ram Setu' among a burgeoning English-educated Indian middle class. On a deeper level, they underscored Ram Setu's centrality in this new culture of placemaking legends dating back to supposedly knowable times. What was, until the previous century, being seen as an unfinished colonial maritime passage had suddenly been flung back to the canvas of an uncolonized past, with warring voices of Indian and Ceylonese historians staking claims thereupon. The geological enigma had now become a historical enigma, in that Ram Setu had conjured a strange paradox of colonial life. Now, a technocratic colonial machinery—India's longest sea-bridge—was not only cohabiting and thriving on an Indic spiritual enclave, but it was also stimulating Indians to reimagine a militaristic image of their sacred geography. This union of strange bedfellows rendered more visible, than ever before, how colonial science could actively catalyse Indian nationalism or—what the intellectual elites of the late twentieth century would both derisively and farsightedly label as—Hindu nationalism.

Unlike the sunken continent of Lemuria, which was still at best a fabulous geography, Ram Setu was distinctly visible and knowable, especially through the placemaking legends and historical speculations that were facilitated by imperial geology,

---

[142]Pillai, *Setu and Rameswaram*, pp. 8–9.
[143]Paul, *The Early History of Bengal*, p. 88.

with the fantastical goal of tracing 'the kinship of all human religious speculations or even so-called *Revelations*'—to quote a leading theosophist's vision of Lemuria. Lurking in the archives of Ram Setu's long nineteenth-century career is the thesis that 'an indigenous process' had been 'released by external [imperial] forces', in a mind shared by 'the rulers and the ruled'.[144]

---

[144]Blavatsky, *The Secret Doctrine*, p. 767; Nandy, *The Intimate Enemy*, p. 3.

A SUEZ-COMPLEX IN
SETHUSAMUDRAM

In 1952, as the first elections were held in independent India, the nation was poised between legacies of grand colonial endeavours and ideologies of Gandhian indigeneity. According to a prominent twenty-first-century biography of its first prime minister, 'a good deal of Jawaharlal Nehru's legacy appears intact—and yet hotly contested. India has moved away from much of Nehru's beliefs, and so (in different ways) has the rest of the developing world for which Nehruvianism once spoke.'[145] Nehru's ineffable influence on India's modern-day infrastructural ambitions is never entirely absent. It lingers in the margins of public discourses, such as those revolving around the recently renewed Pamban Bridge.

A standout moment of the Nehruvian legacy dates to 17 November 1955. That afternoon, Nehru rose to a flag-festooned podium, pitted against the sharp winter breeze, as a congregation of 10,000 Indians witnessed his pouring 'the first bucket of concrete into the foundation of the Bhakra dam in the dry river-bed of the Sutlej and thus set into motion the gigantic concreting work of the ... highest straight gravity dam in the world.'[146] A few hours later, he refused authorization of Bilaspur's Bhakra

---

[145]Tharoor, 'Nehru's Relevance in India Today', p. 229.
[146]'Nehru Opens Work', 1955.

Dam to be named as Nehru dam.[147] Eight years from that day, as the Bhakra Nangal Dam was being inaugurated, Nehru famously labelled it as modern India's 'Temple or Gurudwara or Mosque'.[148]

On the first day of that November, when the Bhakra Dam's foundation was laid, the Indian government had instituted an expert committee to lay the guidelines for heralding the advent of another Nehruvian *temple*—not on land but sea. The newspapers of 18 November that reported on the Bhakra Dam's inauguration also underscored the renewal of Indo-Ceylonese bilateral ties following a three-year interlude.[149] The most prominent vehicle to do so was the Sethusamudram Canal Project. The Sethusamudram Project Committee was established by Nehru's cabinet to deliberate—like several erstwhile colonial administrations—whether it was possible to cut a channel through Ram Setu to join the Gulf of Mannar and Palk Bay. If so, a safe channel could be granted for deep-sea vessels, shortening the passage between the Arabian Sea and Bay of Bengal, as well as the expanse between eastern and western ports of India. The project was not merely infrastructural but largely of a geopolitical figuration. If successfully executed, it could establish an extraordinary maritime, political and cultural proximity between India and Ceylon.

MUDALIAR'S DISPLEASURE

The Sethu Project aroused the imagination of the Indian media and public. It was dubbed as 'the Suez of Asia' with great enthusiasm in the All-India Radio journal *Akashvani*.[150] The proposed canal further aimed at turning Tuticorin into a 20-foot-deep sea harbour,

---

[147]'Bhakra Dam, Not Nehru Dam', 1955.
[148]'When the Big Dams Came Up', 2015.
[149]'Indo-Ceylon Official Conferences', 1955.
[150]Natarajan, 'The Suez of Asia', 1967.

whose vision was as old as plans conceived by the Government of Madras in the early 1920s under teams led by Wolfe Barry, Robert Bristow, the Palmer Committee and B.N. Chatterjee. Could the independent Indian administration succeed in setting the right strategic parameters for its new maritime infrastructure? For the Sethu Canal was more than an engineering challenge; it was imperative for India's modernization, and its economic, geopolitical and infrastructural independence. But did the hero of *Ramayan* have something else in mind?

The Sethu Project seems to have been revived in the Indian political imagination—for the umpteenth time—on 27 January 1954, when a decisive letter was dispatched to the central government by the chief minister of Madras, and Nehru's trusted ally, Kumaraswami Kamaraj. The latter wanted the incorporation of the Tuticorin Harbour Project in the government's second Five Year Plan. Fast leads started rolling. In its meeting of 29 April, the National Harbour Board deliberated on the proposal and expressed its recommendation. Less than a year later, on 8 March 1955, Chatterjee, the Calcutta Port chief engineer, once again entered the dramatis personae. His file on the Tuticorin Harbour Project estimated its cost at ₹40 million. Chatterjee's findings hinted at an essential symbiotic relationship of the Tuticorin Harbour Project with the then-extinct Rameswaram Ship Canal Project—more familiar to the bureaucracy and posterity as the Sethusamudram Project.

The respect enjoyed by Chatterjee ensured that by 19 May 1955, the state and union government machineries had started to mesh. Subsequently, A. Ramaswamy Mudaliar was appointed to lead a new committee, to which were flanked the Southern Railway's chief commercial superintendent, the Calcutta Port's retired chief engineer, the Indian government's nautical adviser, the directorate general of shipping, and senior officials of the Madras government's home department. The Mudaliar Committee inherited the task assumed to have been left incomplete by British surveyors, but one that had actually been either deferred or abandoned on nine separate occasions.

MINISTRY OF TRANSPORT
(Transport Wing)

RESOLUTION

New Delhi, the 1st November 1955

No. 9-PII(23)/55.—The Government of India are pleased to constitute an Expert Committee to examine and report on the feasibility and desirability of connecting the Gulf of Mannar and the Palk Bay by cutting a channel at the approaches to the Adam's Bridge for enabling deep sea ships to navigate in safety from the west to the east coast of India. It has been suggested that the construction of such a passage would increase the potentiality of the port of Tuticorin if it is to be developed into a deep sea port. The composition of the Committee, which may be known as the Sethusamudram Project Committee, will be as follows:—

Shri A. Ramaswami Mudaliar—*Chairman.*

The Chief Commercial Superintendent, Southern Railway.

Shri B. N. Chatterji, Retired Chief Engineer, Calcutta Port.

Captain J. R. Davies, Nautical Adviser to the Government of India, Directorate-General of Shipping, Bombay-1.

Shri R. A. Gopalaswami, I.C.S., Secretary to the Government of Madras, Home Department, Madras—*Member-Secretary.*

2. The terms of reference of the Committee will be as follows:—

(a) What is the extent to which shipping in general is likely to benefit by, and in practice to take advantage of, the shortened sea route *via* the proposed Sethusamudram passage?

(b) Would the advantage, likely to be secured, be commensurate with the expenditure involved?

(c) What are the traffic prospects of the Tuticorin port during the next decade—

(i) if the Sethusamudram passage is provided; and

(ii) if the Sethusamudram passage is not provided.

(d) In the light of the traffic assessment, should the Tuticorin development project be proceeded with? If so, what should be the timing—

(i) immediately by itself and independently of the Sethusamudram project;

(ii) simultaneously with the Sethusamudram scheme; or

(iii) at a later stage and if so, when?

3. The Committee is requested to submit its report to Government by the end of January, 1956.

Fig. 29: Gazette notification for the formation of the Mudaliar Committee, 1 November 1955, published in the *Gazette of India*, 12 November

Handed the deadline of 31 January 1956, the Mudaliar Committee was faced with decades of British surveys and records. But unlike the colonial regime, failure was not an option for the committee. From December 1955 to February 1956, the committee conducted reconnaissance missions around Ram Setu—denoted as 'Adam's Bridge' on official records—to help unravel the mysteries that had left British surveyors in the lurch for decades. On 22 February 1956, the Lok Sabha throbbed with questions about the committee's progress and whether the Sethu Project was indeed the top priority for the transport ministry.[151] The parliamentary secretary faced the heat on account of inevitable delays. In a few weeks, as the Mudaliar Committee's report was announced, it caused a mild tumult in the bureaucracy and government. What was hitherto thought of as a simple plan to dredge a lifeless Adam's Bridge turned out to be a stark warning, especially in the report's subset—the 'Unsuitability of Adam's Bridge' for canalization.[152] The report alerted that 'the idea of cutting a passage in the sea through Adam's Bridge should be abandoned.'[153] It argued that its subsurface geology was impenetrable. The committee was mindful of the history of plans to canalize Ram Setu. They knew that the idea was first conceived in the late 1700s, following James Rennell's surveys. However, after successive setbacks, finally, in 1921–22, harbour engineer Robert Bristow's report had hammered the last nail in the coffin of the plan of dredging the formation in favour of Rameswaram Island as a more suitable site for canalization. Even as early as in AD 1860 Taylor's proposal of a canal route had suggested Mandapam to the west of Pamban Island as the site for dredging. The Mudaliar Committee argued for a resuscitation of Taylor's original ideas.

---

[151]*Lok Sabha Debates,* February 22, 1956, pp. 225–226
[152]Mudaliar, et al., 'Report of The Sethusamudram Project Committee', p. 4.
[153]Ibid., p. 5.

There was also a critical geopolitical reason that Ram Setu could not be dredged. Less than a quarter of a century later, this very stretch would become the international marine border between Sri Lanka and India. But more importantly, the committee's insights turned out to be eerily prescient. A little more than a decade after the report's publication, a 25-foot storm surge flattened Dhanushkodi Island, killing more than 200 people when their train was crossing the Pamban Bridge. The bridge itself was terribly damaged, while the whole town of Dhanushkodi practically became a ghost town. Once the epicentre of commercial activity, it was now a haunted wasteland with remnants of its post office, hospital, customs office, telegraph office, panchayat, dispensary, railway station, cathedral and temple reminding of the ephemerality of its past and the 800 lives that the hurricane swallowed.

CONGRESSIONAL PROCRASTINATIONS

Tensions surrounding the Sethu Project were palpable as the debates commenced in the Lok Sabha. By 1958, parliamentary deliberations had come to accept its monumental implications— geological, locomotive and administrative—and began normalizing the idea of shifting the location of the canal from Ram Setu to Mandapam, near the Pamban Channel. Members of parliament were wholly cognizant of the stakes, even as the Ministry of Transport wavered, offering equivocal responses on deadlines, future surveys and critical data from conjoined studies on the Tuticorin Port Trust.[154] Meanwhile, the estimated budget of the canal spiralled from ₹84 million (from the time of the Mudaliar Committee report) to ₹100 million, if combined with the Tuticorin Port.[155] By June 1964, reports in an American

---

[154]*Lok Sabha Debates,* September 27, pp. 1958, 8861–8862; 8915–8916.
[155]'Sethusamudram Canal Project', p. 90.

Department of Commerce weekly revealed a more shocking escalation. The project's budget had climbed to 'about 210 million rupees (approximately $44.1 million)' with foreign exchange expenditure of 'about $9½ million'.[156] As the relentless rise in expenses became insuperable, the Sethu canal was de-hyphenated from the Tuticorin Port.

The following year, a key committee headed by a project official, a chief engineer, and a superintending engineer was instituted by the government to study the feasibility of integrating it into the fourth Five Year Plan. New studies reported that the soil around Mandapam was composed of 'soft' workable material. Results from littoral studies, radioactive analyses, and rock cutting trails also looked promising. Despite its reimagined parameters, the project retained its original name: the Sethusamudram canal. It was slated to 'confer benefits both national and international' to 'improve world communications and avoid absolute waste of the world's resources of fuel, time, shipping and human energy.'[157] Such grand proclamations occurred not only in the corridors of bureaucracy, but were also trumpeted from the *Akashvani*, a mouthpiece of the Government of India. This unmistakably internationalist messaging of progress and global cooperation was ironic since, three decades later, the anti-Sethu canal campaign would be fought in a starkly different language—an ethno-nationalist rhetoric avowing Ram Setu as a divine legacy. However, back in the 1960s, the Sethu canal embodied the vision of an elusive modernity, precariously poised between promise and conflict, and ambition and controversy, with a future as uncertain as the waters it sought to tame.

The project's glacial pace in the 1960s mirrored India's broader economic slowdown, whose roots could be traced to

---

[156]'India', p. 27.
[157]Ibid., p. 3.

the nation's planning history and grim fiscal reality. The entire allocated budget for minor ports and all-weather harbours in the second Five Year Plan, inter alia, encompassing Paradip, Mangalore, Malpe and the Sethu Canal, stood at ₹50 million.[158] Meanwhile, the estimated cost of the canal alone was double that figure. Financial disparity and chronic underfunding were exacerbated by the tone of the official communications, laden with indefinite expectancy or outright deferral. A transport committee report from 1966 captured this bureaucratic limbo perfectly.

> The Sethusamudram Canal project, which is expected to be taken up in the Fourth Plan, may have a significant impact on the costs of coastal shipping, for, the canal will make, it possible for coastal ships to negotiate the passage between the Gulf of Mannar and Palk Bay and, thus, reduce the lead of shipment between the two coasts by about 600 kilometres. The precise economies that may be possible in the costs of coastal movement on account of the opening of the canal have of course to be worked out in detail.[159]

Despite decades of languishing progress and systemic adjournments, the Sethu Project continued to be a prevailing fixture in Indian political discourse owing to at least two compelling factors.

First, the canal was a long-held aspiration of Conjeevaram Natarajan Annadurai, who served as the final chief minister of Madras State and the first for Tamil Nadu, as well as Muthuvel Karunanidhi, the state's second and longest-tenured chief minister. They wielded substantial clout in successive postcolonial union governments. As founding members of the DMK—India's first Dravidian political party established

---

[158]Roy, *Planning in India*, p. 132.
[159]*Report of the Committee on Transport Policy*, p. 123.

in 1949—they traced their antecedents to the ideology of Erode Venkatappa Ramasamy Periyar's Dravidar Kazhagam, a vehemently anti-Brahminical movement that defied the legacies of Lord Ram, Gandhi and orthodox religious rituals.[160] Periyar was himself arrested in 1954 for his anti-Ram campaigns.[161] Although the DMK eventually distanced itself from Periyar's personality cult, it preserved steadfast resistance to Brahminical ideologies and idolatry. Nevertheless, their championing of the Sethu Project had no anti-religious sentiment—as it was not designed to destroy an avowed structure dedicated to Ram— but was deemed to be a flagship initiative for Tamil Nadu's coastal development and strengthening bonds between Tamil communities on both sides of the maritime boundary. Well into the twenty-first century, the DMK would firmly assert that the Sethu Canal 'will become as famous as the Panama and Suez Canals.'[162] This conviction would keep the project simmering on the political backburner.

The second reason that cemented the project's relevance was the support given to it by Prime Minister Jawaharlal Nehru. On 8 April 1959, Y.D. Gundevia—India's high commissioner in Ceylon and the imminent foreign minister—wrote a sharp note to the PM. Gundevia emphasized a dire need for 'intensive development' in southeastern coastal regions, including the Ramanathapuram (Ramnad) district. The letter painted a bleak picture of poverty in Ramnad and Tirunelveli that was driving an uncompromising flow of illicit immigrants into Ceylon where they faced worse living conditions due to the island's 'extreme Buddhist communalism'.[163] Inter alia, Gundevia raised the urgency of reviving the Sethu Project that was sidelined

---

[160]Periyar, *The Collected Works*, 2005; Kannan, *Anna*, 2010.

[161]Jeyaraman, *Periyar: A Political Biography*, 2013.

[162]*The DMK Election Manifesto*, p. 58.

[163]Gundevia, 'A Note on the Need for an Intense Development', p. 583.

during the second Five Year Plan due to unsatisfactory estimates from the Madras State. Simultaneously, the union government was urged to prepare for the return of Tamil migrants from Ceylon, in parallel to the Sethu Canal being envisioned as the 'one and only big industrial venture' to revivify southern Tamil Nadu.[164] Nehru's response on 19 April aligned with Gundevia's views—with minor reservations. Agreeing with the need for development, Nehru noted that living conditions in districts like Madurai, Ramnad and Tirunelveli were superior to those 'in South-East U.P., parts of Bihar and Orissa and West Bengal.'[165] Nonetheless, Nehru's general concurrence prolonged the importance of the Sethu Project and its unmitigated relevance as a Dravidian dream that was then supported by succeeding Congress-led union governments.

Despite the apparent federal cooperation between Tamil political leaders and the central government, throughout the 1960s and 1970s,[166] an array of committees and panels paved the way for little more than unfulfilled promises over the Sethu Canal. Recommendations invariably concluded with calls for new bodies or assurances that more detailed insights were forthcoming, or acknowledgements that while the project was undeniably 'costly', its 'promising' revenues would outshine the negatives.[167] By 1975, the Tamil Nadu state government began showing signs of frustration. Tamil leaders in parliament reiterated the canal's geostrategic ramifications besides its economic potential. However, each of their inquiries was met with mannerly but firm bureaucratic postponements.[168]

---

[164]Ibid., pp. 584, 586.

[165]Nehru, 'To Y.D. Gundevia', p. 291.

[166]Kumar, *Committees and Commissions*, pp. 95–96.

[167]*Lok Sabha Debates*, 21 March 1966, pp. 3859–3860; 22 November 1967, 1902; 8 June 1971, p. 189; 21 July 1971, p. 328.

[168]*Lok Sabha Debates*, 27 November 1972, p. 225; *Index to Lok Sabha Debates*, 8 February–10 May 1974, pp. 397; 516–517; 896.

The beacon of progress seemed increasingly and tantalizingly out of reach, ensnared in a matrix of red tapes and indecisions.

THE TAMIL RESILIENCE

The Tamil Nadu government's commitment to accelerating the Sethu Project was documented by the *Tamil Nadu District Gazetteers for Ramanathapuram* (1972), penned by scholar A. Ramaswami and published by the state administration. The book offered a curious but seamless juxtaposition of the sacred Ram Setu with plans to dredge the natural tombolo. The document was one of postcolonial India's most remarkable attempts to intertwine sacred legacies and economic progress. It echoed the promotional zeal of the South Indian Railway's campaigns during the Pamban Bridge's opening in the First World War. The Sethu Canal was underscored as 'the Suez of Asia',[169] while blending infrastructural ambitions with localized history. The book documented how the Ramnad district—established in 1910—derived its name from Ramanathapuram, which, in turn, owed its identity to Lord Ramanathaswamy, who, as legend would have it, had 'directed his faithful servant Guha to build a town near the Sethu (Adam's Bridge).'[170]

The *Gazetteers* even delved into medieval Tamil history. It informed that, under the rule of Sadaika Deva II Dalavoy Sethupathi (1635–46), a conflict arose as his illegitimate half-brother, Battana Nayakka 'Thampi' formed a pact with Madurai Nayak king Thirumala Nayak (1623–59) and proclaimed himself the new 'Sethupathi'—lord of the Sethu—as well as the ruler of the Ramnad kingdom.[171] Thirumala Nayak's general, Ramappaiya, who led the siege on Rameswaram, later commissioned an

---

[169]Ramaswami, *Tamil Nadu District Gazetteers*, p. viii.
[170]Ibid., p. 1.
[171]Everett-Heath, *Oxford Concise Dictionary*, p. 438.

account of the battle in *Ramappaiyan Ammanai*. According to the account, Ramappaiya reportedly 'rebuilt the mythological Sethu'—a bridge that had been destroyed by a cyclone around 1480.[172] The conflict culminated in Sadaika II's incarceration and Thampi's short-lived rule as the new Sethupathi. But Sadaika II was eventually freed and reinstated as ruler of Ramnad and the legacy of the Sethupathis was restored.

That the *Gazetteers* sought to capture this tale was ironic. On the one hand, it highlighted the historic desire of Tamils to scale the Palk Strait—in this case as an overland military bridge. On the other hand, it reminded that Thampi's hubris and Ramappaiya's military feat were only transient and easily revocable. Furthermore, the book made clear that the political and symbolic gravity of the title 'Sethupathi' was paramount, since the Sethupathis traced their authority to the belief that Lord Ram himself gave them the sole responsibility 'to guard the Sethu or the isthmus which once connected Ceylon with the mainland.'[173] In the historical imagination of the indigenous Maravas of the region, the rulers of Ramnad were celebrated as 'the guardian of the causeway [on] "Sethu Samudram" (Rameswaram) from time immemorial and hence his name Sethupathi ("Lord of the Sethu").'[174]

The *Gazetteers* even described Dhanushkodi as a prominent 'place of pilgrimage for Hindus', veering into an homage to Swami Vivekananda's momentous visit to Pamban in 1897. Soon later, it noted that Mandapam had developed into the location of an assistant engineer's office for the Sethu Canal, which, if realized, might lead to the dredging of Ram Setu itself.[175] What seemed even more complicated was that the *Gazetteers'* foreword,

---

[172]Ramaswami, *Tamil Nadu District Gazetteers*, p. 81; also see, Taylor, *Oriental Historical Manuscripts*, p. 31,

[173]Ramaswami, *Tamil Nadu District Gazetteers*, p. 433.

[174]Kadhirvel, *A History of the Maravas*, p. 6.

[175]Ramaswami, *Tamil Nadu District Gazetteers*, pp. 874; 875; 931; 914.

authored by the Tamil Nadu chief minister M. Karunanidhi, praised Ramaswami's prose as a ray of 'light on our traditions' reflecting Tamil 'civilization', and capable of illumining 'our thoughts of past with pride and to be hopeful about our future with confidence.'[176] Years later, this foreword would be quoted by Karunanidhi's opponents—at the height of the anti-Sethu-Canal campaigns supported by the Sangh—citing his endorsement of India's religious and civilizational heritage while doubling up as an anti-Brahminical atheist. Notwithstanding the chief minister's compromise to risk this apparent political contradiction in his regime, his stance did not help the cause of the Sethu Canal.

A FEW MORE COMMITTEES

Throughout the 1970s, the idea of the Sethu Project dawdled in the backbenches of India's progressive ambitions. Under Indira Gandhi's administration, the Indian government was economically unprepared to tackle the project. But, in theory, it never allowed the project to become extinct. In early February 1981, during Gandhi's second term as prime minister, the government revived the project by establishing a five-member expert committee to reassess its economic viability. The numbers having ballooned by now, the revised budget estimate pointed to a staggering ₹1,100 million as the cost of canalizing the Palk Strait.[177] News of this came as salt on injury, especially for the DMK members, who had, as far back as 21 July 1971, articulated in the Lok Sabha that Indian strategic needs in the Indian Ocean were tied to the Sethu Canal.

Tamil members had for long fervently advocated for the canal not merely as a shipping project but also 'from the point of view of defence', stressing its potential to enable Indian

---

[176]Karunanidhi, 'Foreword', p. ii.
[177]*Eastern Economist*, 1981.

vessels to navigate between the eastern and western coasts without penetrating international waters.[178] The DMK's urgency was visionary because since 1968 NASA's Gemini spacecraft had been surveilling Ram Setu, whose evidence would later surface under the guise of a commercial fisheries report.[179] Juxtaposed with the bilateral Indo-Lankan agreement of 26–28 June 1974, which formally delineated their international maritime boundary, the seemingly benign overture by NASA would only confirm the notion that Ram Setu was, indeed, a geopolitical flashpoint.

The division of the maritime boundary came on the heels of India's cession of Katchatheevu, executed in 'conformity with historical evidence, legal international principles and precedents', with the international boundary lying 'one mile off the west coast of the uninhabited island' after making 'mutually satisfactory provisions' for 'navigation, pilgrimage, fishing and mineral exploration in the area', to settle disputes 'handed down unresolved and undetermined from the colonial period.'[180] The granting of the island sparked fury among Tamil stakeholders. The Indian government's seeming disregard for Tamil parliamentarians during the critical decision, paired with long-standing inaction on the Sethu Project, ignited discontent. DMK members, joined later by AIADMK and CPI(M), consistently raised the issue of the canal in parliamentary discussions and public addresses in the 1980s and early 1990s.[181] What began as a call for maritime traffic evolved to stress the canal's geostrategic significance, considering China's impact in the Indian Ocean. In 1984, a year into the Sri Lankan civil

---

[178]*Lok Sabha Debates, 21* July 1971, p. 328.

[179]Stevenson and Ruth, 'An index of ocean features photographed from Gemini spacecraft', 1968.

[180]'Indo-Sri Lanka Boundary', pp. 5–6.

[181]*Lok Sabha Debates,* 14 March 1983, p. 400; 5 May 1992, p. 439; 'Namboodiripad Holds Press Conference in Trivandrum', 1989.

war, even a Congress Lok Sabha member from Tamil Nadu's Tiruchendur constituency labelled the Sethu Canal as a 'vital defence need' for India.[182] Despite these impassioned debates, the spate of expert committees, and rising costs, no tangible progress was in sight. More confusingly, a recent Estimates Committee (1981–82) report from the seventh Lok Sabha had even gone on to conclude that the canal was economically and geologically feasible, contrary to previous reports. What was stranger, it once again nominated Ram Setu as the chosen site of canalization.

> The desirability of taking up Sethusamudram Project providing for an artificial canal across the rocky barrier called Adam's Bridge to connect the Indian Ocean with the Bay of Bengal similar to Suez and Panama Canals has been represented before the Committee. It is claimed that the project is economically viable and technically feasible and should be undertaken as a national project in national interest.[183]

Thus, another chapter of uncertainty unfolded as the government established yet another 'expert committee' to reassess the canal's techno-economic feasibility. This time, the focus extended beyond economics to encompass the geostrategic impact of the Pamban Channel, particularly in the light of India's defence needs[184] against the background of the Lankan civil war and naval inroads by the Liberation Tigers of Tamil Eelam, which marked the deliberations with the greatest possible exigency in the intellectual history of the Sethu Canal.

---

[182]'Very Low Frequency Radio Transmitter Planned', 1984.
[183]*Estimates Committee*, 1982, p. 202.
[184]Ibid., pp. 131–132.

SETHUSAMUDRAM SHINING

Whether as tragedy or travesty, by 1988, another redoubtable obstacle emerged in the canal's journey. A United Nations Environment Programme paper authored by C. Sheppard and Susan M. Wells raised serious concerns over the predictable destruction of the Gulf of Mannar's coral reefs due to dredging.[185] While the canal's economic viability had long been questioned, these new environmental concerns threatened to disrupt its future entirely. For the DMK, meanwhile, these delays were politically corrosive. By October 1990, *The Illustrated Weekly of India* cast a grim picture of torpor, reporting that key DMK schemes—including the Salem Steel Plant's development and the Sethu Canal—were flagging despite the party's ostensibly 'friendly' terms with the union government. Allegations against the DMK chief minister, of 'encouraging LTTE militants' amid political turbulence in Madras, stoked public displeasure even more.[186]

The turbulence in Tamil politics coincided with a national catastrophe. India's involvement in peacekeeping in the Sri Lankan conflict, and the horrific assassination of Prime Minister Rajiv Gandhi in 1991, propelled the Sethu Canal's geostrategic value back into the limelight. Just as the canal project seemed to be ensnared in the deceptive tides of domestic politics, an inscrutable twist in its story unfolded under the National Democratic Alliance government steered by Prime Minister Atal Bihari Vajpayee (1998–2004). Vajpayee, a statesman known for his Orwellian doublespeak and complex persona,[187] was an unlikely figure to preside over the project. Often regarded as a paradox—a man of the Sangh Parivar and yet deeply influenced

---

[185]Sheppard and Wells, *Coral Reefs of the World*, p. 90.
[186]Sunil, 'Theatre of the Absurd', pp. 37–38.
[187]Ullekh, *The Untold Vajpayee*, 2018; Choudhary, *Vajpayee*, 2023.

by Nehruvianism—Vajpayee's coalition politics offered a new lease of life to the Sethu Canal. Back in May 1964, following Jawaharlal Nehru's death, a young Vajpayee had eulogized the late prime minister as Mother India's 'beloved Prince' and 'the benefactor of the downtrodden.' He compared Nehru 'to none less than Lord Ram, for like Valmiki's (and the Hindutvawadis's) hero, Nehru was "the orchestrator of the impossible and inconceivable."'[188] Vajpayee's tenure was characterized by several moments of ideological difference with the Sangh Parivar, including his sorrow over the Babri Masjid demolition.

Vajpayee and his inner coterie—especially members of the hardline Hindutvavadi faction headed by L.K. Advani and the Sangh's affiliates—were determined to build a long-cherished Ram Temple at the location of the erstwhile Babri Masjid in Ayodhya. This religio-nationalist agenda was not without magnificent political boons. In 1993, political observers acknowledged the Bharatiya Janata Party to be 'an unstoppable juggernaut', even months before the party suffered perplexing election losses in four states it had formerly ruled.[189] The thundering setback drove a speedy recalibration. Under Vajpayee's leadership, the party adopted a softening of its approach, attempting to blunt the edge of its divisive agendas. To many an eye, Vajpayee appeared as 'a liberal caught in an illiberal party.' However, his own expression bore a more nuanced description: he was 'a swayamsevak [RSS ideologue] first', he used to say.[190] Following his party's 13-day stint in power, in May 1996, Vajpayee renewed his strategy, once again. He courted regional allies like the DMK, Telugu Desam Party and MANAALI Congress—to prevent becoming 'a political pariah on account of its communal ideology'—promising the

---

[188]Tharoor, 'Nehru's Relevance in India Today', pp. 235–236.
[189]Andersen, 'India in 1994', p. 127.
[190]Subramaniam, 'The Making of Atal Bihari Vajpayee', 2018.

suspension of its 'hardcore Hindutva agenda'.[191] This included sidelining contentious matters. Given the DMK's acceptance of this new face of the Bharatiya Janata Party, Vajpayee's political pragmatism was expected to embrace the cause of the Sethu canal.

Vajpayee's backing for the Sethu Project transcended political buccaneering. His allies in the DMK—though staunch detractors of the Sangh's majoritarian Hindutva-outlook—threw their weight behind Vajpayee, helping to project him as 'the man who brought honor to India in war and peace [after the Kargil war].'[192] While being the beneficiary of DMK's critical support, Vajpayee was mindful that the Sethu Project had also received the approval of his predecessor H.D. Deve Gowda, the previous prime minister of India (1996–97). In fact, between 1996 and 1998, the successive administrations of Deve Gowda and I.K. Gujral had engaged in diplomatic negotiations with Sri Lanka's external affairs ministry to address the Katchatheevu affair and the Palk Bay fisheries conflict. Paradoxically, some Tamil fishers' organizations even saw the Sethu Project as a symbol of hope, for they believed it to be a potential solution to avert inadvertent forays of Indian fishermen into Lankan waters.[193] The canal project was all set to be Vajpayee's winning move on the political chessboard, dexterously juggling loyalties, ideologies and tenuous coalitions. Thus, in 1999, he announced that the Sethusamudram Project would commence within three years. The National Democratic Alliance's 2004 election manifesto further reinforced the party's commitment to the project's 'speedy completion'.[194] What was most incongruous, however, was that one of the Sethu Project's proposed alignments

[191]Engineer, 'Communalism and Communal Violence', p. 324.
[192]Subramanian, 'Tamil Nadu', p. 122.
[193]Gaan, *Environmental Security*, p. 194.
[194]Sharma, *Sonia versus Vajpayee*, p. 62.

could lead to the demolition of the structure the Sangh Parivar would later champion as the sacred Ram Setu—a twist in the tale that remained unapparent until the next few years.

Until 2002, the Sethu Project sailed ahead without any controversy of a religious nature. The Sangh Parivar, usually agile at politically cultivating issues of Indic sacred interests, was found to be astoundingly silent on the matter of Ram Setu. The lack of politicization was evident in Finance Minister Yaswant Sinha's budget speech from 2000. On 29 February Sinha informed lawmakers regarding the government's endorsement of 'the undertaking of a detailed feasibility study and environmental impact assessment of the project at a total cost of ₹4.8 crore [48 million].' That all requisite provisions had been made for the 'much awaited [Sethu] project'[195] indicated that, undoubtedly, the first Hindutvavadi political regime of India had entered the new epoch with an avantgarde intellect. But that was not to be. The dawn of the new century would usher in the antithesis to the Nehruvian vision that regarded factories, dams and canals as the modern temples of independent India.

As the new millennium gathered momentum, one saw a dramatic transformation in the Sangh's rhetoric. Instead of invoking ancient texts by sages Vyasa or Valmiki, the Sangh's members turned to the newfound testimony of American scientists. In 2002, NASA issued satellite imagery of the shoals between Dhanushkodi and Thalaimannar on the internet, without attaching any special consequence to the fortuitous capture. Sangh activists, still new to the digisphere, instantly latched onto it, citing it as unimpeachable proof that Ram Setu was a man-made structure—therefore, indeed, a bridge of primitive construction by Lord Ram's army. The two-century-old developmental marine project was now on the cusp of becoming

---

[195]Sinha, 'Budget Speech', 29 February p. 50; Sinha, 'Budget Speech', 27 February p. 37.

the foil to a symbol of divinely conspired engineering. As fate would have it, another front to challenge the Sethu Canal was fast gaining traction. In 2001, the Zoological Survey of India issued a severe forewarning about the ecological risks of canalizing Ram Setu. It reported that dredging the Sethusamudram Sea would trigger a chain reaction of sedimentation that could 'physically interfere with recruitment of coral larvae which require a solid substratum to settle and metamorphose.' This disruption, as it warned, would mutilate the Gulf of Mannar's reefs, eroding the ecosystem through 'physical disturbance, habitat alteration and the subsequent problems associated with sedimentation.'[196] As if religious symbolism was not enough, here was the unlikely ally of environmentalism to afford Hindutva ideologues a newfangled arm to valiantly defend the bridge of Ram.

---

[196]Venkataraman and Sinha, 'Coral Reefs', p. 285.

IN THE SHADOW OF
DIVINITY

The ecological impasse around Ram Setu might remind experts of the Mediterranean story of the 1990s and American urban planning theorist Lawrence E. Susskind's book *Environmental Diplomacy* (1994) that led to an interdisciplinary wave, linking politics, governance, law, environmentalism and activism, based on lessons drawn from the Mediterranean experience.

The partnership between marine scientists and ecologists in the Mediterranean, according to Susskind, was a model of international cooperation. Recalling political scientist Peter Haas (1990) and his category of citizenship—the 'epistemic community'—Susskind related how the Mediterranean Action Plan, initiated under the United Nations Environment Programme in the 1970s, aimed to safeguard Mediterranean environments through multilateral cooperation. The epistemic community that emerged helped institute norms, guidelines and multilateral strategies for addressing Mediterranean pollution, and fostered agreements on protocols and legal frameworks, like those stemming from issues of maritime traffic and land-based pollutants.

Guarded from ideological biases by scientific temper, the community offered 'policy advice about domestic pollution control measures and encouraged their countries to support the norms and principles' needed to safeguard the Mediterranean, notwithstanding the stance of their domestic administrations.[197] The Sethusamudram Canal Project, on the other hand, relegated the scientific community to the margins. Thanks to the Sangh Parivar, the public became aware of the fabulous creationist possibility of Ram Setu being a divine construction. But an equally enchanting and urgent—more empirically certain— environmental story was deprioritized.

GULF, PALK AND BAY

The International Maritime Boundary Line between Sri Lanka and India stretches across 400 kilometres, dividing the terra aqua into distinct regions: the Bay of Bengal, Palk Bay and the Gulf of Mannar. The distance between the two territories narrows dramatically in places—just 16 kilometres at its closest point and extending to 45 kilometres at its farthest. The Palk Bay, along this boundary, is an ecological paradise, boasting of nearly 600 piscine species, over 300 marine algal species, 11 species of seagrass, 5 species of marine turtles and numerous mangrove species. Together, they inhabit a 15,000-square-kilometre marine zone.

The Gulf of Mannar is a great hallmark of India's historical and ecological heritage. More than 2,200 years ago, early Pandya kings established their globally renowned pearl factory at Korkai—the ancient Pandyan capital conjecturally located around the present-day Tuticorin district. This landmark of transnational commerce attracted pre-Christian Romans and Europeans to the Indian subcontinent.[198] Today, the Gulf of Mannar is known as one of India's four key coralline colonies, besides the Gulf of Kutch, the Andaman and Nicobar Islands, and Lakshadweep Islands. At the core of this marine heritage

---

[197]Susskind, *Environmental Diplomacy*, p. 73.
[198]Sen, *Ancient Indian History and Civilization*, pp. 7; 451.

lies the Gulf of Mannar Biosphere Reserve, South Asia's first marine biosphere reserve. And this fragile ecosystem traverses the projected routes of the Sethu Canal.

The biosphere reserve consists of an archipelago of 21 islands spread between Rameswaram (8° 47' N to 9° 15' N) and Kanyakumari (78° 12' E to 79° 14' E), each of about eight square kilometres. Krusadai Island is among the ecologically richest islands in the world. Spanning 10,500 square kilometres, the marine reserve has a 365-km-long coastline, stretching across the Ramanathapuram, Tuticorin, Tirunelveli and Kanyakumari districts. A buffer zone of 10 kilometres from the park's borders protects this unique ecosystem. Many of the islands are deserted. But Krusadai, Musal and Nallathanni still teem with life.

Krusadai itself is the habitat of almost every animal taxonomy, except for amphibians. The environmental history of the region indicates its origins to be calcareous coralline formations, which constitute the bulk of the evolutionary prehistoric foundations of the area of the reserve. Balanoglossus (*Ptychodera fluva*), a living fossil, is among the most remarkable species of the region as it is considered an evolutionary bridge between invertebrates and vertebrates. The reserve is known to host almost 100 coralline species from 37 genera, including conspicuous species such as *Acropora, Montipora, Porites, Astreopora* and *Pocillopora*. Do not think of them as adding to species diversity alone. They also provide the marine ecosystem with the backbone on which the entire spectrum of aquatic life depends.

In 2006, the United Nations Development Programme pointed to the grave environmental concerns facing the region. Among the key threats to the sensitive ecosystem of the reserve was habitat erosion due to pollution and overexploitation of oceanic assets. Seen in the light of the reserve's entangled biodiversity, the threats were all-encompassing. The reserve supports no fewer than 10 true mangrove species and 24 mangrove-associated species. Corals occupy nearly 120 species from over 30 genera. A 1999 Global Environment Facility report placed the biosphere's number of plant and animal species at some 3,600—the number has since been amended to over 4,200. Besides, 13 of India's 14 seagrass species live within the region. Added to that are five species of sea turtles: leatherback, loggerhead, olive ridley, green and hawksbill. Then there are over 120 species of commercially important ornate reef fish, nearly 650 species of crustaceans, over 730 species of molluscs, nearly 450 species of finfish, and nearly 150 seaweed species. The reserve is also frequented by migrant marine mammals, including whales, dolphins and porpoises.

The Gulf of Mannar Marine National Park was established by the Government of Tamil Nadu in 1986 under the Wildlife (Protection) Act of 1972. Its primary goal was to preserve the diverse flora and fauna of the Gulf of Mannar, including coral reefs, rugged shores, tombolos, estuaries, mangrove forests, and seagrass beds. Additionally, the park was designed to protect India's endangered marine species, such as the dugong (*Dugong dugon*), Risso's dolphin, Chinese white dolphin, sea turtles, seahorses, sea cucumbers, green turtle, hawksbill turtle, olive ridley turtle, loggerhead turtle and leatherback turtle. It also serves as a refuge for rare marine species, including the short-finned pilot whale, bottlenose dolphin, false killer whale and Bryde's whale, as well as unique chanks like *Turbinella pyrum*, which is used for conches. The park further safeguards shrimp, lobsters, pearl oysters, sea snakes and a variety of plant species such as rosary pea, wattles, umbrella thorn, nettle and prickly chaff flower. Numerous bird species also find protection here, including the great egret, grey heron, pond heron, western reef heron, greater flamingo and northern pintail (*Anas acuta*), among others.

The Palk Bay is a constricted marine stretch adjoining the reserve. It is approximately 75 kilometres wide and 13 metres deep, with coral projections pushing above the surface in places. It is one of India's five principal coral sanctuaries. The Palk Bay harbours 61 species of algae, and 11 of India's 14 marine seagrasses. The former include 28 species of green algae, 13 species of brown algae, and 17 species of red algae. Along with the Gulf of Mannar, the Palk Bay is rich in underexploited piscine resources, especially sardines, mackerels, seer fish and tunas.

The Palk Bay and the Gulf of Mannar represent the only terrain in the southern Indian peninsula 'where continuous stretches of coral reefs occur near shore.'[199] There are also seahorses and butterfly rays that have been overexploited by destructive fishing practices. These include *Gymnura poecilura*, *Himantura bleekeri*, *Himantura uarnak*, *Pastinachus sephen*, *Amphotistius zugei*, and *Rhinoptera javanica*.[200] Besides, the region also provisionally harbours waterbirds on the Indo-Sri Lanka sea-route during their migratory stints and fleeting habitats. Since around 1960, coralline exploitation has struggled to be 'commensurate with the growth rate and the ability for repopulation of the exploited species.'[201] This has resulted in the archipelago's coralline degradation, particularly in the Tuticorin islands.

BROKEN IMPACT ASSESSMENTS

The Sethusamudram region was identified as a zone of attention in the United Nations Development Programme's Millennium Development Goals in October 2006, with the aim of strengthening local communities. Meanwhile, though the Sethu Project was perceived to be one of the biggest lasting threats to the marine national park since the 1980s, the canal was presented officially as a viable and reasonably low-risk project. One of

[199]Mahadevan and Nayar, 'Distribution of coral reefs', p. 189.
[200]James, 'Notes on the biology and fishery of the butterfly ray', p. 150.
[201]Balachandran and Kannan, 'Gulf of Mannar Marine National Park', p. 1685.

the most glaring weaknesses was its Environmental Impact Assessment that seemed to lack environmental consciousness— at least insofar as the politicized perception of the project went in 2007 after nationwide protests erupted.

The first oversight was the failure to use complete subsurface geological data. The 'L&T Ramboll Detailed Project Report', commissioned in December 2004 by the Ministry of Shipping, seemed to acknowledge these shortcomings, as did the National Environmental Engineering Research Institute's (NEERI) 'Technical Feasibility and Economic Analysis Report' released around the same time. Bathymetric studies were conducted in the Pamban Pass—an integral part of the proposed canal—by NEERI between 2003 and 2004. But geotechnical investigations conducted at three places—drilling at water depths of between 2 and 5 metres around Ram Setu—appeared to be a very limited sampling, far from enough for a project of this size. Bathymetric studies were also conducted by the National Hydrographic Office in 2005, following a study by the National Institute of Ocean Technology from November to December 2004. The findings of these were perceived not to be wholly integrated in the detailed project report. Critical data on water depth and composition seemed to have been overlooked. Also, the environmental impact assessment appeared to have excluded newly acquired environmental data.

More recent data implied grave implications of annual sedimentation of 58.8×10^6 m^3—strong enough to diminish the oceanic depth at 1 cm/year—that the Sethu Canal would have to face.[202] Over 99 per cent of the projected sedimentation had been previously ignored. These nuances were not considered as major obstacles to the canal by environmental impact assessments, besides lacking in data from vital investigations on sedimentation

---

[202]Chandramohan, Jena and Kumar, 'Littoral drift sources and sinks along the Indian coast', 2001; Ramesh, *Sethusamudram Ship Canal Project*, 2006.

over the last decade.[203] Based on the existing impact assessment, annual maintenance dredging was projected to be 0.1 million cubic metres. But this estimate was probably based on secondary data and the confirmation bias likely created by a hydrodynamic modelling study carried out by Indomer Hydraulics which had incorrectly determined that because the Palk Strait's sediment outflux and influx were comparable, it would require negligible maintenance dredging.[204]

Future tests conducted by the National Institute of Ocean Technology indicated that the substratum was more rigid than previously estimated, necessitating blasting and thereby increasing both the overall project costs and its potential risks. In early 2010, the National Institute of Oceanography's environmental assessments at the proposed canal site yielded striking findings. The study revealed a phase reversal of tides at the southern and northern ends of the proposed canal, causing the gulf waters to exhibit a 'see-saw' effect, where water levels alternately rose and fell at these two points. This phenomenon also contributed to an 'enhanced tidal current', which could significantly exacerbate sedimentation—an impact that had not been previously accounted for.[205]

---

[203]Rajamanickam, 'Sethusamudram Canal', 2004; Ramasamy, Ramesh, Paul, et al., 'Land Building Activity along Vedaranniyam', 1998; Chandramohan, Jena and Kumar, 'Littoral drift sources and sinks along the Indian coast', 2001; Sanil Kumar, Anand and Gowthaman, 'Variations in Nearshore Processes along Nagapattinam Coast', 2002; Ramesh, 'Sethusamudram Shipping Canal Project and the unconsidered high-risk factors', 2004; Ramesh, 'Is the Sethusamudram Shipping Canal Project Technically Feasible', 2005; Ramesh, 'Sethusamudram Shipping Canal Project', 2005; Rajendran, 'Assessing the Stability of the Sethusamudram Shipping Canal Project', 2005.
[204]Ramesh, *Sethusamudram Ship Canal Project*, 2006.
[205]Joseph, *Investigating Seafloors and Oceans*, p. 184.

OF CYCLONES AND SALINITY

As the project's lacunae began being noticed, others started to scrutinize its lack of sensitivity to cyclonic agency. Of over 60 cyclones that hit Tamil Nadu between 1890 and 2000, 36 were brutal, surpassing wind speeds of 90 km/hour. This only endangered the project's destiny, combined with the fact that the Indian Meteorological Department has designated the Sethu Canal route as a high-risk zone as its return period of wind speeds of 65 km/hour was less than 3 years, and the return period for cyclones was less than 4.5 years.[206] Such granular data called for more robust projections of tsunami impact. The feasibility studies preceded the tsunami of 26 December 2004. Naturally, the rapid impact assessment proposed to the Ministry of Environment and Forests, and the L&T Ramboll detailed project report, modified in February 2005, undermined the question of tsunamis. That was despite research findings that warned of the Palk Bay region's increased susceptibility to large subduction-zone events like tsunamis and earthquakes.[207]

Furthermore, there was the issue of unplanned dispersion of dredged matter from dumping sites. In the December 2004 tsunami, subaquatic sediments were cast ashore and, as the ocean receded, it imbibed fine heavy minerals, clays and silts into the marine bed, significantly transmogrifying the continental shelf. Nearly four-fifths of the canal's estimated budget was because of dredging and dispersal, and the sites

---

[206]Ramesh, 'Is the Sethusamudram Shipping Canal Project Technically Feasible', 2005; Ramesh, 'Sethusamudram Shipping Canal Project', 2005; Jeyanthi, 'Cyclone Disaster Management', 2002; Ramesh, *Sethusamudram Ship Canal Project*, 2006.

[207]McCloskey, Nalbant and Steacy, 'Earthquake risk from co-seismic stress', 2005; DoD, 'Preliminary Assessment of Impact of Tsunami in Selected Coastal Areas', 2005.

chosen for dredge-dumping sites were, ironically, susceptible to monsoonal erosion and prolonged ecological decrepitude.[208] This was closely linked to the coral population along channel route, comprising 'major groups of biological resources like sea fans, sponges, pearl oysters, chanks and holothuroids', that could become extinct because of the dredging in 'an area of about 6 km² along the channel alignment in Adam's Bridge and about 16–17 km² in Palk Bay/Palk Strait area.'[209] Aligned to this was the question of marine chemical properties (chemical oxygen demand, biochemical oxygen demand, oil, grease, chlorides, sulphates and nutrients) and biological properties (coliform count, phytoplankton and zooplankton), whose imbalance could disrupt the ecosystem. The impact assessment addressed physical properties (pH, electrical conductivity, salinity, turbidity and temperature), but had not factored in sediment quality. Another hitherto elided impact of tsunami on the region was that almost 49 per cent of coral colonies in the Gulf of Mannar had shrivelled to 36 per cent, while the Palk Bay's cover contracted from about 27 to 19 per cent, alongside about 7 per cent damage to the entire coral system.[210]

It also seemed to environmentalist critics that there was inadequate transparency in honouring the ministry's guidelines, like restrictions on 'discharge of bilge, ballast, treated sewage, solid wastes, oily wastes and spillage of cargo,'[211] dredging suspension during fish breeding seasons and observance of

---

[208]Ramesh, 'Is the Sethusamudram Shipping Canal Project Technically Feasible?', 2005; Rajamanickam, 'Sethusamudram: Can it remain safe and stable', 2005; Rajendran, 'Assessing the Stability of the Sethusamudram Shipping Canal', 2005; Rajendran, 'Sethusamudram shipping canal project', 2005; Seralathan, 'Disposal of dredge spoil', 2006.
[209]Rodriguez, *Review of the Environmental Impacts*, p. 18.
[210]Kumaraguru, Jayakumar, Wilson and Ramakritinan, 'Impact of the tsunami of 26 December 2004 on the coral reef environment', 2005.
[211]MoEF, 'Letter No. J-16011/6/99-IA-III'.

recommended dredge dispersal mechanisms from dredged sites.[212] The collective impact of these shortcomings was mortifying for environmentalists, especially when all the ideological fuel seemed to be monopolized by secular or religious expressions in the social discourse. There was no likely intended malfeasance in Sethu Project's feasibility reports. But there was evidently a lack of awareness of the total systemic damage, extending to the depopulation of molluscs and polychaetas owing to dredging.[213]

DENTED AND SEDIMENTED

By and by, the canal project was turning into a scheme of computing 'the inherent value of nature' hastily shoved in an 'economic calculus'. If the Sethu Project was undertaken, coral resuscitation could take as long as five years after dredging—as evident in coral rejuvenation at Indonesia's Banda Island after volcanic lava damaged its coral reefs, or bleaching of corals in the Lakshadweep Islands that took almost as long to recover.[214] Even chances of regeneration are generally slim.[215]

A Lankan rapid assessment of the Sethu Canal's environmental impact (at the Lankan reef sites of Eluvaitivu, Analaithivu, Pungudutivu, Karathivu and Kankeasanthurai) showed between 35 and 58 per cent living coral cover in 2005,

[212]Seralathan, 'Disposal of dredge spoil', 2006.

[213]Ramakrishna and Alfred, *Faunal Resources*, p. 257.

[214]Iyer, *Towards Water Wisdom*, p. 247; Tomascik, Van Woesik and Mah, 'Rapid Coral Colonization', 1996; Arthur, Done, Marsh and Harriott, 'Benthic recovery four years after an El Niño-induced coral mass mortality in the Lakshadweep atolls', 2005.

[215]Hughes and Tanner, 'Recruitment failure', 2000; Lourey, Ryan and Miller, 'Rates of decline and recovery of coral cover', 2000; Pandolfi, Bradbury, Sala, et al., 'Global trajectories of the long-term decline of coral', 2003; Lambo and Ormond, 'Continued post-bleaching decline', 2006.

which was found to have shrunk to between 27 and 49 per cent in 2021.[216]

A key structural component of corals—Scleractinia—depends on photosynthetic symbionts, like zooxanthellae. Sedimentation impedes symbiotic photosynthesis, intensifying mucus secretion, and worsening energy and health. Chronic sedimentation only further worsens the recovery period of corals lost due to dredging. And increased sedimentation assaults coral juvenilia, expediting depopulation.[217] As the photosynthetic potential of symbionts is choked, siltation on sedentary organisms, like corals, pearl oysters, algae, gorgonids, echinoderms, annelids, prochordates and the embryonic mass of marine creatures, disastrously alters oxygen and pH levels due to mineralization, spreading chain reactions of death waves through the ecosystem. Hence, the continual danger of anthropogenic waste demands stronger legal applications, especially in the Palk Bay region, which harbours one of the richest seagrass and seaweed ecosystems globally.[218]

Seagrasses regulate erosion, deposition and sedimentation, facilitating natural piscine nurseries and hatcheries for turtles and dugongs.[219] Turbidity caused by dredging, changing levels of

[216]Weerakoon, Goonatilake, Wijewickrama, et al., *Conservation and Sustainable Use of Biodiversity*, 2020; Arulananthan, Herath, Kuganathan, et al., 'The Status of the Coral Reefs of the Jaffna Peninsula', 2021.

[217]Riegl and Branch, 'Effects of sediment on the energy budgets', 1995; Philipp and Fabricius, 'Photophysiological stress in scleractinian corals', 2003; Esslemont, Russell and Maher, 'Coral record of harbour dredging', 2004; Weber, Lott and Fabricius, 'Sedimentation stress in a scleractinian coral', 2006; Bak and Meesters, 'Population structure as a response of coral communities', 1999; Flood, Pitt and Smith, 'Historical and ecological analysis of coral communities in Castle Harbour (Bermuda)', 2005; Gilmour, 'Experimental investigation into the effects of suspended sediment on fertilisation', 1999; Fabricius, 'Effects of terrestrial runoff on the ecology of corals and coral reefs', 2005.

[218] Jagtap, Komarpant and Rodrigues, 'Status of a seagrass ecosystem', 2003.

[219]Gacia and Duarte, 'Sediment retention by a Mediterranean *Posidonia*

salinity, diminishing light quanta, alteration of seabed biomass, tissue nutrients, chlorophyll quanta, metallic concentration, and the like, pose lethal threats to seagrass meadows.[220] Ecosystem symbiotically linked to seagrasses are also adversely affected, changing regimes of siltation and deposition, leading to eutrophication—disproportionate concentration of nutrients— that causes the supersession of seagrasses by microalgae.[221] Naturally, these intricacies of the Sethusamudram Sea's ecosystem were not everyone's cup of tea, nor was the task of mapping matrices of corals and seagrasses, studying their annual cycles, executing high-precision and staggered empirical tests, or instituting a robust environmental management and dredge-dispersal mechanism.

Mercifully, not all was inglorious in the shadow of Ram Setu. Whenever the travesties of the Sethusamudram's environmental impact assessments are discussed, one must be equally mindful of the great milestone that a committed group of geologists and civilians saw through in the resurrection of the almost drowned Vaan Island.

---

oceanica meadow', 2001; Duarte, 'The future of seagrass meadows', 2002; Waycott, Longstaff and Mellors, 'Seagrass population dynamics and water quality', 2005; Sheppard, Lawler and Marsh, 'Seagrass as pasture for seacows', 2007.

[220]Hemminga and Duarte, *Seagrass Ecology*, 2000; Duarte, 'The future of seagrass meadows', 2002; Zimmerman, 'Light and photosynthesis in seagrass meadows', 2006; Gacia, Kennedy, Duarte, et al., 'Light-dependence of the metabolic balance', 2005; Waycott, Longstaff and Mellors, 'Seagrass population dynamics and water quality', 2005; Filho, Creed, Andrade and Pfeiffer, 'Metal Accumulation by *Halodule wrightii* populations', 2004.

[221]Marbà and Duarte, 'Coupling of Seagrass', 1995; Wear, Sullivan, Moore, et al., 'Effects of Water-column Enrichment', 1999; Peralta, Pérez-Lloréns, Hernández and Vergara, 'Effects of Light Availability', 2002.

AN ISLAND RESURRECTED

By the late twentieth century, the reserve had already seen the ghastly submergences of the Vallanguchalli and Poovarasanpatti islands. As late as 2015, Tuticorin's Vaan Island—one of the Gulf of Mannar archipelago's 21 uninhabited islands—had shrivelled from 20 hectares (1969) to 16 hectares (1986) to 2.5 hectares (2005) to the eerie figure of 1.5 hectares (2015). By then, the Vaan had been dissevered into two, one part already engulfed by the ocean.

Due to overly exploitative coral harvesting, aggravated by a 2016 global coral bleaching incident, the island's coral blanket was seen to diminish from 33.5 per cent in 2005 to 23 per cent in 2016.[222] Everyone knew that the Vaan would also sink by 2022. But just then the most unexpected thing occurred. Since 2017, Vaan Island began reviving. It recovered by over 50 per cent thanks to the ingenious reconstruction of its coralline bed through natural coral recolonization via 10,600 artificial reef modules.

In 2017, the Ministry of Environment, Forest and Climate Change commissioned new research by the Tuticorin-based Suganthi Devadasan Marine Research Institute. The team was joined by engineers from the Indian Institute of Technology (Madras). Together, they revealed that the Thoothukudi (Tuticorin) islands, including Vaan, had witnessed the greatest land cover erosion (71 per cent), followed by Keelakarai (43.49 per cent), Vembar (36.21 per cent) and Mandapam (21.84 per cent), in the last half a century, primarily because of exploitative mining, fishing, rising sea levels and climate

---

[222]Sivarajah, 'Gulf of Mannar isle splits in two, may sink', 2013; Raj, Mathews, and Edward, 'Vaan Island of Gulf of Mannar', 2015; Chaitanya, 'Gulf of Mannar's Vaan Island', 2021; Edward, Jamila, Mathews and Wilhelmsson, 'Status of corals of the Tuticorin coast', 2005; Chaitanya, 'Gulf of Mannar's Vaan Island', 2021.

change. For centuries, coral harvesting had built Tuticorin's old coral houses. Formed of calcareous lifeless reef, islands like the Vaan were paradises for coral harvesters, who extracted annual coral quantities of nearly 25,000 metric tons, in the 1970s and 1980s, from the Sethusamudram region. Coral mining was delegalized in 2001 as the Government of India listed corals in Schedule I of India's Wildlife Protection Act. In 2005, the Supreme Court passed a stay on coral mining. However, by then, 32 square kilometres of the Gulf of Mannar had already vanished.

Other islands in the Tuticorin group told similar dreary tales. Koswari had shrunk from 20 to 7.70 hectares, and Kariyachalli, from 21 to 6 hectares. If these islands are not attended to urgently, they might drown by 2036. Then there are the Vembar group of islands (Upputhanni, Puluvinichalli and Nallathanni), the Keelakarai islands (Anaipar, Valimunai, Poovarasanpatti, Appa, Thalaiyari, Valaim and Mulli), and the Mandapam islands (Manoliputti, Poomarichan and Pullivasal) that are feared to drown over the next four–six decades.[223] Nonetheless, there is also the hopeful paradox of four Mandapam islands—Shingle, Hare, Manoli and Krusadai—that have grown by 17 per cent. Morphology and geomorphology from these, combined with data from successful tests at Vaan Island, harbour the solutions for restoring the disappearing reefs and islands of the Sethusamudram Sea.

A major finding from the Vaan experience is that the reduction of human interference in the environment can control macro- and meso-plastic pollutants and refine the quality of piscine life. This was evident in several spots of the Gulf of Mannar where macro- and meso-plastic levels reduced by about 51.5 per cent and 28 per cent, between February and May 2020. Simultaneously, the average fish density in Tuticorin islands was

---

[223]Chaitanya, 'Gulf of Mannar's Vaan Island', 2021.

found to grow by 22 per cent, and the parrotfish population (*Scarus ghobban*) also rose by almost 40 per cent.[224]

Tales from the Vaan and the other Tuticorin islands may appear as digressions in the Ram Setu saga. But these too are manifestations of a sacred ecosystem that millennia of human stories have bestowed with holy forms. Unbeknownst to political watchers from the Indian heartland, Susskind's environmental diplomacy had taken a new avatar in the Gulf of Mannar. And so, the plot of 2007 had thickened. The new millennium had begun with the promise of Ram Rajya. But—to turn one observer's wry aside into a question—was it mostly Raj, and almost no Ram? Or, as another asked: whose Ram Setu is it anyway? And, finally, a third added: what is Ram Setu anyway?

[224]Narayani, 'Lockdown improved coastal ecosystems', 2020.

ANGLING IN THE
TIME CONFLICT

Pamban's dwellers are captives of the Indian Ocean's hydrological anarchy.[225] Common catastrophes— earthquakes, aquamarine instability, soil erosion and shifting deltas—exert far greater influence on their lives than political ideologies. Ram Setu itself embodies the ephemeral nature of their dwellings, livelihoods and fishing resources. An interesting example of the region's environmental caprice can be seen in the hamlet of Ramakrishnapuram, close to Rameswaram. Climatic variations that affect oceanic currents, and oscillatory movements of Ram Setu, alter the direction of fish fleets otherwise trapped by beach-seines off the coast of Ramakrishnapuram. During certain seasons, the fish swing out of their course cutting across Ram Setu to another village before they reach Ramakrishnapuram. This ostensible ecological nuance is a vivid sign of the vulnerabilities of the human and psychological terrain at hand. The name of Ram—believed to be greater than the Lord himself—does not intervene in this aquascape. Maybe this is what the most profound meaning of the Lord's name entails. And this is only the tip of the iceberg.

The volatility of the geopolitical equation between Sri Lanka and India smudges dichotomies between the licit and illicit, the local, the national, the regional and the international, in

---

[225]Wink, 'From the Mediterranean to the Indian Ocean', p. 439.

and around Ram Setu. The ocean does not understand fishing regulations laid down by nation-states. Pamban's fishers, who understand little else besides the ocean, are rendered the villains or victims of innocent trespasses across the international maritime boundary. As two postcolonial states assert their independence by inscribing cartographies over the Sethusamudram Sea, the diurnal forays of fishermen from either side globalize the regional waterscape by subverting the national seas into a shared ocean. Unlike oil, minerals, or fish, neither the ocean nor Ram Setu can be quantified for use and exchange values.

The Sethu Canal Project was to become the perfect specimen of human incomprehension of the deep mysteries of oceanic life and how they are entangled with human civilization's devotion, atheism, nationalism, secularism and constitutionalism. The project threatened to disrupt the symbiotic relationship that has prevailed for centuries between the human and non-human communities in and around Pamban and Jaffna. The proposed canal, that never even reached the halfway mark, was also a siege on the sovereignty of the ocean itself, that, unlike hard surfaces, is not subject to phrasal turns like *the land beneath our feet*.

ANGLERS OF PAMBAN UNITE

As early as 2004, when the first feasibility studies of the Sethu Project were conducted, fishers of Tuticorin and Ramanathapuram realized that it would turn into their nightmare. Being the harbinger of a modernity that they were suspicious of, the canal was seen as much more than a threat to their economic survival as a million-strong community. Environmentalists had already termed it as 'one of the most controversial projects that independent India has undertaken.'[226] Tensions over the Sethu Project became more palpable when the Tamil Nadu government

---

[226]Puthucherril, 'A Case Study of India's Policy and Legal Regimes', p. 486.

conducted gatherings of fisherfolks in January 2005 to give them a platform to voice their dissent. At one such gathering in Ramanathapuram, flying chappals disrupted the meeting, leading to police using force to disperse the crowd. AIADMK leaders alleged that the crowd was politically motivated. The gatherings at Nagapattinam and Tiruvarur fared no better, as Tamil Nadu administrators wound up the hearings by 'citing public disturbances at the venue and during the proceedings as the cause.'[227]

In 2004, O. Fernandes, the co-convener of the Coastal Action Network—a nongovernmental organization representing fisherfolk's bodies and environmental protestors—had petitioned the Madras High Court seeking the invalidity of public hearings conducted by the state. He claimed that the hearings were based on an unsatisfactory 'Rapid Environment Impact Assessment Report' when, in fact, they should have considered the 'Comprehensive Environment Impact Assessment Report'. According to the Coastal Action Network, the authorities had rushed through the process in unconstitutional haste. Consequently, the 'hearings were marked by pandemonium, shouting matches for political parties that forced through narrow political interests.'[228] But the resistance was dealt a hammer blow when, on 17 December, the High Court bench quashed the petition.

The bench ruled that the Tuticorin Port Trust, the Sethu Project's nodal agency, had submitted all requisite records to the Tamil Nadu State Pollution Control Board before initiating the public hearings. The bench added that environmental sustainability could not be made a cause of protest to obstruct India's infrastructural and scientific advancement. Accordingly, the Sethu Project was to be treated as a cornerstone of the

---

[227]Moorthy, 'Working the Federal Polity', 2004.
[228]Puthucherril, 'A Case Study of India's Policy and Legal Regimes', p. 486.

nation's future, a vision to 'turn India into a powerful and modern industrial state' in an age that accepted 'power, not poverty or weakness'; and that India's destiny was to become a 'highly industrialized and prosperous' society to compete with the Chinese and Japanese, without losing the favour of 'Westerners'.[229] The court directed district collectors to expedite the hearings. The verdict reverberated like a death knell through the coastal villages. Beaten but not broken, the fishers withdrew from the political scene reeling under the weight of their fears. Though the battle for the Palk Strait was far from over, the clock seemed to be ticking faster than ever.

Without hopes of legal redressal, fisherfolks' groups like the Minority Communities Fishermen's Association, the Country Boats Fishermen's Panchayat and the Singaravelar Fishermen's Forum, scattered across Rameshwaram, Pamban, Tuticorin, Thracepuram and Vercode, aligned against the Sethu Canal Project. These were joined by the All-Fishermen Associations, the Fishermen's Association, the Country Boat Fishermen Association, the Mechanized Boat Owners' Association, the Vercode Fishermen's Association, and the Democratic Fish and Fishery Workers' Association, coalescing into a formidable front to resist the unstoppable upheavals to the dignity and livelihood of Tamil fishers.

The fishers had not forgotten the loss of Katchatheevu—awarded to Sri Lanka in the 1970s—and the more recent establishment of the Tuticorin New Harbour, which nearly eradicated local rowing boats or *thoni*s (as known in Tamil). The loss of dignity did not end there. Commercial prawn farming became the dominant method of fishing compared to traditional modes. Pazhaverkadu stood as an extreme case, where the once thriving fishing community was left to be helpless spectators as prawn farms gobbed up the sea and pollutants seeped into the

---

[229]'O. Fernandes vs. Tamil Nadu Pollution Control Board', 2004

waters. With the canal, the marine pH levels would turn acidic, leading to the depletion of pearl banks, seagrasses, seaweeds and the already fragile coral colonies. And with them would go the species that spawned and fished in these waters, including dugongs, dolphins and lobsters.

BETWEEN SCYLLA AND CHARYBDIS

As Tamil political parties gauged the weight of fishers as a constituency, allegations flew thick and fast, and alliances fragmented. The party Marumalarchi Dravida Munnetra Kazhagam and the Communist Party of India (Marxist) accused the AIADMK-led Tamil Nadu government of sabotage through misinformation and fanning the flames of discontent in a public that was already up in arms. The claim was supported by the union minister for shipping, road, transport and highways, also a DMK leader. It was whispered that Chief Minister Jayalalithaa was 'supposedly unhappy' because the project was being executed by a Congress-led administration at the centre.[230] The political volleys only served to deepen the trust deficit between Tamil fisherfolk and the ruling establishment. In the eyes of the former, political parties and corporate stakeholders seemed to be secretly united, unmoved by fears of human and non-human lives that would be ruined by the fallout of the canal.

Lurking in the promise of the canal was the spectre of displacement. It would prohibit fishermen from casting their nets 'for about 167 km, starting from Adam's Bridge to the Bay of Bengal, for a width of 0.3 km, about 51 sq km of the total area.'[231] The Sethusamudram Corporation seemed to coldly advise fishermen to find other means of livelihood. The canal would immediately affect 100,000 people across 130 villages

---

[230]Ram, 'Sethusamudram Project', 2005.
[231]Subramanian, 'Fishermen's Protest', 2005.

in the Sethusamudram Shipping Canal zone—40 in the Gulf
of Mannar and 90 in the Palk Bay—whose subsistence was
drawn from fishing, seaweed harvesting, chank gathering and
coral quarrying. Their predominant lifeline was their fishing
catch, amounting to about 80,000 tons a year.[232] The National
Fish Workers' Forum estimated that about 500,000 fishermen,
across almost 140 fishing bases from five Tamil coastal districts,
would be deprived of livelihood by the canal. That number was
revised to 'approximately fifteen lakh [1.5 million] fishermen.'
Like the Katchatheevu affair, which became a *'fait accompli'*,[233]
the fishers were once again likely to be stranded between Scylla
and Charybdis.

The Sethusamudram Corporation, meanwhile, publicized
the grand benefits of the canal, promising savings of more than
₹500,000 per voyage, sustained economic growth along Tamil
Nadu's coast, accelerated maritime exports and geostrategic
vantages. This would come at the cost of restricting fishermen's
mobility, fishing schedules and general freedom, while subjecting
them to being branded as smugglers and imprisoned if they failed
to abide by the rules. In any case, the fishers' schedules had
been tightened to a 5.00 a.m.–9.00 p.m. fishing window during
good weather, while for about half a year, fishing activities were
restricted by climatic vagaries. The canal would not only change
all that but also compel them to stay awake throughout the night,
so that they could protect their boats and nets from colliding
with large ships and being shredded by marine traffic. That
was not all. The canal's annual maintenance dredging indicated
more devastation. The amount of silt and clay expected to be

[232]Sacratees and Karthigarani, *Environment Impact Assessment*, p. 53; Victor,
'Sethusamudram Ship Canal Project', 2010.
[233]Raju, 'Sethusamudram Ship Canal Project', p. 82; Raju, 'The (In)Security
of Fishermen in South Asia', p. 168; 'Abandon Sethusamudram project',
2014; Divan and Rosencranz, *Environmental Law and Policy*, p. 938; Gaan,
Environmental Security, p. 194.

dredged annually, estimated at 0.1 million cubic metres, along with plans of reclaiming land in Mandapam, Ramanathapuram and Pamban, threatened to trample beaches or asphyxiate the sea itself. As the dredgers readied to bisect the aquascape from its natural inheritors, a conflict was festering along the Tamil coastline.

THE GREAT COASTAL REVOLT

On 2 July 2005, Madurai's air crackled with tension as Prime Minister Manmohan Singh prepared to inaugurate the Sethu Project. The absence of the Tamil Nadu chief minister marred the ceremony otherwise billed as a monumental leap for India's infrastructural expansion. Nearer the sea, groups of fishermen were erupting in revolt. The resistance was severe at Thracepuram, where black flags flew atop every fisher's residence on 1 and 2 July, each wearing a grim face of defiance. Fishermen in Tuticorin swept rallies in the town as they declared fishing strikes. The revolution had been brewing for some months. Four days before the project's launch, Tuticorin's fishers had derailed a public hearing organized to discuss the canal's implications. They accused the administration of carrying out absurd hearings that helped it greenlight the destruction of their livelihoods. And a month later, the conflict had escalated and spread to other parts.

On 2 August, as dredging began, over 1,500 fishermen and activists gathered at Arcottuthurai to block the operations near Point Calimere, in Nagapattinam. About a hundred policemen, forming a human wall, attempted to prevent the fishermen from making it to their boats. Coast guard vessels patrolled the sea waters to thwart the protest. Nevertheless, over the next three days, fishers poured into Athur, Tiruchendur and Tuticorin in droves, clamouring for a complete overhaul of the Sethu Project. They also levelled charges about the state's use of tsunami protection measures as an excuse to ignore illicit garnet sand mining in the coastal villages and rampant coral harvesting in the Gulf of Mannar. Thracepuram emerged as the nucleus of the anti-Sethu-Canal campaign, with the rage of the fishers having extended to the Tuticorin New Harbour Project. They pledged that if tenders for global investment opened, they would circle the dredgers in the Palk Bay in an act of protest unto death.

Gradually, the protests fanned out to Jegadapattinam, Kameswaram, Pushpavanam, Serudur, Arcottuthurai, Pamban, Rameswaram, Ramanathapuram, Pudukottai, Nagapattinam, Vizhundhamavadi, Tirunelveli, Tuticorin and Kanyakumari. Fishers stood in solidarity as they asserted their rights to the sea and the coast that were being threatened by foreign trawlers. They also alleged that Tuticorin's coastline was being rebranded as tourist spots in a convergence of interests of the state with the World Bank and global firms.[234] The narrative of the fishermen's protests sought to paint state-led tourism as a Trojan horse, with the secret goal to displace fishers and destroy their autonomy.

The protestors were not without their detractors who dismissed the uprisings of July–August 2005 as part of India's 'long and often wildly misapplied tradition of civil disobedience,'[235] especially since the Sethu Canal was seen by powerful corporate, political and intellectual elites in Delhi as India's geostrategic empowerment in maritime geopolitics. It was argued by this lobby that fishermen's livelihoods would be affected only in Arimunai and Dhanushkodi, and would be confined to 'negligible' numbers and 'temporary' shifts.[236] Meanwhile, Lankan environmentalists countered in favour of the Tamil fishers by arguing that about 35 to 70 per cent of Lankan resources were harvested on the Indian side of Ram Setu; thus canalization could wipe out the ecosystem, on a road

---

[234]Subramanian, 'Fishermen's Protest', 2005.
[235]Pai, 'Non-State Threats', p. 171.
[236]Suryanarayan, *Conflict Over Fisheries*, p. 148.

to extinction for oceanic life.[237] The bilateral defiance could well have become a saga of indigenous resilience pitted against the stampede of an illusory developmental ideology.

Amid this escalating crisis, retired major general S.G. Vombatkere, wrote a powerful open letter to the president of the Indian National Congress, the Indian prime minister, and the Indian president in 2007. His words echoed grim tales from Dhanushkodi's fraught coastline as fierce protests by Hindutva-oriented religious rights organizations broke out in several parts of urban India—including Tamil Nadu. The loud and uncompromising representation put forth by affiliates of the Sangh had been more effectual in galvanizing a volatile cocktail of religion, politics and ecological activism than the fishermen could do for their survival. Vombatkere's voice had the sobering clarity to reveal that the religiously motivated anti-Sethu-Canal protestors—for whom Ram Setu was a sacred bridge—had succeeded in deflecting the most pressing issues of the fishermen and coastal communities. And so, the major rued that:

> The issue at hand in the current Ram Setu controversy is whether the strip of submerged land connecting India with Sri Lanka is natural or created by human intervention, and not whether Lord Rama is a real or mythological character. The scientific data shows that the strip of land is natural. Anybody who denies the existence of Lord Rama in the minds of the people is certainly misguided and perhaps also ill-motivated ... those who now oppose the Sethusamudram project on religious grounds have gained media attention and those who have from the outset been opposing it on grounds of human displacement, ecological reasons and even on economic viability grounds have been sidelined and forgotten. The displacement of thousands of

---

[237]Withanage, 'Sethusamudram', 2010.

fisherfolk and their loss of livelihood and the undoubted environmental damage that will occur due to dredging the channel to create a canal do not need elaboration, except to say that if these costs are taken into consideration, the project may actually prove economically unviable.[238]

Given the lack of the Indian state's engagement with questions of fishers' livelihoods, religion continued to take up centre stage as a potent ally for arguments of the canal's economic unviability. In this new alliance, fishermen and environmental activists were demoted from being stars to bit actors, distant and nearly peripheral. At the altar of political expediency, Ram Setu, the oceanic wonder and the metaphysical reverie, was redefined once again as Hindu civilization's great symbol of technological mastery, and the Indian Ocean was reimagined as the unchanging testimony to Lord Ram's perennial reign.

One way or another, the Sethu Project was meant to be stalled. But the fishermen's woes would not end there. Of late, the Lankan administration has been particularly stern about tackling the Palk Bay fisheries conflict—a nearly five-decade-long micro-political battle involving Indian fishermen on the one hand, and Lankan fishers and the navy on the other. The conflict dates roughly to the 1970s if not further back. It emerged as an outcome of Indo-Lankan entangled political, economic and environmental histories. Besides its vulnerable ecological heritage, the Palk Bay was the background to the Sri Lankan ethnic war that lasted from the early 1980s to 2009—a war that did not leave Indian Tamil fishers untouched.

In a startling move in 2018, the Lankan government revised its Regulation of Foreign Fishing Boats Act of 1979 to increase the fines for the foreign vessels—likely to be predominantly Indian—found fishing within Lankan territorial waters. Those

---

[238]Vombatkere, 'Letter to President', 2007.

arrested would be liable to penalties between SLR 6 million and 175 million. For India, this law was susceptible to be perceived as creating a threat for the Tamil fishing community. But Colombo, being cautious to avoid provoking New Delhi's ire, offered mixed signals to Indian mandarins. Neither the escalation of fines nor the subsequent appeasement of Indian authorities was an enduring solution to the Palk Bay conflict that had turned the Sethusamudram region into the killing waters of the Indian Ocean.

ORIGINS OF THE FISHERIES CONFLICT

India's fishing industry, which contributes one per cent of its total GDP and five per cent of agricultural GDP, is heavily dependent on Tamil fishers—a community of about a million, that contributes nearly one-fifth of the total national fishing produce. The first known strain felt by Tamil fishers in independent India was in the 1960s, when Indo-Norwegian trawlers arrived in the Palk Bay. They introduced a highly unsustainable capital-intensive form of fishing that aided India's fishing exports. India and Sri Lanka were yet to wake up to the reality that trawling in the Sethusamudram Sea began because the United Nations Food and Agriculture Organization and the Government of Norway had abolished trawling in Norwegian waters.[239]

Throughout the 1970s and '80s, the Tamil fishing industry boomed as fleets and gear improved, ushering in the nylon revolution and the 'pink gold rush' or the 'blue revolution'.[240] These paralleled increasing trespasses by Indian fishers onto the Lankan side, as new fishing methods commanded returns more commensurate with the sea's estimated wealth. As the

---

[239]Srinivas, 'The Palk Bay Dispute', 2021.
[240]Kurien, 'Entry of big business into fishing', 1978; Bavinck, *Marine Resource Management*, 2001.

Tamil Nadu state doled out greater subsidies, privatization of the fisheries increased, traditional vessels were motorized, and the foraging of Indian fishers in the Lankan marine territory became normalized.

Tamil Nadu's trawlers increased from about 2,300 in 1980 to nearly 6,000 trawlers in 2010. The major Tamil site of fishing harvest was the Palk Bay. From 1980 to 1984, the Palk Bay contributed to more than 25 per cent of Tamil Nadu's total fishing catch. Between 1988 and 1992, the quantity went up to 35 per cent. By 1996, it had grown to 37 per cent. Concurrently, the Lankan fishery suffered significant shortfalls. Between 1983 and 2000, the catch from the Jaffna peninsula fell from nearly 49,000 metric tons to a little over 2,200 metric tons.[241] Simultaneously, the harvest from other Tamil districts also deteriorated.

Today, Rameswaram itself accounts for about 5,500 vessels, of which about 2,500 are directly reliant on the Lankan marine territory. The Tamil fishing enterprise comprises a total of 5,800 trawlers, almost half of them in the Palk Bay, in addition to nearly 12,500 motorized boats and more than 1,000 artisanal boats.[242] A combination of adversity and scarcity has led Indian Tamil fishers to adopt non-compliance as a 'more profitable' stance, given the Tamil Nadu government's incentivization of trawlers in Indian (and Lankan) marine territory without due consideration of international principles for protecting marine biodiversity and ensuring fair distribution of oceanic resources.[243]

---

[241]Central Marine Fisheries Research Institute, 'Marine Fisheries Information Service', 1981; Central Marine Fisheries Research Institute, *Marine Fisheries Census*, p. 4; Gupta and Sharma, *Contested Coastlines*, p. 121; Siluvaithasan and Stokke, 'Fisheries under fire', p. 244.

[242]Vivekanandan, 'Crossing Maritime Borders', 2001; Adams, 'Indo-Lanka Fishery Issues', 2015; Prasada, 'Indian Poaching in Lanka's Waters', 2021; Vincent, 'Palk Bay Fishing Problem', 2020; Nath, 'Tamil Nadu Government Calls for Retrieval', 2022.

[243]Shekhar and Prakhar, 'The Indo-Lankan Fishing Water Conflict', 2020.

Artisanal fishers have had to bear the brunt of competition and confrontation from big Indian merchants and the Lankan navy. Official Indian records suggest that from 1983 to 2009, about 250 Indian fishers lost their lives indirectly or directly at the hands of the Lankan navy. Thousands of others suffered economic losses, even after the civil war. In 2012, about 200 Indian fishermen were arrested. The number grew to about 680 the following year; about 790 in 2015; and about 250 by July 2016. From 2015 to 2018, nearly 1,400 Indian fishers and 250 fishing boats were taken into custody by the Lankan navy.[244] In 2020, nearly 80 Indian fishers were incarcerated. Ironically, in December 2021, when Sri Lanka was on the brink of a fiscal collapse, before being rescued by the International Monetary Fund and Indian support, the Lankan navy intercepted about 70 Indian fishermen, and seized 21 trawlers off the Tamil Nadu coast, over suspicions of illegal fishing in Sri Lankan waters.[245]

The Palk Bay conflict is a legacy of ruthless patrolling policies assumed by the Sri Lankan navy since the civil war: of 'shoot first and question later.'[246] More than 75 per cent of shooting, apprehensions and incarcerations by the Lankan navy relate to Rameswaram fishers, who are generally owners of mechanized trawlers (32–42 footers) and artisanal boats. Other Tamil districts that are most vulnerable include Kottaipattinam, Jagadapattinam and Kodikarai (Point Calimere). While a part of the reason for the accidental forays of fishers from these regions is their impoverished gear and stubborn navigational choices, the larger cause is the high concentration of shrimps in Lankan territory. Nearly 500 vessels set sail from Rameswaram every day, traversing the Indian Ocean into forbidden waters, driven as

---

[244]'Attack on Indian Fishermen', 2015; 'Release of Fishermen in Custody of Sri Lanka', 2018.
[245]'As more Indian fishermen are detained by Sri Lanka', 2021.
[246]Manoharan and Deshpande, 'Fishing in the Troubled Waters', p. 79.

much by desperation as by history. As piscine resources in Indian waters have themselves undergone depletions, Indian fishers foray into the perilous fishing zones off Jaffna—a territory they still consider a part of their ancestral Tamil psychogeography.

Back in 1983, the Tamil Nadu government had passed the Fisheries Regulation Act, which restricted mechanized fishing operations to 12 nautical miles from the coast. It was intended to safeguard artisanal fishermen, whose livelihoods relied on nearshore waters. But enforcing the act was a different story altogether. Even today the aggrieved fishers ask: Why legislate if one cannot enforce?

DIN OF METAL ON DARK SEAS

Fast forward to 2017, the Indian government launched the Blue Revolution Scheme with a budget as huge as ₹16,000 million. Accordingly, deep-sea fishing vessels were to substitute traditional trawlers. But the reforms could not untangle the thicket of tensions in the Palk Bay. In 2022, as the Russia-Ukraine War led to the inflation of already crippling fuel prices, Tamil Nadu's fisheries minister announced a controversial plan: the extension of the daily fishing duration from 16 to 21 hours. The bid to expand the state's fishing schemes was another major blow to small fishers. The 1983 act was devised considering mechanized boats with engine capacities of about 70 HP. But by the early twenty-first century, the boats had evolved capacities of 240 HP, while Chinese-made engines could scale a staggering 600 HP. Their merciless speeds meant that mechanized boats could push further into the sea and siphon off marine resources at breakneck speed.

The Indian government, deeply cognizant of the fishermen's strife, is yet to see real success ahead of two decades of bilateral diplomacy with Sri Lanka over the Palk Bay conflict. Even before the termination of the civil war, an ambitious effort to defuse the Indo-Lankan crisis was launched in 2004 by the two administrations via a Joint Working Group on Fisheries. More recently, prime ministers Narendra Modi and Mahinda Rajapaksa engaged in a bilateral dialogue on 26 September 2020, assuring de-escalation of the Palk Bay conflict. On 30 December 2020, when the working group met again, the meeting was attended by the foreign ministries, naval representatives and members of the coast guards. Nevertheless, fresh tension was on the cards. Soon after the meeting, India's Fisheries Secretary raised the alarm. The Lankan navy had arrested 40 Indian fishermen and confiscated six boats.

Reportedly, an annual average of 68—between 11 and 167— Indian fishers face incarcerations each year. Meanwhile, the bilateral developments, though technologically and politically brilliant, have failed to become the much-need balm for the collective consciousness of the Tamil fishers. Lacking representation in the air-conditioned rooms where corporate interests dominate decisions on Pamban's future, Tamil fishers continue to stray or be led astray, like un-exorcised spectres of the politically treacherous waters. As night falls, their engines hoot against a backdrop of shattered stillness on the sea. The Palk Bay remains a theatre of war and unfulfilled dreams. The din of metal upon the dark waters becomes the nightmare of a submarine civilization. Its realities lie censored from public discourses on Ram Setu.

PERFORMING PUJA
IN MID-SEA!

The April of 2008 would go down in the annals of India's
judicial history as the month when the Supreme Court
posed one of the most philosophical questions on Ram Setu.
'Who does puja in the middle of the sea?' asked the honourable
court.[247]

It was an insinuation to The Places of Worship (Special
Provisions) Act, 1991. Less known to the public back then, the
act proscribed the 'conversion of any place of worship', while
safeguarding the 'maintenance of the religious character of any
place of worship as it existed on the 15th day of August 1947'.
But where the act would come under serious scrutiny was that
it defined a 'place of worship' as 'temple, mosque, gurudwara,
church, monastery or any other place of public religious worship
of any religious denomination or any section thereof, by
whatever name called'.[248] By that logic, the great Indian spiritual
and soteriological traditions of worshipping mountains, rivers,
forests, and even winds, fires and rains, seemed not to count
as worthy 'places' of worship.

Nevertheless, could one really blame the court? The
honourable court's question sincerely hoped to establish the
'religious character' of Ram Setu in statutory terms. To many

---

[247]Mahapatra, 'SC: Is Sethu a place of worship?', 2008.
[248]'The Places of Worship', p. 3.

pragmatic and analytical observers, Ram Setu did not still qualify as a conventionally cognizable *place*. More critically, no one indeed worshipped there or, at least, no one literally travelled on a pilgrimage to the middle of the Setu to offer oblations. But, did that not imply that Ram Setu was not really a *constructed* place *in the first place*?

NASA VOTES FOR RAM SETU?

It would be impossible to understand the ramifications of the question posed by the honourable court without reflecting on the kerfuffle that broke out in 2002, when Ram Setu's satellite images photographed by the National Aeronautics and Space Administration were released onto the then relatively new worldwideweb. These spread with lightning speed across the nation, aided by Hindutva groups, who manoeuvred them 'as evidence of the remains of the mythical bridge built by Rama'.[249]

As the images became viral, the Union Ministry for Coal and Mines—under the administration led by Prime Minister Atal Bihari Vajpayee—nominated the Geological Survey of India to execute Project Rameswaram, a palaeogeographic investigation into Ram Setu to uncover the structure's history. According to believers of sacred legends, the *bridge* should have been millions of years old. According to evolutionary common sense, however, the species of homo sapiens was about 200,000 years old, while the Indian subcontinent first became populated about 100,000 years ago. In other words, the Geological Survey of India had been tasked with an extremely grave project. The destiny of the institution itself appeared to be at stake as the movement to reclaim Ram Setu as the glorious architecture of a Hindu past gained greater momentum.

The Survey conducted reconnaissance, drilling, depth

---

[249]Ramachandran, 'Myth vs Science', 2007.

measurements, seabed sampling, sonar imaging, radiocarbon and thermoluminescence dating, between late 2002 and early 2003. Their findings did not seem to disprove—at least not by then—that Ram Setu was a natural formation. Coral dating evidence pointed to the age of Rameswaram Island as being approximately 125,000 years old. This was astonishingly less than the figure of 1.75 million years, otherwise believed by Hindutvavadi activists back then, to be the age of the structure, since *Ramayan* was set in the Treta Yuga.[250] Moreover, Rameswaram's geomorphology seemed to indicate that the island was formed by tectonic shifts, airborne abrasions and littoral sedimentation. Palaeogeographic reports added that about 6,000–7,000 years ago Rameswaram Island's adjoining sea was 17 metres below the present level; 60 metres below, 10,000 years ago; and almost 120 metres below, during the previous glacial maxima, about 20,000 years ago. Arguably, the seabed at and around Ram Setu was raised to near the present level between 12,000 and 18,000 years ago.[251] In the syntax of geologists, this was to be considered the *age* of Ram Setu, correlating to the period of its reef formation. The Archaeological Survey of India also appeared amenable to the theory that Ram Setu was a marine formation—created from calcareous precipitates—upraised between 18,000 and 7,000 years ago due to tidal movements from the Palk Bay to the Gulf of Mannar.

Around the same time, the Marine and Water Resources Group of the Indian Space Research Organization deployed Indian Remote Sensing Satellite data—IRS-P4's Ocean Colour Monitor findings from April 2002, and IRS-1D's LISS-III shots from March–May 2000—to reveal that the Setu comprised 103

---

[250]Sen Gupta, 'Sethusamudram Project and BJP's Pseudo Science', 2007.
[251]Rajamanickam and Loveson, 'Results of radiocarbon dating', 1990; Prabakaran and Anbarasu, 'Coastal Geomorphology', 2010.

small and linear patch reefs formed of coralline accruals.[252] Anticlimactically, the Vajpayee administration—even before the decisive 2004 general elections which would see the exit of the Bharatiya Janata Party from the government—approved a sum of ₹35,000 million for the Sethu Canal Project, that could otherwise be seen to signal Ram Setu's destruction. While the political elites of Tamil Nadu were quick to celebrate it as the realization of 'more than 100-year-old dream of the nation',[253] providence had other plans.

In the middle of 2004, when the newly appointed finance minister of the United Progressive Alliance-led government instituted 'a special purpose vehicle to raise funds for the Sethusamudram ship canal'—then evaluated as being worth ₹24,270 million—the project's capital cost had already more than doubled since 1996.[254] In July 2006, dredging operations commenced in the Palk Bay, with great pomp and show. The spotlight of the ceremony was on six dredgers: Dredger XVI from the Dredging Corporation of India, Pacifique operated by Belgium's Dredging International, Banwari Prem and Triloki Prem belonging to Vector Shipping Services, Darya Manthan from Hong Kong's Chellaram Shipping Limited, and Professor Gurjanov managed by Russia's Baltdraga Limited.[255] Said to be about 17.5 per cent complete in July 2007, the project reportedly saw nearly one-fourth of itself to be concluded by September. But what seemed to discolour the reports was the fact that, since

[252]Bahuguna, Nayak and Deshmukh, 'IRS views the Adam's bridge', 2003; Rao, Girishkumar, Ravichandran, et al., 'Do cold, low salinity waters pass through the Indo-Sri Lanka Channel during winter?', 2011; Stanley, 'Ecological Balance of Sethusamudram Canal', 2004; Murali, 'Applications of remote sensing', 2005.
[253]Sarma, 'What is this Sethusamudram Project?', 2005.
[254]Gupta, 'P. Chidambaram', p. 33; Gupta, 'The Palk Straits Canal', p. 18; 'Sethusamudram Ship Canal Project', p. 50.
[255]Narain, 'Will the Sethu Channel be a Security Risk?', 2008; Narain, 'Informal Hindu Alliance Starts Fussing', 2008.

March 2006, protestors affiliated with the Sangh Parivar had unleashed a defiant and deafening—albeit mostly nonviolent— campaign against the canal, repurposing the hitherto challenged theories of Ram Setu's divine, demi-divine, and semi-human construction.

As the Sangh's supporters cited the 2002 satellite images released by the National Aeronautics and Space Administration, officials from the latter came ahead to respond. In 2007, Mark Hess, a NASA spokesperson, dismissed the ruse that the American space research organization owned any 'direct information about the origin or age of a chain of islands' or if 'humans were involved in producing any of the patterns seen.'[256] Another disclaimer warned that 'to interpret our response as a scientifically rigorous conclusion as to the nature of the Palk Strait islands is both a misinterpretation and misreporting of our response and is inappropriate considering the limitations of our data.'[257] By and by, the Geological Survey of India, the Archaeological Survey of India and the Indian Space Research Organisation too began to solidify their stance against the theory that Ram Setu was a monument of civilizational construction. But the tides had already changed their course over the previous year.

RAM SETU BACHAO ANDOLAN

The Sangh's anticipatory counter-offensive had begun, as Ram Navami celebrations broke out on 6 April 2006, in a nationwide movement to salvage Ram Setu. In a few weeks, 3.6 million defiant Indian signatures were amassed. On 27 September an 11-member delegation, led by the founding president of the Sangh-affiliated Hindu Munnani, petitioned President A.P.J. Abdul Kalam to stop the supposed scheme to eradicate 'Shri

---

[256]Kumar, 'Photos No Proof of Ram Setu', 2007.
[257]Narain, 'Adam's Bridge Issue', 2007.

Ram Setu'.[258] Various other affiliated organizations, including the
Tamil Nadu Sewa Bharati, Hindu Mahasabha, Tamil Nadu Hindu
Munnani, Delhi Hindu Manch, Vishwa Hindu Parishad, Tamil
Nadu Panchayat Presidents' Federation, Sanatan Dharam Sabha
and Hindu Jagran Manch, also dispatched their representatives.
Interestingly, the meeting also featured senior advocates of the
honourable Supreme Court.

Reportedly, President Kalam seemed convinced of 'the
historicity of the Setu', and he had resolved to personally ensure
the protection of Hindu sentiments. The meeting appeared to
offer something for everyone. As the delegates told the Sangh's
inhouse publication, the *Organiser*, the Sethu Canal could help
India save 400 nautical miles, 20 tons of fuel per transit, ₹70,000
per vessel, and about ₹210 billion in foreign exchange, annually.
Suddenly it seemed that the Sangh's rallies were not against the
canal itself. In fact, the delegates seemed to suggest that the
project even made 'good economic sense'.[259] President Kalam's
eloquence had acted as a much-needed emollient to quell the
fears of the Sangh as having been, mostly, unfounded. All that
was needed now was a new alignment for the canal.

Only a dull story would have ended there. By February
2007, the shankaracharyas of all four sacred Indian mathas
united to confer with President Kalam. Hitherto, the ends were
satisfying, though the means were yet to be exhausted. So, the
shankaracharyas now presented a petition to President Kalam,
wherein they hybridized religious imagery with geological
pragmatism and political realism. Accordingly, Ram Setu
was an 'architectural wonder' built by *Ramayan's* Nala and
Nila. As claimed, because Ram Setu was centred on primal
'Vaastushastra', it had withstood the 2004 tsunami, protecting
Kerala and neighbouring regions. Besides, Ram Setu was also

---

[258]'Ram Setu Resolution', 2007; 'Protect Shri Ram Setu', 2006.
[259]Ibid.

a great barrier that militants of the Liberation Tigers of Tamil Eelam had not been able to breach.[260]

President Kalam calmed the shankaracharyas with his profound patience. 'Being a native of Rameshwaram,' he said, he would diligently 'probe into what was occurring there.' The shankaracharyas were probably less placated than the president had hoped for. They had already galvanized the support of the Maharashtrian political party, Shiv Sena, to accomplish the 'task of creating awareness and revolutionizing the thinking pattern of Hindus.'[261] And there were other allies awaiting in the wings.

The birth of social media ensured that the movement to save Ram Setu, whether it was to be harmed at all, captivated the Indian diaspora. On 27 March—Ram Navami Day—several international organizations displayed banners in support of the 'Save Ram Setu' campaign ('Ram Setu Bachao Andolan'). These included the American Hindu Human Rights, the Hindu Forum of Britain, the Netherlands-based Global Human Rights Defense, and Esha Vasyam. By November, the diasporic movement had gained further momentum with the backing of the Hindu Council of Africa, Hindu Council of Australia, Hindu Council of Holland, Hindu Forum of Belgium, Hindu Conference of Canada, Hindu Collective Initiative of America, Caribbean Sanatan Dharma Mahasabha, Mauritius Sanatan Dharma Temples Federation, Federation of Hindu Temples in France, and Italian Hindu Union. The flag-bearers of each organization vowed to lead rallies in the Indian diaspora.

Fuelling their revolutionary zeal from India was a petition in the Madras High Court, in May 2007, filed by the Janata Party president and Sangh supporter Subramanian Swamy. It sought the honourable court to 'restrain the Centre from in

---

[260]'Shankaracharyas unite', 2007.
[261]Ibid.

any manner causing damage to the "Ram Sethu"', while also petitioning the court for guidelines to the centre to investigate the origins of Adam's Bridge. The petition further sought the judiciary's wisdom in designating the structure as a 'monument of national importance'.[262] If there was an incident in history that paralleled the moment, it was perhaps that of Madam Bhikaiji Cama hoisting a prototype of independent India's flag at the International Socialist Conference at Stuttgart, in August 1907—the first instance of an Indian flag unfurled on foreign soil. Like Cama, the diasporic personification of the Indian freedom movement, Swamy became her twenty-first-century counterpart—almost exactly a century later—except, while he was the virtual leader of the intellectual movement to protect Ram Setu in India, his mantras were being chanted in the newly mobilized diasporic entities of the Andolan.

AFFIDAVIT AGAINST VALMIKI?

The Sangh, which had hawkishly studied the triumph of the movement to save Ram Setu, knew which way the nation's morality had swung. Elites in the United Progressive Alliance, however, were more content with old-fashioned footnoted scholarship. In August 2007, in the affidavits filed by the government in the Supreme Court, it was argued that Ram Setu was a natural structure 'caused by tidal action and sedimentation.'[263] This was no falsehood or tardy legalese. But it was not the idiom that the nation—at least the looming majority that clamoured and was heard more—wanted to hear.

Even so, the government's principal witness, the Archaeological Survey of India, testified that since the structure was not provable as being human-made, it failed the criterion to

---

[262]Gotlob, *History and Politics*, p. 47.
[263]Ramachandran, 'Myth vs Science', 2007.

be assessed under the Ancient Monuments Archaeological Sites and Remains Act of 1958.[264] The United Progressive Alliance's loss of political capital could have been controlled had it ended there. But the testimony went on to argue that since the Survey was a 'science and technology department', its view was that '[t]he *Valmiki Ramayan*, the *Ramcharitmanas* by Tulsidas, and other mythological texts, which admittedly form an ancient part of Indian literature, cannot be said to be historical records to incontrovertibly prove the existence of the characters or the occurrence of the events depicted therein.'[265]

If there was ever a recipe for outrage, here was an incredible one. As soon as the news of the affidavit broke out, Ram Setu Raksha Manch activists undertook systematic disruptions of train and road services across Indian cities. Mumbai, Delhi, Bhopal, Patna, Bhubaneshwar, and highways branching from the national capital region to Jaipur and Agra were decked with traffic jams. The overseas media, especially operating out of Britain, found a golden opportunity to hastily register it as the victory of a Hindutvavadi theatre over science and archaeology, while conveniently forgetting how accepting the British regime had been towards the legend of Ram Setu.[266] The Sangh retaliated by impugning the central government for ignoring 'the sane advice of the Acharyas, Tsunami experts, scientists, environmentalists, scholars and reject[ing] the appeals from eminent persons like former Justices Krishna Aiyer and K.T. Thomas,' besides scorning 'the freedom struggle which according to Mahatma Gandhi was aimed at establishing Ram Rajya.'[267] And the Congress president—a naturalized Indian of Italian descent—was derided by a chief minister in a Bharatiya

---

[264]Nanjappa, 'What ASI has to say about Ram Sethu', 2007.

[265]Sharma, 'In Affidavit to SC', 2007.

[266]'Hindu groups oppose canal project', 2007; 'Report on Hindu god Ram withdrawn', 2007; 'Gods row', 2007.

[267]'Ram Setu Resolution', 2007.

Janata Party-ruled state: 'Ram was born here. He wasn't born in Italy.'[268]

The Sangh even mobilized Muslim and Christian spokespersons to protest the supposed destruction of *their* sacred 'Adam's Bridge'. The result was that the affidavit was publicly tainted as 'blasphemous' and 'sacrilegious' from several quarters.[269] Sangh activists pledged to negotiate for nothing short of Ram Setu being declared a national heritage. And even Congress leaders came ahead to glorify Lord Ram. One such leader, the minister for law, asserted:

> Lord Rama is an integral part of Indian culture and ethos and cannot be a matter of debate or subject matter of litigation in court ... As Himalaya is Himalaya, Ganga is Ganga, Rama is Rama. It is a question of faith. There is no requirement of any proof to establish existence based on faith.[270]

Confronting the backlash, the government retracted the affidavit from the honourable Supreme Court. The minister for culture nobly volunteered her resignation, as a party colleague, no less than the then minister for commerce, bitterly observed that had he been in charge, he would surely have resigned.[271] Evidently, prior to the submission in court, the Ministry of Culture had tried to eliminate three clauses in the document that could offend Hindu sentiments. Of these, only two were stricken down. The one that flew off into the court proceedings was that of the purported denial of Ramayan's historicity. With the withdrawal of the affidavit, the officials of the Archaeological Survey of India who had drafted the document were rewarded with suspensions.

---

[268]'Government in a Fix', 2007.

[269]'Ram Setu Resolution', 2007.

[270]Qtd. in Venkatesan, 'Parts of ASI Affidavit to be Withdrawn', 2007.

[271]PTI, 'Ambika Offers to Resign', 2007.

INCARNATIONS OF SCIENCE

Fascinatingly, 'while the Indian state, invoking secularism, continually counterposed "religious belief" to "scientific facts",' the Sangh contended that Ram Setu was human-made and 'therefore amenable to historical proof.'[272] But did that not imply that the structure was, therefore, not of some supernatural design but born of mortal agency?

Regardless of that fallacy, key members in the government reportedly vouched for their Hindu credentials.[273] 'Science and rationality have taken a beating,' one commentator noted. Another dubbed the movement to save the 'so-called "Ram-Setu" bridge' a specimen of the Sangh's 'obscurantist saffron agenda' alongside the 'sham of "nationalism"' that had triumphed over 'the Indian Constitution and secular rational norms.'[274] Although the leftist parties were united in their contempt for the Sangh's campaign, the Communist Party of India (Marxist) endorsed the affidavit's withdrawal, while deriding the Sangh for parading 'mythology as history' to turn Ram Setu into a 'faith accompli'.[275]

Despite the criticism that the 'Ram Setu Bachao Andolan' was an annihilation of scientific temper, more careful observers were able to discern that science was not absent but had been reconfigured as a performance. The steady periodicity with which critics—particularly the left intelligentsia—lampooned the Hindutvavadis probably acted as a boon for the Sangh. The latter now hybridized its unapologetic nationalist agenda with the 'post-tsunami environmental awareness that the natural bridge had also been a protective barrier to the full impact of the waves.'[276] Likewise, the America-based Hindu rights

---

[272]Menon, 'Ram Setu', 2013.

[273]Nagi, 'Nervous Govt now chants "Ram naam"', 2007.

[274]'Myth vs Science', 2007.

[275]Yechury, 'Faith Accompli', 2007.

[276]Eck, *India: A Sacred Geography*, p. 424.

organization Esha Vasyam argued that 'Ram Setu is as holy to Hindus as the Western Wall is to the Jews, the Vatican to Catholics, Bodh Gaya to the Buddhists and Mecca to Muslims,' wedding religious sentiment to fears of '[colossal] environmental damage such a project will bring about.' And the Hindu Forum of Britain claimed that the so-called scientific grounds of the Sethu Canal had been made 'obsolete by the tsunami of 2004, which radically altered the environment and conditions' of the Sethusamudram region.[277]

Given the Andolan's chutzpah, the prestigious British journal *Ecologist* styled the canal as a destroyer of India's 'cherished beliefs and a delicate ecosystem'—a deed of 'unpardonable sacrilege' that would warrant 'disaster not only for the invaluable biodiversity of the area, but also, through the destruction of fisheries and the salinization of freshwater wells, for the human population' and the 'complex ecological communities'.[278] A popular British travel account, *An Indian Odyssey* (2008), fashioned as a spiritual voyage on the tracks of Lord Ram, went a step ahead to underscore the canal's 'potential to become a new Ayodhya—if governments are unwise enough to drive the project ahead with the lofty disdain for Hindu sentiment that they are currently demonstrating.'[279] Such opinions were doubtless fostered by the Sangh's fierce ideological affirmations that had conditioned the rhetoric of the campaigns against the canal.

According to the Rashtriya Swayamsevak Sangh's Hindi weekly *Panchjanya*'s editor, the idea of the canal itself was 'an old game' to 'humiliate Hindus. Make them feel small and indefensible. Colour them as heathens and pagans, who worship stones and snakes,' sans history.[280] Additionally, the Sangh was

---

[277]'The protest over Ram Setu', 2007.

[278]Bunyard and Vyas, 'A Bridge too Far', p. 12.

[279]Buckley, *An Indian Odyssey*, p. 302.

[280]Vijay, 'Why the Ram Setu must not be destroyed', 2007.

also careful not to waste prospects of expressing distress over how the Congress had deliberately ignored Tamil fishermen's predicaments and warnings issued by the tsunami expert Tad S. Murthy, the retired naval captain H. Balakrishnan, eminent jurists like justices K.T. Thomas and V.R. Krishna Aiyar, and even a former director of the Geological Survey of India, S. Badrinarayanan.[281]

'THERE IS ONLY ONE SETU'

A subtle dotted line bridged the incidents of 2007 to the classic question posed by the Supreme Court bench, in April 2008, to the Hindu Munnani: 'Who does puja in the middle of the sea?' It was not to a petitioner but to the conscience of a society. But the Hindu Munnani's advocate, Soli J. Sorabjee, famously chose to interpret the question literally.

His argument was equally piquant. It was beyond the ambit of the judiciary, he argued, to 'historically and scientifically' question Ram Setu. 'The Court's role is to determine whether the aforesaid belief is genuinely or conscientiously held over a period of time by Hindus and if that be so it falls within the ambit of the freedom of religion guaranteed by Article 25,' under the Constitutional 'right to worship', added Sorabji. Debatably, the 'impairment or even partial destruction of Ram Setu' qualified as a breach 'of the guarantee of freedom of religion'.[282]

Equal to the task, the bench retorted whether, by that rationality, the Himalayan or the Tirumala range or Mathura's

---

[281]*Ibid.* The band of interdisciplinary experts who supported the anti-Sethu-Canal campaign, in their implicit support to the 'Ram Setu Bachao Andolan', were able to rescue the movement from, what S. Balagangadhara would call, the radical unintelligibleness of 'heathen' and Indic ideas to an intellectual public sphere dominated by secular Protestant ideologies; see Balagangadhara, *The Heathen in his Blindness*, pp. 229–235; 274.

[282]Venkatesan, 'Sethusamudram case in the Supreme Court', 2008.

Govardhan Hill, believed to be sacred to Hindu culture, would all qualify as impenetrable to progress and development. Soli's peer, advocate K. Parasaran, resorted to an appeal to psychogeography— not known till date to be one of the informal fallacies. In that light, Ram Setu's placemaking powers were equivalent to the idea of Ayodhya's Ram Mandir. Parasaran's concluding words prognosticated that any injury to Ram Setu might 'cause a wound again in the minds of so many Hindus to leave a permanent scar.' Echoing his sentiments, Sorabji added: 'Without Lord Ram and *Ramayan*, Hindu religion will be a husk.'[283]

The legendary courtroom dialectics would be remembered for years to come, and eventually enter the world of fiction, in the film *Ram Setu* (2021). In one of the film's final scenes, the hero— the eccentric, though brilliant, government archaeologist— delivers a theatrical monologue to thwart a nexus of large nefarious capitalists and the state machinery supposedly out to ruin Ram Setu.

> Milord! To protect a symbol of Bharat's historic loss of prestige—the Qutb Minar—the metro railway network had to be rerouted; although the monument symbolizes loss, we still see it as our historical heritage. The epitome of global artistic excellence, indeed the wonder, that some people also call the symbol of love—the Taj Mahal—was protected by rerouting the Taj Corridor and by shutting down the factories around it that were said to emit pollutants that could tarnish the monument's white marble ... But why is our government so zealous about breaking apart the oldest symbol of love and monument to a woman's self-esteem—the Ram Setu? ... [B]reaking Ram Setu is a blatant attempt to smear the global legacy of Shri Ram, because as long as the monument remains untouched, it

---

[283]PTI, 'Ram Setu May Leave Babri-like Scar', 2008.

will remind the world that whenever someone tries to sully a woman's self-esteem or oppress her, a Lord Ram will cross the ocean with his *vanar sena* [hominoid army] to destroy the Ravans. There may be hundreds of thousands of Ram Temples in the world, but there is only one Setu. Only a Talibanist mentality can seek the plan the destruction of Ram Setu ... the kind of progress that comes at the cost of desecrating cultures and civilizations should be anathema to governments. (Aryan Kulshreshtha, in the film *Ram Setu* [2022]; translation mine)

Though not a true historical depiction of the court proceedings, the above speech—from a film that oddly failed to recoup its budget—captured the essence of the Ram Setu debates that sought to position the 'bridge' as a performed entity. The performance superseded ideological warfronts and courtroom spectacles. It represented a crucible to test the very fabric of India's collective consciousness. Underneath the clever judicial arguments and ethics of environmentalism lay those simmering questions that no one dared to ask—of Ram Setu's ability to remould not just the past and present but also the future. Unfazed by the political pageantry that was unfolding in the Indian heartland, the ancient bridge wriggling at the periphery whispered its own hauntingly ambiguous truths that neither science nor scripture could wholly encapsulate.

Or so one would have thought had the nation's most eminent economists not jumped onto the bandwagon.

On 23 September 2007, one of India's most popular economics columnists penned a virtual obituary for the ₹25-billion-worth Sethu canal. The article that dubbed it as 'a 150-year-old idea for 150-year-old ships'[284] was published in *The Times of India*, which had about three million subscribers. On

---

[284]Aiyar, '150 year dream for 150 year old ships', 2007.

26 September another leading Indian daily ran a similar story anchored by a bewitching passage.

Scattered rocks in shallow sea, a religious fable, an ambitious minister, and riotous crowds? Sounds like a promo of a Bollywood potboiler. Sadly, for India, it's not reel-life, but a continuation of bad policymaking and insouciant politicians stealing a march over scientific and economic opinion.[285]

Since June 2007, a barrage of fiscal critiques had already begun pummelling the Sethu Canal. The project's detailed report, first drawn up in December 2004, was questioned on grounds of inadequate economic foresight. A canal, intended to revolutionize shipping via a navigable channel through the Palk Strait, now became a quagmire, uniting unlikely allies— scientists, Christian missionaries, Vishwa Hindu Parishad activists, conservationists and fishermen. By July 2008, this would go on to become a global coalition. Scientists, economists and environmentalists from Mauritius and Austria to Kenya and to the United States joined Hindu activists in their fight. Critics, even those grudgingly giving credence to the project's promise of enormous economic benefits, were willing to concede that the destruction of Ram Setu would leave a trail of destruction— whether they believed in the legend of the divine bridge or not.

The first cracks opened in March 2007, when reports began trickling in regarding how expensive a voyage the Sethu Project would prove to be. The promised fuel savings for east to west shipping routes were found to be grossly overstated. As for the passage through the canal, the tariffs appeared too steep, enough to dissuade most shipping companies. But even before one could rationally agree to disagree over the economic figures, something rather surreal had already set the brakes on the project's progress.

---

[285]'Rocks in Sea', 2007.

A TROJAN HORSE
FOR LORD RAM?

In January 2007, the Sethu Canal hit a bed of rocks below the Palk Strait's apparently shallow waters. The Dredging Corporation of India's prized asset, DCI Aquarius, deployed to pound through the shoals proved no match for the unyielding rocky bed near Ram Setu. Designed for dredging soft rocks, Aquarius not only failed miserably but also lost a spud, which snapped under the strain.

Bought in 1991 from the Netherlands, Aquarius cost around $200,000. In 2007, it was estimated at more than ₹8 million.[286] A 150-ton floating tug crane, named Thangam, was summoned to save it. When Thangam faltered as well, so did the realist explanations of the curious incident. A former director of the Geological Survey of India attempted to offer a pragmatic critique. He lashed out at the Ministry of Shipping for not appointing experts from the Survey's marine geology division. But more mayhem awaited in the wings. The Dredging Corporation now chose to appoint 'Hanuman'—a 200-ton crane from Vizag—on the project. Its mission was to rescue the broken parts and spud of Aquarius. Alas, even 'Hanuman' floundered.

As late as May 2012, there were reports that Aquarius's

---

[286]Narain, 'Silence, Controversy Shroud Sethu', 2007.

broken spud had turned into a 'nightmare for fishermen',[287] as nearly 50 mechanized vessels had drowned in the Palk Strait after accidentally colliding with its relics. So shocked were the project officials back in 2007 that they had forgotten to mark the zone where Aquarius's spud had been lost, endangering not only the prospects of canalization but also lives and assets on Indian marine territory. The local fisherfolk populace already knew that 'dredging could release toxins buried in the sea.' After the fate suffered by Aquarius, Thangam and Hanuman, they went on to claim that being 'dodged by bad luck in its initial stages' made it evident that the project's misfortunes were 'a sign from God' that the divine bridge should not be disturbed.[288] The panchayat president of the Ramnad district summed up the situation by reflecting that because two 'mishaps' had befallen in a fortnight, there was no doubt left that 'the bridge was indeed built by Ram himself, and it deserves to be preserved as a national monument.'[289] It was as though mother nature had herself paved the threshold to a profound slippery slope, as hundreds of thousands of Hindutvavadi activists prepared in the backdrop to chant slogans opposing the purported obliteration of their sacred monument on the sea.

AN AMBITIOUS ECONOMICS

The Sethu Project's deadline was November 2008—a highly ambitious one, perhaps even ominous. For, until the late summer of 2007, the Sethusamudram Corporation was unable to secure even one client for its proposed sea routes. In September, as the Supreme Court hearing approached, the situation only aggravated. The Dredging Corporation, which was still excavating

---

[287]'Broken spud a nightmare for fishermen', 2012.
[288]Abram, Edward and Ford, *The Rough Guide to South India*, p. 609.
[289]'Hanuman heads for Palk Strait', 2007.

the path of the canal—at least in theory—was yet to replace the vital spud lost earlier. The Sethusamudram Company's rather optimistic claims that it had dredged 43 per cent of Palk Bay seemed much less flattering compared to the truth. Its personnel were disenchanted, having gone unpaid for more than a year. They sought retribution by leaking reports that the dredging had only scraped the top in most places.[290] The projected losses of the Sethusamudram Corporation were estimated to have risen to nearly ₹5 million, while the Dredging Corporation itself was known to have sunk about ₹145 million.[291]

So, this was the bleak stage on which the rest of the drama of the Sethu Project was slated to unfold. As one sharp critic remarked, 'the repeated claims' by the Sethusamudram Company, 'that it will save up to 30 hours of shipping time, sounds suspiciously like a shoe sale that offers a discount of up to 50 per cent.'[292] Until then, the company's broadcasters had promised that, following the canal, travelling around the Indian peninsula would be reduced by 400 nautical miles and 36 hours. The average time gain was estimated to be between 24 and 32 hours. However, a new detailed project report drawn up by L&T Ramboll adjusted time savings to a little over 22 hours,[293] since the real gain for ships from Tuticorin to Kolkata would only approach that figure after estimating pilotage. Seen more realistically, connecting Europe and Kolkata could save merely 8.4 hours, while those from Africa would, in fact, travel for an excess of 3.5 hours before reaching Kolkata.

As regards fuel costs and time-charter savings of coastal (Indian) and noncoastal (overseas) ships, while coastal ships were newly estimated to save an average of $18,000, noncoastal

---

[290]Ibid.

[291]Ibid.

[292]John, 'Sethusamudram Canal', p. 2993.

[293]Rodriguez, John, Arthur, et al., 'Review of Environmental and Economic Aspects', p. 40.

ships could only save as much as $4,000, if not less, if they used the canal. So, although noncoastal ships stood to gain only 28 per cent of the gains estimated for coastal ships, the former would have to expend the same tariff, even while contributing to over 70 per cent of the traffic and 60 per cent of the expected revenues.[294]

New insights emerged from an independent study titled *Review of Environmental and Economic Aspects of the Sethusamudram Ship Canal Project*, later republished as *Review of the Sethusamudram Ship Canal Project: Mitigation and Monitoring Measures as a Management Strategy for the Gulf of Mannar* (2007) by the Gulf of Mannar Biosphere Reserve Trust. The findings revealed that only a minor portion (35 per cent) of the cargo anticipated for the canal would originate from coastal ships, while the majority (65 per cent) was projected to come from Europe, America, Middle East and Africa.[295] This put noncoastal ships at the risk of losing about $5,000 after factoring in slower speeds and amplified fuel outlays in ecologically vulnerable straits. Expenses were also bound to rise because high-end low-sulphur marine diesel oil was obligatory in environmentally vulnerable zones like the Gulf of Mannar Biosphere Reserve. Furthermore, since the first detailed project reports of the project, marine diesel prices had only escalated, threatening to become another agent in the canal's economic impracticality.

LOSSMAKING FOR 200 YEARS?

The economic perils did not end there. The Sethusamudram Company had expended precious resources and time in

---

[294]John, 'Sethusamudram Canal', 2007.
[295]Rodriguez, John, Arthur, et al., 'Review of Environmental and Economic Aspects', p. 40.

generating the opinion that the canal would create tremendous economic and logistical gains without being able to channelize enough evidence to rationalize the canal's economic and infrastructural longevity. By September 2007, fears of underestimated maintenance dredging costs—estimated to be 2 million cubic metres, annually, in the Palk Bay—were running rife. As the 'likelihood of overestimation of the revenues and underestimation of costs' became common knowledge, there was growing trepidation regarding the project's costs and revenues that were also likely to increase and drop, respectively, by up to 20 per cent.[296] And, supposing one were to go ahead and dispose these misgivings, the Sethusamudram Company and the Ministry of Shipping would still have to confront the indeterminable challenge of growing interests on financing loans.

When the project commenced in 2004, its financing costs were calculated based on an Indian rupee loan at an 8 per cent interest rate and a US dollar loan at a 4 per cent interest rate. By 2007—coinciding with the onset of a global recession— interest rates had increased, with the Indian debt rising to 10.25 per cent and the US dollar debt reaching 8 per cent. The loan was structured for repayment over 13 years in three instalments, including a two-year moratorium, along with a 1.2 per cent commission payable to the Government of India for countersigning the loan. After the moratorium, repayment was scheduled over an eight-year period. Due to the revised interest rates, the project's estimated cost was expected to rise by ₹2 billion, alongside an increase of over ₹3 billion in total repayment obligations.

The *Review of Environmental and Economic Aspects of the Sethusamudram Ship Canal Project* estimated that only 30 per cent of the anticipated savings for non coastal vessels—including reductions in fuel consumption, travel distance and time—could

---

[296]John, 'Sethusamudram Canal', p. 2995.

be realistically achieved. As a result, nearly 60 per cent of these ships might have opted to bypass the canal entirely. As the canal's critics underscored, its drawbacks included bad projections for capital and maintenance dredging costs, unanticipated cost inflations due to augmented rates of international and domestic interests, and wrong projections of savings in distance, time and fuel. Accordingly, the Sethu Canal could handsomely recover its costs in a little over two centuries. The alternative for it was to face the label of being a child of 'faulty design' that was deeply hazardous to, among everything else, the 'social fabric not only of India but also of Sri Lanka'.[297]

Five years from then, the project would record an escalation of ₹2.4 billion.[298] Even as economists publicly refused to ally with religious protestors against the project, providence seemed to unite their ends, if not means, ensuring that the canal would 'become one more public sector white elephant.'[299] Comparisons with the Suez and Panama canals made the Sethu Project look even more unflattering. The former could support the passage of vessels weighing up to 65,000 deadweight tons and 150,000–200,000 deadweight tons, respectively. The Sethu Project was powered to be adequate for only ships weighing up to 20,000–30,000 deadweight tons. 'Very Large Crude Carriers like Suezmax, Panamax and Aframax would not be able to pass through the canal.'[300] Political opponents highlighted that 'Poompuhar Shipping Corporation vessels, which transported coal from the eastern ports of Pradeep, Haldia and Visakhapatnam could not pass through the channel.' Arguably, the canal's terminal 'north of Tuticorin, would not even be beneficial to vessels leaving Tuticorin port towards south to European, central east Asian

---

[297]Ramesh, 'Will to Disaster', p. 2652.
[298]Kumar, 'Ram Sethu', 2012.
[299]Aiyar, '150-year Dream', 2007.
[300]Zadoo, 'Big vessels may have to skip Lanka canal', 2007.

and southeast Asian countries.'[301] Gradually, a whole dramatis personae of critics virtually assembled to make the project an albatross around the neck of the Indian government.

Yet, there was something so resilient in the idea of the Sethu Canal that, in September 2014, under the Narendra Modi administration, the shipping ministry assigned the Rail India Technical and Economic Service to weigh alternate alignments.[302] The coming years did not brighten the canal's prospects, though. In 2018, the project's budget escalation was reported to be ₹4.5 billion.[303] But even that seemed to be a puny amount compared to the drastic valuation by the Axis Bank (formerly UTI Bank)— the project's official loan manager—as far back as September 2007. As stated by the bank's capital markets vice president, as early as 2005, the ₹24 billion project had escalated to 35 billion; and to 40 billion in 2007.[304] Ironically, even as the honourable Supreme Court deliberated on Ram Setu in the autumn of that year, it was plain to see that the Sethusamudram Company itself would be one of the greatest losers in the gamble if the court did not rule in favour of religious protestors. As one critic sardonically quipped, one did not 'have to be a North Indian "Ram bhakt" to be worried about the Sethusamudram Canal Project.'[305] If so much was stacked against the project, how could the 'Ram Setu Bachao Andolan' not profit from it?

PROVING HOMER AND VALMIKI

By the beginning of October 2007, it became manifest that officials of the Archaeological Survey of India would have to scapegoat themselves for having 'bungled' on the matter of

---

[301]'Jayalalithaa calls Sethusamudram project useless', 2014.

[302]'Shipping project', 2014.

[303]Rishi, 'Sethusamudram project cost rises by Rs 4500 cr', 2018.

[304]'Ram Setu project faces cash crunch', 2007.

[305]Hazra, 'Ram Setu', 2007.

Lord Ram's historicity.[306] It was now reported that, despite the dissension of the minister of culture, anonymous agents in the administration had chosen to retain sections in the affidavit submitted to the court that the minister had suggested for omission. What made the ministry's situation worse was that, even professional historians—otherwise in doubt of Ram's historicity—appeared to agree that the affidavit was mistimed, logically misplaced and superfluous to its expertise in historicizing Indian religious traditions.[307] The institution had previously conducted pathbreaking research in churning empirical studies on the Buddha's birthplace in Kapilavastu and Ashoka's pilgrimages. Then why the reluctance to historicize Ram?—or so asked Hindutvavadis.

In March 2008, a massive vehicle rally was organized by the Ram Setu Raksha Manch in Delhi, attended by 10,000 devotees and 5,000 vehicles. It commenced from Ramlila Grounds and ended 7 kilometres away, at Rajghat. Led by the Manch and the Vishwa Hindu Parishad, the protest clamoured with the slogan 'Shri Ram is in every drop of our blood.'[308] Not only the opposition, but also members of the government were in no mood to tether the religious tide. A government publication titled *Images India* was introduced in parliament in December 2008. Published by the National Remote Sensing Agency, it contained a foreword by the ISRO chairman that craftily endorsed the Sangh Parivar's axiom that Ram Setu 'may be man-made.' A Bharatiya Janata Party spokesperson (later the minister of environment, forest, and climate change), gushed, 'science has prevailed upon the politics of Congress,' now obliged to 'accept not only Lord Ram but also Ram Setu.'[309]

---

[306]TNN, 'Scholars Divided on Setu Issue', 2007.

[307]Ibid.

[308]'VHP warns against destroying Ram Setu', 2008.

[309]IANS, 'Ram Setu "man-made," says Govt publication', 2007.

Earlier in July, the government had appointed a committee led by the environmental scientist R.K. Pachauri, to study alternate alignments for the canal, which, by March of next year, revealed that almost all alignments in the Palk Strait were marred by ecological hazards. Eight months later, Subramanian Swamy, the eminent co-petitioner in the 2007 Ram Setu case—and by now the author of *Rama Setu* (2008)—once again moved the honourable Supreme Court. While repeating his demand for legalizing Ram Setu's heritage, he argued that the government had censored reports on the ecological unfeasibility of alternative alignments of the Sethu Canal. The court was to deliberate on the matter until February 2011 when it again adjourned its verdict on the project, bringing the canal to a halt yet again.

Interestingly, the momentum of the religious protest movements was such that almost none of the Hindu rights activists probably publicly acknowledged that half of Ram Setu lay in Lankan historic waters—and that half was resolutely referred to as Adam's Bridge. More importantly, any bid to have Ram Setu declared a national heritage 'monument' could not be officiated simply based on a Supreme Court judgement but would require legitimacy from the Lankan side. Even the precious right to religious freedom, safeguarded by the Indian Constitution, was inadequate when it came to securing India's geopolitical control over Ram Setu beyond the International Maritime Boundary Line. From time to time, critics of the 'Ram Setu Bachao Andolan' pursued this argument.

In a petition filed in February 2021, the president of the Dravidian Historical Research Centre argued that even 'the Supreme Court has no powers beyond the Indian borders.'[310] In the previous summer, the DMK Lok Sabha member from Sriperumbudur constituency had appealed to Prime Minister Narendra Modi to finish constructing the Sethu Canal before

---

[310]'Ram Setu Not an Ancient Monument', 2021.

the 2024 Lok Sabha elections, raising alarms regarding growing Chinese influence in Sri Lanka. Besides, the left-liberal intelligentsia was also concerned as to how the overseas media would respond to India's claims of Ram Setu's historicity. Time and again, Indian historians and geologists had raised sceptical eyebrows at the idea of a divine bridge on the Sethusamudram Sea, only to join committees appointed to survey the region's past and present, before once again resuming a noncommittal stance.

In March 2017, the Indian Council of Historical Research, under the Ministry of Human Resource Development, had notified that it would conduct the 'Ram Setu Pilot' project. Its chairperson had even added: 'We have seen that the Greek mythology of Helen of Troy is in fact proven to be true. So, we will speak about "Ram Setu" after the collection of evidence.'[311] But, by April 2018, the council's members turned into reluctant naysayers. The council's newly appointed chair justified its withdrawal from the project in that, 'It is not the work of historians to carry out excavations and work like that. For that, there are apt agencies such as the Archaeological Survey of India.'[312] So who was to resurrect the real story of Ram Setu?

There was clearly an intellectual void left by the lack of serious takers for full-fledged research on Ram Setu. And who would rush to fill this? A group of scientists from America consented with alacrity. And so, on 11 December 2017, the Science Channel owned by Discovery Communications plunged into the drama with a 150-second teaser on an episode on Ram Setu, for its series, *What on Earth*. Those theatrical 150 seconds would leave an enduring impact on the psyche of millions of Indians, who heard scientists claim, therein, that geological explorations into Ram Setu had exposed the remnants of an ancient human-made bridge. The scientists presented a spectacular theory, that the

---

[311]Gohain, 'Is Ram Sethu a Natural Shoal', 2017.
[312]PTI, 'ICHR Not to Conduct Study', 2018.

rocks on top of the sandbars were 3,000 years older than the 4,000-year-old sand bed of Ram Setu, and this, apparently, showed that the former were allochthonous bodies exported from elsewhere. The phrases that mostly resounded in the ears of Indian devotees were: 'building such a long bridge [thousands of years ago] would have been a superhuman achievement.'[313] The dramatis personae of the teaser included Alan Lester, a University of Colorado geologist, Erin Argyilan, an Indiana University geoscientist, and Chelsea Rose, a Southern Oregon University archaeologist. Upon watching the teaser, an eminent Indian earth scientist remarked sceptically that it was 'not clear from the commentary what the dating methods and their error margins were.'[314]

One of the immediate outcomes of the mood created by the documentary was that, in early 2018, India's ruling regime virtually renamed parts of Ram Setu on Google Maps imagery as Sri Hanuman Pratima and Setu Chandra Dweep. This reflected a larger drift in nationalistic reclamation of lost emblems of civilizational heritage. In the case of Ram Setu, however, these names deceptively suggested that parts of it were at least mentally habitable, where Hindu icons could be deified. More curiously, neither Hindutvavadis nor secularists recognized that British colonial geology and modern-day American science had implicitly allied with this nationalist consciousness that sought to be identified as a post-facto anticolonial ideology.

In an irony of ironies, American scientists were more than content to play to a gallery of Indian devotees, while serious Indian scientists believed that the corrosion of the Palk Strait and reconfiguration of coral clusters may have resulted in the creation of a 'bridge'. Calling Ram Setu a human-made structure, therefore, seemed to some Indian geologists to be a specimen

---

[313]Qtd. in Krishnan, 'A Bridge that Lord Ram Built', 2017.
[314]Rajendran, 'A Post-Truth Take', 2018.

of regressive 'post-truth' defying the 'transformative power of science'.[315] Nevertheless, the winter of 2017 was now to join a list of euphoric Indian months, that included the September of 1995, when hundreds of idols of Lord Ganesha suddenly deciding to drink milk from the hands of Indians—unless one was a cynic and simply attributed it to capillary action. A voice as influential as *The New York Times*—generally known to be an adversary of Hindu nationalism—stressed that 'for centuries, pilgrims from the Indian cities of Chennai, Mumbai and Patna, and a few from London, have travelled to the tip of [the] thumbnail island in southern India ... where Sita quenched her thirst, the spot where Rama bathed.'[316] Not surprisingly, then, Prime Minister Modi's 2017 speech during the opening of a new Ayodhya-Rameswaram rail connection recapitulated the fabled event 'of a little squirrel of Rameswaram that helped [Lord Ram] in building Ram Setu.'[317]

It was merely a matter of time now for the government to appoint a new team that was only likely to unearth evidence to substantiate the 'archaeological remains' of Ram Setu— believed then to be no less than a monument. A submarine archaeologist from Assam University (about 3,500 kilometres from Ram Setu)—who was previously an advisor in the 2007 Dwarka excavations to excavate the supposed remains of Krishna's drowned city—came forward to draft a proposal for archaeological studies at Pamban. The historian Romila Thapar meanwhile dubbed it as an 'ideological excavation'.[318]

Back in March 2017, the Indian Council for Historical Research's chairman had even gone on to compare Ram Setu to Homer's legendary Helen of Troy, who was (according to the

---

[315]Ibid.

[316]Schultz, 'In India, A Ghost Town', 2017.

[317]Modi, 'Dr. Kalam inspired the youth of India', 2017.

[318]Schultz, 'In India, A Ghost Town', 2017.

chairman) historically demonstrable. This was notwithstanding the fact that European archaeologists and historians strongly differed on such claims.[319] The chairman's remarks also ran counter to a former chairman of the council who was firm in his view that Ram Setu could throw up 'no evidence from an archaeological point of view'.[320] Simultaneously, the stance by a large section of Indian historians that there was 'no historical evidence for Rama's birthplace' or even birth[321] was vigorously challenged by the historian Meenakshi Jain, who admonished the effort to undermine 'different streams of belief', as legends also 'convey a message that we should try to grasp.'[322]

What was otherwise a great debate among Indian scholars to shape the future of new Indian epistemologies did not go undetected by the overseas media. An anthropology magazine ran a polarizing story titled 'God or Geology', terming India 'increasingly intolerant, nationalistic, and zealous' with its global reputation 'marred by recent attacks on religious minorities and lynchings of suspected beefeaters.'[323] Such oversimplified views of foreign journalism on the debates around Ram Setu were based on old-archaic binaries of science and religion—an intellectual baggage of the European Enlightenment. But Indian media moguls did not lose the opportunity to milk the tide

---

[319]Haywood, 'Was Helen really to blame', 2016; Nolan, 'Troy: Fall of a City', 2018; Dunn, 'Did the Trojan War actually happen', 2020; Jarus, 'Ancient Troy', 2022.

[320]Bardi, 'God or Geology', 2017.

[321]Thapar, 'Where Fusion Cannot Work', 2007; Parkin, 'Historian Romila Thapar', 2022.

[322]Schultz, 'In India, A Ghost Town', 2017. Jain may be placed alongside an emerging school of popular Indian historians comprising Sanjeev Sanyal, Rajeev Malhotra, Vikram Sampath and J. Sai Deepak, whose unorthodox, Hindu-centric and civilizational contentions on Indian history have been undermined in Western and liberal Indian academics.

[323]Bardi, 'God or Geology', 2017.

either. Ram Setu had already entered a galaxy of 'post-truth'.[324] Occasionally, it also collapsed into a theatre of the absurd, as in satires like the one that fictionalized a press conference by the chief minister of Delhi and Aam Aadmi Party chief equipped with 300 pages of evidence charging that a terrible scam in the Treta Yuga had led to Ram Setu's damage in the Kali Yuga.[325] Thankfully, the said article was published as a piece that explicitly announced itself as parody, lest it be considered the truth. It was probably almost believed as such.

LORD RAM—A 'CIVIL ENGINEER'?

The revival of the Ram Setu discourse in the Indian public imagination meant more political fodder. And so, in late 2018, the then ruling establishment broadcast that the prime minister had delivered on its 2014 election manifesto promise to protect the sacred bridge.[326] Instead of renewing plans of the Sethu Canal Project, the government commissioned a new broad-gauge rail connection between Rameswaram and what was now the ghost-town of Dhanushkodi, especially to rejuvenate the latter, which had practically been deserted since the cyclone of 1964.

In 2019, the prime minister ushered in another new project in Ram Setu's vicinity, this time to renovate the 104-year-old Pamban Railway Bridge.[327] The announcement of the foundation ceremony came barely weeks after the Indian Railway Catering and Tourism Corporation Limited unveiled its 'Ram Setu Express-Tamil Nadu Temple Tour', that offered pilgrims a tour of 18 temples in renowned Tamil temple towns at less than

---

[324]Rajendran, 'A Post-Truth Take', 2018; Rajendran, 'The Geo-heritage Value of Ram Setu', 2022.

[325]Upadhyay, 'Mocktale: Kejriwal Alleges Huge Corruption', 2016.

[326]Shekhar, 'Affidavit on Ram Setu in Supreme Court', 2018.

[327]'New Pamban bridge to come up in two years', 2019.

₹5,000 ($67).[328] Styling itself after the legendary bridge, the tour package was bound to act in the public imagination as an aide-mémoire of Pamban's sacred geography.

The Bharatiya Janata Party's decisive electoral victory in the summer of 2019 and return to power with a greater majority meant that the Ram Setu discourse was nowhere near oblivion. In August 2019, the minister of human resource development grabbed the headlines for his speech at the 65th annual convocation of the Indian Institute of Technology (Kharagpur). Addressing a hall of engineers and engineering students, the minister monumentalized Ram Setu. 'If we talk about Ram Setu,' he rhetorized, 'was it built by engineers from America, Britain or Germany?' In the same vein, he termed Sanskrit to be 'the first language in the world' or '*Dev-vaani*' (word of God).[329] Whether or not it was intended as thus, the minister's remarks appeared to be a belated rejoinder to an old tirade by the late DMK leader M. Karunanidhi.

At the height of the anti-Sethu-Canal protests, in 2007, when Karunanidhi was the Tamil Nadu chief minister, he had polemically asked: 'Who is this Raman? In which engineering college did he study and become a civil engineer? When did he build this so-called bridge? Is there any evidence for this?'[330] The statement came days after the Government of India—then helmed by the Congress-led United Progressive Alliance—retracted its controversial affidavit from the Supreme Court. Karunanidhi, a staunch adherent to the Periyarite ideology, saw *Ramayan* as nothing but 'a piece of fiction that allegorically represented the conflict between Aryans and Dravidians.'[331] Karunanidhi's Tamil opponent and successor, AIADMK leader

---

[328]Prasad, 'IRCTC Ram Sethu Express tour package', 2019.

[329]'Ram Sethu was built by Indian engineers', 2019.

[330]Express News Service, 'Where is proof Ram built bridge', 2007.

[331]Ibid.

and next Tamil Nadu chief minister Jayalalithaa, would remain steadfast in her antagonism to the Sethu Project. Although she cited environmental concerns, the 'livelihood of hapless fishermen', and a $100 million deficit borne at the altar of an insolvent project, her opposition meant a de facto alliance with the 'Ram Setu Bachao Andolan'.

However, despite the rather ecumenical acceptance that the anti-Sethu-Canal movement had garnered since 2007, over the next decade and a half, the government seemed to act too tardily on conferring heritage status on the structure in the eyes of disciplinarians. In October 2020, an incensed Swamy took to media outlets to question the prime minister as to why his regime was procrastinating the fulfilment of its promise. Being asked if he now felt undermined having once spearheaded the campaign against dredging Ram Setu, Swamy exclaimed: 'I don't need the credit,' referring to his 15-year-long crusade. 'Lord Ram does!'[332]

On the one hand, the frustration may have looked exaggerated, because, in December 2020, reportedly plans of the Sethu Canal were 'slowly dying due to litigations in the Supreme Court.'[333] The demise of the idea of the canal should have signalled a reprieve for Ram Setu. But Swamy's fears were not unfounded. The ambiguity and fragility of almost any evidence that had stemmed from Ram Setu in the last 150 years could be interpreted in multiple ways.

'FOREIGN HAND' TO THE RESCUE?

As if to illustrate Ram Setu's versatility, in February 2021, the president of the Dravidian Historical Research Centre leapt to challenge Swamy's theories. He moved the honourable Supreme

---

[332]'I don't need credit, Lord Ram does', 2020.
[333]Shivakumar, 'Is the Sethusamudram project being laid to rest', 2020.

Court of India to dispute the veridicality of Ram Setu. The president marshalled evidence from the nineteenth-century German geologist Johannes Walther's *Report*, which was, alas, spaciously and selectively cited as evidence against the dominant Hindu imagination of the sandbars of Sethusamudram Sea.

The petition appended that the 'national [Tamil] poet' Subramania Bharati believed *Ramayan* to be fictional. However, the petitioner probably prevaricated on the fact that, after his appraisals of Victor Hugo, Shelley and Goethe, Bharati had concluded that no 'modern vernacular of Europe can boast works like ... *Ramayan* of Kamban' (the twelfth-century Tamil version of the epic).[334] Given the shortsighted binary frame within which the Ram Setu drama played out, the staple recourse was to see it as a battle between tradition and modernity, or superstition and progress, or secularism and religion, or truth and falsehoods. In almost all these seemingly honourable battles, the casualties were not mistruth, misinformation, naivete, fallaciousness, or social anathemas, but the reputation of the participants and the most critical questions surrounding Ram Setu.

Take the above petition, for example. It was disputed by representatives of the ruling regime not with historical counters but ideologically loaded moral aspersions. Ironically, so engrossed were the seemingly Hindu-centric defendants in attacking the petitioner that they even argued that Walther's study 'was conducted in the time of British Raj which had anything but scorn for the native Bharatiya'[335]—not even bothering to discover that Walther's findings, in fact, were radical in that they unambiguously claimed to have found evidence of a human-made bridge having existed at least twice between ancient India and Sri Lanka.

Similar gaffes were not rare but perhaps the norm in Ram

---

[334]Bharati, *Essays and Other Prose Fragments*, p. 62; Ramaswamy, *Passions of the Tongue*, p. 54.

[335]MahaKrishnan, 'Ram Setu', 2021.

Setu's twenty-first-century intellectual history. Back in December 2015, a Bharatiya Janata Party Lok Sabha member had raised the matter of the Sethu Project in parliament, only to claim that the previous United Progressive Alliance-led administration had chalked out a 'deal with foreign forces' to destroy Ram Setu. The member added that the Setu was a storehouse of huge 'lithium deposits [sic]'—mistaking it for thorium, the real metal found underneath the tombolo.[336] The above comment would probably not have been made in parliament were it not for the Sangh-affiliated Rameswaram Ram Setu Raksha Manch's allegation that a 'foreign hand' desired Ram Setu's destruction so as to usurp its 'deposits of around 3,60,000 tonnes of thorium'. Apparently, as the Sangh activists claimed, the thorium reserves could 'produce electricity for India for the next 400 years, at least, even if the annual consumption is four lakh watts.'[337] No one asked why the current ruling regime had not done anything, then, to harvest that electricity, while safeguarding the sacred tombolo's coral foundations.

It was as though the strawman, 'foreign hand', was a more crucial subject than Ram Setu itself. Indications of its importance lay in a peevish letter written by the Tuticorin Port Trust chairperson, V. Sundaram, on 1 July 1982, to the chief of the Lakshminarayanan Committee (1981) tasked by the government to study the canal's feasibility. Sundaram raised apprehensions over what he called 'the surreptitious subterranean efforts being made by the Catholic Church in Tamil Nadu to influence the Government of India to somehow destroy the Rama Sethu Bridge just in order to give a death blow to an ancient symbol of Hindu religion.'[338] The letter was later reproduced in Swamy's petition against dredging Ram Setu, and he cited it to berate

---

[336]Maurya, 'Need to Ensure Safety of Sacred Ram Setu', 2015.
[337]'Foreign hand behind Ram Setu demolition', 2008.
[338]Qtd in Swamy, *Rama Setu*, p. 218.

'Indian tutees in an Anglo-Indian educational system' and 'toadies of British imperialists'[339] reared on East India Company historians Charles Grant and James Mill, or historical fallacies like the Aryan invasion theory.

The agony of passionate believers in the legend of Ram Setu could be understood. But the polarization between British epistemology and postcolonial Indian nationalism was far too simplistic and misleading. If anything, the British regime had, overall, catalysed the solidification and percolation of the legend, not only in India but also in the Anglosphere. Nevertheless, the amnesia of twenty-first-century proponents of the legend was compounded when the Sangh's supporters branded the Sethu Project—or the practically extinct plan to dredge Ram Setu—as the spewing of 'information created by colonial mindset' that was, accordingly, 'dictated by the British' and imposed in schools and colleges to degrade India's ancient legacies.[340]

Meanwhile, atheists and self-avowed secularists were not far behind in the game of post-truth either. Back in May 2007, the DMK Lok Sabha member for Sriperumbudur (Tamil Nadu) had boldly proclaimed in the House that the 'Sethu Samudram [sic] Project is around 150 years old project. It is the dream of the people of the Tamil Nadu ... conceived by the Britishers,' and, for that reason, the sandbars between India and Sri Lanka should be called Adam's Bridge, 'not Ram Sethu'. This ostensibly non-sequitur assertion was seconded by the Congress member for Palani (Tamil Nadu), who affixed the incomplete fact that the project 'was first proposed by a British, Mr. A.D. Taylor of the Indian Marines during 1860'; this was then corroborated by the Communist Party member for Tenkasi.[341] Each of these assertions were probably ignorant of the contradictory nature

---

[339]Swamy, *Rama Setu*, pp. 20; 37–38; 39; 171.
[340]Sharda, *RSS 360°*, p. 69; Nalapat, 'Stop Delegitimizing the Vedic Age', 2019.
[341]'Shri Vijay Kumar Malhotra Called the Attention of the Ministry', 2007.

of the history that they referred to. Since at least the 1830s, the colonial Madras government was painfully aware of the pure impenetrability of Ram Setu even to the best of imperial capital and technology.

Given this scheme of easy binarizations and hurried virtue-signalling from all ends of the spectrum, it was no longer possible to see 'communalism and secularism as sworn enemies but as the disowned doubles of each other.'[342] Thus, when, in 2023, the Tamil Nadu assembly approved a motion to renew plans for the Sethu Canal, even proletarians in the electorate were alert to the fact that the Ram Setu alignment was manifestly unfitting for the project. Meanwhile, the unusually quiescent stance of the central government—headed by the Bharatiya Janata Party and its allies for a third term since the summer of 2024—on Ram Setu's heritage status continued to puzzle many observers and, certainly, hardline Hindutvavadi factions.

The Supreme Court's recommendation to the government to elucidate its position on whether—and if so in which alignment—the Sethu Canal will be constructed, remains unconcluded. So does the government's view of commemorating Ram Setu as a national monument. But even a Hindu-centric Indian regime cannot move unilaterally on Ram Setu, half of which lies in Lankan marine territory. The multifaceted, and sometimes contradictory, history of Sri Lanka's dissenting stance on the Sethu Canal would complicate the intellectual contours of Ram Setu, which now extended beyond Indian geologists, historians, archaeologists, fisheries, fiscal narratives and electoral semiotics.

Could the Lankan posture be harnessed as a wild card—an alternative *foreign hand*, so to speak—and if so by whom? Was Ram Setu not merely a national conundrum but the Trojan

---

[342]Nandy, 'The Twilight of Certitudes', 157; Nandy, 'An Anti-Secularist Manifesto', p. 245.

Horse of global geopolitical intrigue? Was the triumph of Ram bhakts on the Indian electoral scene not the end but only the beginning of another long-drawn battle? And, if so, on which side were Ram and his valorous vanar sena going to enlist?

KATCHATHEEVU—THE 'BARREN' BOON

'There is perhaps no country in the world'—a reviewer of C.M. Enriquez's *Ceylon* (1927) once gloated—'about which more has been written than the Island of Ceylon.' For Lanka 'was well known in the early ages by the peoples of India, Burma, China, Siam, and Cambodia as a "Pearl drop on the brow of India,"' even prior to 'the Christian Era to the Greeks and Romans who gave it the name "Taprobane." The Serendib of the Arabs and Persians, it is the scene of many of the adventures recounted in the familiar story of Sinbad the sailor.'[343] Yet, Ceylon's limited geographical span portended that its future presidencies could nurse resentments owing to the fact that India was far more significant in the British colonial imagination by the sheer dint of its volume and unfathomable diversity.

A MILLENNIAL KINSHIP?

Not surprisingly, latter day Sri Lanka has chosen to remain tacit over the fact that Rabindranath Tagore—who authored the national anthems of Bangladesh and India—also arguably composed the Lankan anthem's musical score. As one Indian psychoanalyst jovially remarked, Lankans 'may not always live

---

[343]'Review: Ceylon, Past and Present', p. 467.

happily with the Indian state, but they seem to live happily with India's national poet'[344]—whether or not they actively remember or acknowledge that fact of life.

Nonetheless, Sri Lanka and India are connected by millennia of cultural and commercial traffic.[345] Since a Free Trade Agreement was signed between them in March 2000, Sri Lanka turned into India's premier partner for direct investments in the South Asian Association of Regional Cooperation. On 28 December 2005, the Indian government organized a banquet for Lankan president Mahinda Rajapaksa, attended by the Indian president A.P.J. Abdul Kalam and other key delegates. Both sides were pleased by Rajapaksa's remark: 'Your Excellency, we are your closest neighbours. Our immutable and inalienable geographical links come alive even in the satellite pictures taken from outer space.'[346] Subsequently, the foreign ministries of the two nations consented to co-monitor environmental impact assessments for the Sethu Canal that Lankans had hitherto disputed due to foreseeable harm to 'local fishers, Colombo's transshipment trade, and local environments', although freethinking Lankan observers continued to claim that the project would 'boost the economy of the coastal areas of northwestern Sri Lanka.'[347]

Only a year before the double black swan events of the global pandemic and the Sri Lankan economic disaster of 2020–22, Indo-Lankan economic collaborations were estimated to stand at a staggering amount of $5 billion.[348] In May 2022, India stepped forward to offer aid to the Lankans, with a one-billion-dollar

---

[344]Nandy, 'Nationalism, Genuine and Spurious', 3500.

[345]Bajpai, *India, Sri Lanka, and the SAARC Region*, 2020.

[346]Qtd. in Begum, 'Growing Mutuality in India Sri Lanka Relations', p. 169.

[347]Bradshaw, White, Dymond and Chacko, *World Regional Geography*, p. 299; Yogasundram, *A Comprehensive History of Sri Lanka*, p. 359.

[348]Taneja and Bimal, 'India-Sri Lanka Trade Relations', 2020.

credit line.[349] The development was perceived as the threshold
of a new era in the kinship of the two nations and their peoples.
But it also served, for some watchers, as a tangential cue to
recall the fraught relationship that they had shared since the
1960s. A key nucleus of the cold sea winds that has thawed the
relations between the two postcolonial nations is the barren
island of Katchatheevu—which is unbeknownst to many, yet
practically a boon in disguise, at least as far as the bridge of
Lord Ram is concerned.

Approximately 20 miles north of the tip of the Dhanushkodi
peninsula, in India's Tamil Nadu state, and 20 miles to the
southwest of Sri Lanka's Delft Island, lies the contested isle of
Katchatheevu. The name translates to 'barren island' in Tamil.
It is a 285-acre uninhabited isle formed by a volcanic eruption
in the fourteenth century. Shrouded in obscurity, Katchatheevu
has a knack for resurfacing, such as in late 2023 and the summer
of 2024, when Prime Minister Narendra Modi referenced it in
his speeches in the Lok Sabha.

THE COLONIAL GAMBIT

Katchatheevu is a 'square-shaped island' about 'one-fifth as large
as New York City's Central Park ... one-half mile long and barely
one-half mile wide.'[350] In British India, it was used as a military
base by the colonial army. Today, it is the location of a small
Catholic church (12 ft by 14 ft) devoted to St Anthony, the
patron saint of fishermen and travellers. Built in 1905 by Tamil
merchant Seenikuppan Padayachi, the church was intended
as a retreat for Indo-Ceylonese fisherfolk caught in turbulent
weather or in need of drying fishing lines. It is visited by Tamil
and Lankan pilgrims every year, at the end of March, for a
week-long religious festival.

---

[349]'Operational details of USD 1 billion credit line', 2022.
[350]'Crisis over 160 acres', 24.

Katchatheevu is believed to have served as a smugglers' base until its geopolitical dividends became amplified in February 1968, when Prime Minister Indira Gandhi ceded about 350 square miles of arid territory in the Rann of Kutch region in Gujarat to Pakistan.[351] Sensing a parallel prospect in the Gulf of Mannar, Ceylon staked claims over Katchatheevu on account of the St Antony's Church's affiliation with the northern Jaffna's diocese of the Roman Catholic bishop. Although Katchatheevu was a moorland of cacti without drinking water and too insignificant to be seen on most postcolonial maps, Lankan demands for the island eclipsed the then burning crisis of stateless Tamil refugees that confronted both India and Sri Lanka.

Eventually, in 1974, Katchatheevu was conceded to Sri Lanka by the Gandhi-led Indian administration in furtherance of the mutual goodwill she shared with the then-Lankan prime minister Sirimavo Bandaranaike. The cession arose out of the Indo-Lankan Maritime Agreement that promised to resolve the century-old Palk Bay fisheries conflict. The Indian press celebrated it as a riposte to 'the canard that India behaves overbearingly towards its small neighbours.' Though India was believed to possess 'an unassailable case', it claimed to have forfeited Katchatheevu to have 'harmonious relations with Sri Lanka.'[352]

The cession preceded the 1976 exchange of letters between the two nation-states that delineated the maritime boundary line in the Sethusamudram littoral region. However, since the onset of the Lankan civil war in 1983, Katchatheevu became the unofficial theatre for clashes between Indian Tamil fishermen and a predominantly Sinhalese Lankan navy. These conflicts have resulted in the loss of livelihoods, properties and lives of Indian fishers due to unintended forages across the

---

[351]Phadnis, 'Kachcha Thivu', 783; 788; Anand, 'The Kutch Award', 1968.
[352]*Indian and Foreign Review*, p. 24.

international maritime boundary line. But recently, Sinhalese fishermen have voiced concerns that the Lankan administration could be politically persuaded to lease the island to India as a compensatory measure.

The Lankan navy's antipathy towards Indian fishers' rights, alongside continuous inadvertent border crossings by both Indian and Lankan fishers across the International Maritime Boundary Line, constitute glaring evidence of the mutual derecognition of the geopolitical barriers in the psyche of Tamil (and even Sinhalese) fishers on both sides of the border. The 1974 and 1976 agreements were unable to specify, in an enduring manner, the geographical coordinates of 'the fishing rights of the fishermen of Tamil Nadu.'[353] This made Katchatheevu a fulcrum of transgressive mobilities of Tamil fishers.[354] The impact of Indo-Lankan nation-state-level bilateral trade and traffic is at variance with the domestic and civil society perceptions of Indian and Lankan political attitudes regarding each other. In the process, Katchatheevu has become an Achilles' heel of nationalist discourses from both postcolonial nations. Posing the question of who possesses Katchatheevu ignores the entanglements of the island—its potential to be simultaneously performed as a geopolitical territory in bilateral political and nationalist rhetoric while it is precariously experienced as a shared maritime geoheritage of Tamil legacies across the Indo-Lankan International Maritime Boundary Line. At the root of this informational kerfuffle lies the fact that India's cession of Katchatheevu occurred without Indian parliamentary proceedings, which eventually aggravated the challenges of Pamban's fisherfolks and other native stakeholders. Hence, Tamil fishers' memories of Katchatheevu's loss have never really gone underground.

---

[353]Joshi, 'Assessing Indian-Sri Lankan ties', 2022.
[354]Stephen, *Fishing for space*, 2015.

Katchatheevu was historically a territory constituting 69 seaside villages and 11 islets of the Ramanathapuram (Ramnad) zamindari. The zamindari was instituted in 1605 by Madurai's Nayak dynasty and was owned by the Sethupathis—a title literally meaning 'the protector of the Sethu' (Adam's Bridge). The Sethupathi ruler, Koothan Sethupathi—who ruled Ramnad between 1622 and 1635—commissioned a copper tablet whose inscription confirms that the jurisdiction of the territory extended up to Thalaimannar in Ceylon.

Katchatheevu returned substantial economic yields for its Sethupathi rulers, who were not at pains to avoid alliances with the Dutch and British. The Dutch East India Company leased the island, in 1767, from the then Sethupathi ruler, Muthuramalinga Sethupathi. Subsequently, in 1822, the British East India Company rented it from Ramaswami Sethupathi. In 1845, three proclamations by the governor of Ceylon Colin Campbell that defined the boundaries of Jaffnapatnam, omitted Katchatheevu, since the island was not considered a part of British Ceylon.[355]

In July 1880, Muthuswamy Pillai and Muhammad Abdul Kader Maraickar of the Madras Presidency signed a registered lease deed for five years granting Edward Turner, the special assistant collector of Ramnad (under the Zamin's Court of Wards). The lease permitted root collections for manufacturing dyes, from Ramnad's 70 villages and 11 islands, including Katchatheevu. Similarly, in 1885, the merchant Ramaswamy Pillai drew up an agreement for a comparable venture and duration in favour of the manager of the Ramnad Estate, T. Rajarama Rayar. It also included Katchatheevu as part of the lease. In 1913, a lease executed between the Ramnad king and the scrtary of state for India granted exploitation rights over chank shells within the specified limits, explicitly recognizing Katchatheevu as being located in the Indian side of the Palk

---

[355]Jayasinghe, *Kachchativu*, p. 74.

Bay. This reaffirmation of its status as being part of India rather than Ceylon was not without its precedents.

That prevailing common sense was solidified by the judgement in the Annakumaru Pillai vs Muthupayal case (1904). The Madras High Court's verdict in this case denoted that Katchatheevu was 'an integral part of His Majesty's dominions' while its adjoining chank beds constituted 'the territories of British India'.[356] This, and a 1922 report from the Imperial Records Department on the 'Ownership of the Island of Kachitivu', further corroborated India's historical claim to the island, highlighting Katchatheevu's ownership by the Ramnad king.[357]

The first colonial efforts to demarcate the fisheries' line between India and Ceylon dates back to 1920.[358] On 24 October the following year, Indian and Ceylonese delegations attempted to bargain a 'Fisheries Line' to limit the over-exploitation of maritime wealth. The negotiations overlapped with the question of Katchatheevu's jurisdiction. The Ceylonese side, led by the principal collector of Customs, B. Horsburgh, disputed the Indian administration's claim over the island—though it belonged to zamindari of the Ramnad king—by marshalling evidence of the island and St Anthony's Church being assets of the Jaffna Diocese. As an interim measure, it agreed that India and Ceylon would settle on a maritime border three miles west of Katchatheevu, which then nominally placed the island in Ceylonese territories. Thus were sown the seeds of division between the two imminently independent nations. Although the agreement had no official seal by the secretary of state, a makeshift maritime border was born.[359] The Indian

---

[356]Suryanarayan, *Conflict Over Fisheries*, p. 69.

[357]Fraser and Tytler, '... Proposed Delimitation of the Gulf of Manaar and Palk Strait', 1922.

[358]De Silva, 'Sharing maritime boundary with India', 2008.

[359]Jayasinghe, *Kachchativu*, pp. 13–15; De Silva, 'Sharing maritime boundary

delegates were cautious enough to preempt that the Fisheries Line could not officially deemed as an international boundary to avoid prejudicing 'any territorial claim which the Government of Madras or the Government of India may wish to prefer in respect of the island of Katchatheevu.'[360]

Subsequently, the extension of the British government's lease of Katchatheevu up to 1936 effectively excluded British Ceylon from staking any claims on the island. The status quo persisted until 1947–48 when both India and Ceylon gained independence from British colonial rule.[361] In 1947–48, a lease was granted exclusively for Katchatheevu to the dewan of Ramanathapuram, V. Ponnuswamy Pillai, by the Indian merchant Mohammed Meerasa Maraickar. This lease signified a transfer of rights over the island, once again highlighting India's jurisdiction over Katchatheevu.

The colonial Indian administration saw the territory's historical waters as encompassing the 'waters between the mainland [India] and Ceylon', primarily aiming to safeguard British imperial interests in the abundant fisheries of the region. The stance was consistent with latter-day 'international law requirements of long and undisturbed exercise of rights and the international recognition of these rights.'[362] Hence, India's legal jurisdiction over Katchatheevu was uncontroversially recognized until the late 1960s—although the decolonization of India and Ceylon paved the way for the germination of disruptive antigens induced by the colonial regime back in the 1920s.

OF CACTI AND SALTWATER

Following Ceylon's independence, on 4 February 1948, affluent

---

with India', 2008.
[360]Suryanarayan, *Conflict Over Fisheries*, p. 73.
[361]Rajappa, 'Why this double standard?', 2013.
[362]Mani, 'India's Maritime Zones and International Law', p. 380.

Lankan Tamils, and Tamils in general, underwent a major shift in their status in the newly formed state. Sinhalese majoritarianism left Tamils feeling culturally and politically disenfranchised.[363] Some respite came for the Tamils in 1964, when Indian prime minister Lal Bahadur Shastri and Lankan prime minister Bandaranaike reached a pact to repatriate 500,000 Lankan Tamil labourers to India—one that never materialized due to Lankan apprehensions about the loss of Indian labourers from Sinhalese tea estates.

Sri Lanka's Tamil-Sinhalese tensions climaxed in the early 1970s with the advent of the radical Sinhalese communist group, Janatha Vimukthi Peramuna, purportedly induced by North Korean influence.[364] Between 5 April and 30 June 1971, the group orchestrated an armed insurgency against Bandaranaike's Ceylonese United Front government. Since 1972, following the new Lankan constitution and Buddhism's official political status in the nation, Lankan policies tended to impair existing frictions between the Tamil and Sinhalese communities, essentially contributing to the emergence of the Tamil militant organization Liberation Tigers of Tamil Eelam.[365] Given their Indian roots, Tamils were suspected as political allies of India in its alleged intentions of Sri Lanka's colonization.

In 1971, when Bandaranaike solicited India's help in suppressing the Lankan agitation, the Indian navy answered by ordering its western fleet to watch Colombo and its adjacent ports. Gradually, India's intervention became undesirable to the Lankan establishment, alongside the increasing involvement of American and Russian naval troops in the Indian Ocean. At international forums, such as the Non-Aligned Heads of State

---

[363]Oberst, 'Federalism and Ethnic Conflict in Sri Lanka', 1988; Hiranandani, *Transition to Eminence*, p. 185.

[364]Manoharan, *Counterterrorism Legislation in Sri Lanka*, p. 22.

[365]Kearney, 'Language and the rise of Tamil separatism in Sri Lanka', 1978.

Conference in Cairo in October 1964, the Lusaka Conference
of Non-Aligned States in September 1970, and the Singapore
Conference of Commonwealth Prime Ministers in January 1971,
Sri Lanka and India favoured the declaration of the Indian
Ocean as a zone of peace, leading to the United Nations General
Assembly ratifying it in December 1972.[366] Katchatheevu's
cession to Sri Lanka two years later was, in no uncertain terms,
a political goodwill gesture to retain Lankan reciprocity—also
bearing in mind the fact that Lankans superstitiously believed
Katchatheevu to contain petroleum reserves.[367] Even recently,
Sri Lanka has reportedly rented land around Katchatheevu
and Needantheevu to Chinese corporations, presumably under
assumptions of a similar nature.

For the Indian government, which was preoccupied with the
problem of homeless Lankan Tamils, Katchatheevu possessed
'no strategic importance' since the Nehruvian regime. To
'mandarins in Delhi', it was virtually 'a "barren rock" in midsea
far from being worth fighting for with a friendly country.'[368]
When the issue of the 'Kachcha Thivu [*sic*] Island Dispute' was
first raised in the Lok Sabha, in 1956, Indian prime minister
and minister of external affairs, Nehru, immediately vetoed
against 'the Government of India or the Government of Ceylon
coming into conflict over a tiny little island,' while reminding
the parliament that, either way, Katchatheevu would remain
in the ownership of the Ramnad king.[369] For Nehru, the island
was far from national prestige. However, for the Ceylonese, it
was an ideal territory for implementing *uti possidetis juris*—the
legal principle of having colonial boundaries as boundaries of
postcolonial sovereign nation states. While India was of the

---

[366]O'Neill and Schwartz, 'The Indian Ocean as a "Zone of Peace"', 1974.
[367]Vivekanandan, 'Crossing Maritime Borders', p. 78.
[368]Raghavan, 'Internal Conflicts', p. 146; Vivekanandan, 'Crossing Maritime Borders', p. 78.
[369]*Lok Sabha Debates*, 14 April 1956, pp. 2220–2222.

view that the island should be jointly administered, Ceylon's demands grew stronger, although Katchatheevu was invisible 'on most maps'.[370] In 1968, the Colombo-based daily *Sun* produced the prickly byline: 'Ceylon Government takes over Kachcha Thivu [*sic*].' It catalysed renewed 'controversy between India and Ceylon regarding the political status of the island', inducing the Indian government 'to abjure the ambivalent attitude it had taken during the last decade on the issue and to expedite a solution of this question in consultation with Ceylon.'[371]

When the Indira Gandhi administration agreed to the cession of the island, Indian commentators held that the Sethu Project—which, by now, had been debated in the Indian parliament for about 20 years—could see the light of the day soon. As far back as 1974, rumours of a possible Chinese investment in Sri Lanka—particularly Katchatheevu—were afloat, but the Indian euphoria dismissed it as 'fantastic', hoping to focus instead on Lankan reciprocity of the goodwill act.[372] However, the Katchatheevu kerfuffle was far from resolved. According to Article 5 of the cession agreement, Indian fishermen and pilgrims were permitted to 'enjoy access to visit Katchatheevu' without being 'required by Sri Lanka to obtain travel documents or visas for these purposes' as also announced in the Lok Sabha by the Indian external affairs minister on 23 July 1974. Article 6 of the agreement states that 'the vessels of Sri Lanka and India will enjoy in each other's waters such rights as they have traditionally enjoyed therein'[373]—a principle that would be later disregarded by naval authorities of both nations.

Nevertheless, a 1976 agreement by the two nations comprising an exchange of letters between the foreign ministries

---

[370]Jayasinghe, *Kachchativu*, p. i.

[371]Phadnis, 'Kachcha Thivu', p. 783.

[372]*Indian and Foreign Review*, p. 24.

[373]'Agreement Between the Government of India and ...', 1994; *Lok Sabha Debates*, 23 July 1974, columns 197–201.

would complicate matters. Accordingly, the Indian fishing boats and fishers were no longer permitted to 'engage in fishing in the historic waters, the territorial sea and the exclusive economic zone of Sri Lanka,' and Lankan fishers and boats were to follow suit with respect to Indian 'historic waters, territorial sea and the exclusive economic zone of India, without the express permission of Sri Lanka or India, as the case may be'.[374] Anticipating this kind of imbroglio, the Tamil political party DMK had objected to Katchatheevu's cession in the Lok Sabha, back in July 1974, terming it an 'unholy and disgraceful act of statesmanship, unworthy of any government'.[375]

In a classic legal precedent from the Berubari Union Case (1960), India's apex court had opined that no Indian territory could be awarded to another nation without amending the Indian Constitution[376]—a clause overlooked in the cession of Katchatheevu. In the decades to follow, Tamil Nadu would go on to see the 1976 agreement as illicit, especially since it was transacted during the Indian Emergency when the Tamil Nadu assembly remained suspended. And the Lankan view refused to buy the narrative that India 'gifted' Katchatheevu to its littoral neighbour 'through goodwill', for fostering 'bilateral relations'.[377]

Even so, until about the outbreak of the Lankan civil war (1983–2009), Tamil fishers could visit Katchatheevu without being castigated by the Sinhalese navy. Arrested Tamil fishers used to be released by the Lankans after routine investigations and minor seizures—a regimen that was reciprocated by the Indian navy in cases of arrested Lankan fishers. As the Lankan civil war became more intense, and as the LTTE began acquiring popular support from Tamil organizations and political elites,

---

[374]'Exchange of Letters', p. 40.
[375]*Lok Sabha Debates*, 23 July 1974, column 187.
[376]'Berubari Union and ... vs Unknown', 1960.
[377]Jayasinghe, *Kachchativu*, p. 1.

the Tamil Eelam naval wing ('Sea Tigers') became more aggressive, inducing the Lankan navy to adopt more stringent measures not only against suspected LTTE forayers but also straying Tamil fishers, thus turning the Palk Bay fisheries into Sethusamudram's 'killing waters'.[378]

In 2008, towards the end of the Lankan civil war, Tamil Nadu chief minister J. Jayalalithaa appealed to the Supreme Court of India to review the 1974 and 1976 agreements, that had distressed Tamil fisheries and lives of fisherfolks on both sides of the border. Her appeal was followed by a petition to Prime Minister Narendra Modi on the same matter. Recently, Tamil Nadu chief minister M.K. Stalin has also presented a memorandum to Prime Minister Modi concerning Katchatheevu.[379] On the other hand, back in 2014, Mukul Rohatagi, the former attorney-general for India, had opined that India would have to practically resort to war in order to retrieve Katchatheevu, since the island's cession was not contested between the governments of India and Sri Lanka but was a matter of internal federal disagreements between the state of Tamil Nadu and the Indian government.[380] While for Tamil politicians, Katchatheevu has been an emotional issue, the Government of India has maintained official restraint owing to its neighborhood-first policy. Besides, the matter is 'sub-judice in the Hon'ble Supreme Court of India'.[381]

Both India and Sri Lanka are party to the Vienna Convention on the Law of Treaties (1969) which compels them to honour the agreements of 1974/76. The convention's article 56 explains that neither nation can unilaterally withdraw from the agreements without ratification by the other as prescribed by article 65(1).[382]

---

[378]Gupta and Sharma, *Contested Coastlines*, p. 94.
[379]'Press Release No. 351', 2014; 'Demands Made in Memorandum', 2022.
[380]Janardhan, 'Explained: An Island Marooned', 2014.
[381]Joshi, 'Assessing Indian-Sri Lankan Ties in Choppy Waters', 2022; 'Katchatheevu Island', 2019.
[382]*Vienna Convention*, pp. 19; 22.

Furthermore, the withdrawal of either party from the agreement will require a resolution under UN Charter's article 33, with the likelihood of intervention by a mediating state or the International Court of Justice, as accorded by article 37.[383]

It is far from adequate, however, to reduce the histories and possible routes of negotiations around Katchatheevu to merely geopolitical contingencies. The more sustainable way out of this interregnum perhaps lies not in state-based solutions—like the shared administration of Katchatheevu—but rather a bilateral rebuilding of civil society consensuses on the contested memories revolving around the island. And the niftiest precedent for such a consensus was seen during the anti-Sethu-Canal movement which—in a bewildering turn of events—came to be supported even by the Lankan society and government.

LANKANS VERSUS CANAL

The Lankan administration and civil society had sought information 'about the Indian project to dredge the Palk Strait' as far back as January 1999[384]—when AIADMK leader Jayalalithaa and NDA leader Vajpayee lauded the project's economic potential. The defence minister of India, George Fernandes, cherished it as a personal dream but the Lankan intellectual class called it a 'deadly project'.[385] Sri Lanka, under the third and final regime of Sirimavo Bandaranaike, vociferously backed the claim, owing to environmental anxieties and concerns of territorial sovereignty. Lankans saw it as a 'threat that had always been visible on the horizon, excepting to those who did not wish to see it, perhaps because dredging takes place under

---

[383]'Pacific Settlement of Disputes', 2021.
[384]Balachandran, 'Lankans Filled with Misgivings about Fernandes' Dream Project', 1999.
[385]Rajasingham, 'A Canal ... and an island ...!', 1999.

the sea.' The Palk Strait's commercialization could, reportedly, influence a 'devaluation' in Lankan geostrategy, turning it into 'another pearl dangling on her Indian Ocean string'.[386] That could potentially give India a 'remarkable leverage in its relations with China, Japan and the US.'[387]

Lankans warned that if Ram Setu was damaged, 85 islands along the northwest Lankan coast and portions of Jaffna risked drowning. That could end up destroying their 'living sea walls against tides, storm surges and hurricanes' and 'giant sand factories, creating limestone from dissolved minerals in sea water, and leaving behind sands to keep shoreline from eroding.'[388] Besides, Sri Lanka risked losing over half its maritime trade. The canal's traffic was also projected to breach the limit of 12 nautical miles of international territorial waters implicitly set by the 1974/76 Indo-Lankan agreements and the United Nations Convention on the Law of the Sea. Prominent Sri Lankan intellectuals opposing the Sethu Canal included Professor K.N.J. Katupotha of Sri Jayewardenepura University and attorney Chandaka Jayasundere, who authored the white paper *Sethusamudram Ship Canal Project: Where Does the Law Stand?* Meanwhile, India's shipping minister asserted that Sri Lanka's concerns had been addressed.[389]

In response to Sri Lanka's opposition, an Indo-Lankan Inter-Ministerial Committee was established in 2004 to oversee the environmental impact of the Sethu Canal. This committee was headed by Sri Lanka's Ministry of Foreign Affairs, with support from the Ministries of Environment and Natural Resources, Ports and Aviation, Fisheries and Aquatic Resources, Defense, and Science and Technology. During Sri Lankan president

---

[386]'New Avatar Looms', 2014.
[387]Sivaram, 'Geo-Strategic Implications of Sethusamudram', 2004.
[388]Rajasingham, 'A Canal ... and an island ...!', 1999; Balachandran, 'Lankans Filled with Misgivings about Fernandes' Dream Project', 1999.
[389]Warrier, 'Which Tamils are they talking about?', 2005.

Chandrika Kumaratunga's visit to India that year, and later in discussions between Sri Lankan president Mahinda Rajapaksa and Indian prime minister Manmohan Singh, both leaders emphasized the need for India to take measures to mitigate environmental risks.[390]

India was conscious enough to add that the Sethu Canal would 'not displace Colombo in terms of importance as a port, since the bigger Indian vessels will still need to sail around Sri Lanka (because of a lack of canal depth) and dock at the Colombo port.'[391] Yet, in 2006, the *Naval War College Review* of the American Department of the Navy and the Defense Technical Information Center juxtaposed 'Indian assistance in upgrading and developing the Iranian port of Chahbahar, the headquarters of Iran's third naval region' and the Sethu Canal to 'enable warships from India's eastern and western fleets to quickly reinforce one another.' The canal was described as 'analogous to the 1914 completion of the interoceanic Panama Canal by the United States.'[392]

By 2007, the canal's 'immense strategic significance' became staple knowledge.[393] Even the Liberation Tigers of Tamil Eelam—adversaries in a prolonged ethnic war with the Sri Lankan state—viewed the canal as a nemesis. A 2008 report on endangered cetaceans (whales and dolphins, including *Balaenoptera acutorostrata, Sousa chinensis, Kogia sima* and *Peponocephala electra*) in Sri Lanka's Bar Reef Marine Sanctuary warned that the canal could jeopardize the ecosystem northwest of the Jaffna peninsula.[394] Lankan arguments against the canal now built up a fresh plank of resistance borrowing data from

---

[390]Jayawardena, 'Present Status of the Sethusamudram Project', 2010.

[391]Gupta, 'The Palk Straits Canal', p. 18.

[392]Berlin, 'India in the Indian Ocean', p. 82.

[393]Jain, Agarwal and Singh, *Hydrology and Water Resources of India*, p. 863.

[394]Bröker and Ilangakoon, 'Occurrence and conservation needs of cetaceans', 2008.

the Indian environmentalist resistance. These highlighted that Tamil Nadu's mangrove wetlands were spread across major and minor regions, with 700 hectares in the Palk Strait, 148 hectares in the Gulf of Mannar marine area, and 30 hectares in the Gulf of Mannar island region. Besides, the Lankans pointed out that the Gulf of Mannar housed rare native mangrove species such as *Pemphis acidula*, along with approximately 90 aquatic species, over 180 terrestrial species, and a variety of avian life. Additionally, Lankan environmentalists noted that the region's coral ecosystem spanned 104 species across 38 genera, and it remained vulnerable to the threat of cyclonic storms, which could be aggravated by the canal.[395]

As if this was insufficient, the canal was slated on grounds of violating the Law of the Sea, given its hypothetical breach of principles of 'good neighbourliness', non-injury to neighbours, and mutual environmental responsibilities.[396] The Law of the Sea's articles 136 ('common heritage of mankind'), 197 ('protection and preservation of the marine environment'), 192–195—that reinforce article 123—that expect 'states bordering an enclosed or semi-enclosed' to co-operate environmentally with multilateral support, 200 (mandating joint monitoring of 'pollution' and 'pathways, risks, and remedies'), and 279 and 283 that stipulate measures in case of conflicting statutory interpretation,[397] were boldly underscored as legal barriers to the canal. Being parties

---

[395]Selvam, Gnanappazham, Navamuniyammal, et al., *Atlas of mangrove wetlands of India*, 2002; Thirumalaiselvan, Rajkumar, Vinothkumar, et al., 'Seagrass, seaweed and mangrove ecosystem', 2020; Balachandran, 'Shore birds of the marine national park in the Gulf of Mannar', 1995; Pillai, 'Recent corals from the south-east coast of India', 1986; Patterson, Venkatesh, Mathews, et al., 'A field guide to stony corals (Scleractinia) of Tuticorin', 2004; Ramesh, 'Is the Sethusamudram Shipping Canal Project Technically Feasible?', 2005; Ramesh, 'Seven scientific inconsistencies in the Sethusamudram Shipping Canal', 2005.
[396]Mendis, 'Sovereignty vs Transboundary Environmental Harm', 2006; Gunasekara, 'Security Dimensions of Sethu Samudram Ship Canal Project', 2016.
[397]'United Nations Convention on the Law of the Sea', pp. 49; 85–88; 118–129

to the 1992 Rio de Janeiro declaration, India and Sri Lanka are adherents to its principles that imply that in the case of uncertainty in issues of environmental security, either nation could invoke its articles 287, 288 and 290 to plead before the International Tribunal of the Law of the Sea.[398] However, India's position is somewhat legally diminished due to the unfortunate reality of Indian Tamil fishers continuing to stray into Lankan waters, triggering what might perhaps be construed via strict juridical lenses as a breach.

THE STRATEGIC MISE-EN-SCÈNE

Along with legalese, Sri Lanka was able to posture its 'smallness accompanied with weakness' to stress India's additional 'duty to brief Sri Lanka that the Sethu canal has no economic or military danger,' especially since the canal could make India a beneficiary of unchecked political.[399] Sinhala Buddhists, 'fresh on the heels of victory over the LTTE', seemed to tout the canal as being 'symbolic not of the prospect for a renewal of Indo-Lankan relations' but a reminder of 'memories of Indian military intervention in the 1980s and 1990s, regarded by many as a modern instance of the recurrent narrative theme of the *Mahavaṃsa*, the invasion of Lanka by bellicose forces from across the northern sea.' Even in the early twentieth century, Lankans compared the Indian Peace Keeping Force of the 1980s to the 'army of Rama's incarnation'.[400] For Hindutvavadis, the Sethu Project ramified Ram Setu's destruction. But for Lankans, the canal itself was a modern Setu.

Coincidentally, the lead-up to the Lok Sabha 2014 general

---

[398]'Rio Declaration on Environment and Development', p. 3.
[399]Gunasekara, 'State responsibility over SethuSamudram', 2012; Gunasekara, 'Security Dimensions of Sethusamudram Ship Canal Project', p. 20.
[400]Henry, *Ravana's Kingdom*, p. 174.

elections in India witnessed an unprecedented buzz in Sri Lanka regarding the canal's environmental sustainability, a reversal of opinions of the region's increased maritime security, prospects of Sethusamudram Sea being used for American naval deployments, and India's perceived recalcitrance to share environmental assessment data.[401] Ironically—or perhaps not—in 2015, a year after the Indian elections, the *Historical Dictionary of Sri Lanka* penned by a Lankan scholar noted that the Sethu Canal was halted by 'Hindus' to save a 'shrine associated with the *Ramayana*', without mentioning the influential Lankan role in that event.[402]

The Lankan perception of the Sethu Project eventually 'evolved into a geopolitical and security concern of Chinese influence in India's southern shores.' Until July 2020, the Lankan establishment had flaunted 'the Chinese built and operated' port in Hambantota as 'the next commercial city in the island with highways, strategic port, international airport', besides the Mattala airport, and Chinese footprints in Lankan highways, hotels and stadia. However, by September 2021, Sri Lanka had entered a 'strategic trap' that could easily transform the island 'into Chinese colonies or Chinese zones of activity.'[403] Defence analysts in New Delhi seemed anxious over a $12 million renewable energy project in northern Jaffna (50 kilometres from the Indian coastline) handled by a Chinese firm. India too flexed its diplomatic brawn in the Indian Ocean by engaging Australia's 'posture' in the Indian Ocean region to restrain China's unimpeded influence in the region.[404]

[401]Srinivasan, 'Sri Lanka concerned at Sethu project impact', 2013; Vasan, 'Maritime Counter-Terrorism', p. 57; Moorthy, 'Fishing Issue', 2013; 'Doomed: Sethusamudram ship', 2013.

[402]Peebles, *Historical Dictionary of Sri Lanka*, p. 320.

[403]Abeyagoonasekera, 'Sethusamudram to Samudra Manthan', 2020; 'Chinese-built Hambantota Port', 2020.

[404]Pasricha, 'India Feels the Squeeze in Indian Ocean', 2021.

One of India's possible answers to the geopolitical impasse around Katchatheevu lies in an inventive merger of its naval strategy with American Indo-Pacific strategy, where climatology and environment also occupy critical commitments.[405] It is still too early to dismiss the hope that Chinese and American involvements in the Indian Ocean region are poised to trigger unlikely meeting grounds to resolidify Indo-Lankan ties, while reshaping the geostrategic ecosystem Ram Setu.

BRIDGING BILATERALISM?

In 2018, the head of Strategy and Security Studies at the Chennai-based Centre for Asia Studies, who also served as the regional director of the National Maritime Foundation, emphasized the ongoing necessity of establishing a land bridge connecting Pamban and Mannar rather than opting for a canal. In 2022, another Indian observer pitched the idea of 'a railway tunnel under the seabed between India and Sri Lanka', predicting 'new capacities for Indian business and the overall Indian economy' to forge 'a BIMSTEC economic community on the lines of the European Union or ASEAN'. A railway bridge between the two nations could empower Lankan markets—with merchandises like tea and textile or services like tourism and ports—while accruing to India strategic closeness to Sri Lanka's deep-sea ports. If only '5 deep-sea ports of Sri Lanka can get connected to the Indian economy, it will be as if India will have saved ₹50,000 crores ($6.25 billion) in developing deep-sea ports of its own' while planning the historic tunnel project.[406]

While these ideas joined the pool of suggestions, Prime Minister Modi was again solicited by Tamil political leaders in July 2022 to revive the Sethu Project, considering that

---

[405]Luthra, 'The new US Indo Pacific Strategy', 2022.
[406]Hegadekatti, 'An Indo-Lanka tunnel to integrate island to BIMSTEC', 2022.

the 'conflict with China' on India's northeastern front had augmented the Sethusamudram region's 'critical importance from the security point of view'.[407] In January 2023, the Tamil assembly approved a motion in favour of the canal—five years after its budget escalation approximately stood at ₹4.5 billion. Hearing this, Lankan environmentalists once again cried foul.[408] Lankan critics invoked fears of losing Hambantota to India's strategies of curbing Chinese influence in the Indian Ocean. 'Are we to be,' asked the Lankan naysayers, 'a colony of India, as we have always been, with Portuguese, Dutch and British?'[409]

Even so, Lankan antagonism to the Sethu Canal has been an unexpected coalitionist for the 'Ram Setu Bachao Andolan'. This is despite the fact that for the Sinhalese, Ram may not be always a hero while Ravan, likelier than not, is one. While the Sethu Canal denotes a symbol of the destruction of Ram Setu in India, paradoxically, Lankans have only ever seen it as a renaissance of the *Ramayan* legacy. Meanwhile, India's cession of Katchatheevu has meant that both Tamil and Lankan fishers would go on to oppose developmental activities around the isle. Profusely stocked with cacti and saltwater, the virtually infertile island's political fertility has only been enriched by every passing decade that has made it the abject and unacknowledged nucleus—or an invisible boon—around which Indian and Lankan actors have rallied to combat the Sethu Canal Project—bolstering the movement to prevent Ram Setu's 'destruction' by choice or default. Does not this fortuitous, yet extraordinary, turn of history inspire Lankan and Indian civil societies to press their administrations into a bilateral epistemic community to protect the joint geo-heritage of the Palk Bay, the Gulf of Mannar, and Ram Setu?

Could not this triumvirate of geological contact zones

[407]Qtd. in Bhattacharya, 'Eyeing China', 2020.
[408]Rishi, 'Sethusamudram project cost rises by Rs 4500 cr', 2018; Balachandran, 'SL Concerns Over Proposed Sethusamudram Ship Canal Project', 2023.
[409]Sirimal, 'Indian EAM's Visit to SL', 2023.

foster the memorialization of the legend of Ram Setu to resolve Katchatheevu and the Palk Bay fisheries conflict? And does not this unique conjunction of history, geopolitics and cultural heritage escort the saga of the sacred bridge as a new shibboleth to transform the Sethusamudram Sea into a flashpoint of Indo-Lankan union?

EPILOGUE

And so, we return to the threshold where we began: the words of the saint of Dakshineshwar, ensconced in an ashram swathed by the shadows of enigmatic coconut trees. Sri Ramakrishna held, with his distinctive humour, that since Ram, the avatar, had to behave as his human persona, he required the creation of a solid causeway to march across the Sethusamudram. His devotee, Hanuman, meanwhile, was not bound to such material obligations, for he could just leap across the sea by virtue of his immense faith in the name of his Lord.

CAN THE SACRED BE HISTORICAL?

The unlettered Paramhansa was capable of living in profound negative capability or uncertainty in his personal-impersonal *history* of Ram Setu[410]—that never degenerated into a narrow sectarian view. He could not care less for the various names that people gave to benign everyday elements: like water. Some called it *'paani'*, others *'jal'*, while others named it 'aqua'. Ultimately, it served all. This was his principle—of seeing through the world of names, forms and transactions, as also applied while narrating the anecdote from *Ramayan*. And with the seeds of such faith and luminosity that the enchanted bridge was to grant, this author set out to aid you on the journey he has, by now, taken several times.

---

[410]See the third epigraph to this book.

As the German theoretical physicist, Werner Heisenberg, once expressed, 'What we observe is not nature in itself, but nature exposed to our method of questioning.'[411] By that logic, Ram Setu's meanings are produced and reproduced by the questions we ask of it. To ask , 'Is Ram Setu real?' perhaps dilutes not only the autonomy of a discipline like archaeology but also the sacredness of the *bridge*. Ram Setu's incommensurable magical realism is tarnished when we usher in what Alan Watts saw as the 'theological imperialism' (of Judaism, Christianity or Islam) that forced religious followers to revere the corresponding prophets and messiahs as 'historical' personages.[412]

Perhaps this would be seen as a book for burning, a heretical misadventure, a grain of sand in the eyes of every conceivable electoral and political persuasion. But their fears will only be the outcomes of overinterpretations, fragmentary misinterpretations, and discriminative readings. It was probably the fear of a similar nature that led to the banning of this author's documentary on Ram Setu at a state broadcasting network two years ago.

Nonetheless, as a 52-year-old lecture by Srila Prabhupad—the founder of the International Society for Krishna Consciousness—would have it, Lord Ram acquired a throne befitting gods since his powers were 'inconceivable' and could not be cheaply conjured or be spoken of.[413] Accordingly, it was both inconceivable and true that an oceanic bridge was constructed without pillars or piers in a prehistoric epoch when humankind had barely learned to speak. Asking about the underlying nature of Ram Setu—call it what you must—and imposing immediate answers perpetuates the fallacy that the universe is obliged to make sense to us or that we have

---

[411]Heisenberg, *Physics and Philosophy*, p. 58.
[412]Watts, 'Democracy in the Kingdom of Heaven', 2022.
[413]Prabhupad, 'Ramakrishna is God. We don't admit it', 1973.

participated in our mutual co-creation. While these assumptions may not be entirely false—unlike what Albert Camus's vision of the 'benign indifference' of the universe will have us believe—the idioms used to express them, from time to time, require far greater scrutiny than we have cared to afford. Any attempt to render visible Ram Setu's formless yet palpable sacredness obscures the question of its historicity, while attempting to draw its precise historical correlates and time of origin obscures its spiritual infinitude.

FAITHS TRANSCENDING POLITICS

The constant thread running through the intellectual history of Ram Setu is that of the human subject's desperation to prove the existence of a form—the exactitudes of its name (*naam*), form (*roop*), transactability (*vyavahaar*)—in the most precise idiom of intellectual echo chambers cocooned from all others. But what if the bridge is not made of forms but born in formlessness? What if, when we try to ascertain its form beyond a point, the structure's enchantments choose to perish? The legend of Ram Setu may well be taken as a nascent equation to determine not the physical but the metaphysical laws of the 'bridge'. But what laws must it obey in the transactional world? It is to be answered thus.

Ram Setu rises in solidarity with the oppressed, instead of itself rising as the oppressed.

Lord Ram's Setu deserves a world better than that of the ridicule thrown at it. It is not India's debt to its enchanted bridge but the debt of twenty-first century humankind to memorialize it—with compassion, acceptance, repentance and atonement. For it is a bridge of catharsis, not triumphalism. It is not a historical monument meant to spawn war cries and fear-mongering chants. It is a timeless edifice to be harboured spiritually, to solidify the virtues of sagacity, sacrifice, solidarity, sufferance and *shanti*. The secrets of Ram Setu will become caricatures if coloured by an era when a majority of public opinion takes its cue from national interest, which, in turn, gets dyed by the views of majoritarian physicalism and material reductivism. The bridge's intellectual history deserves remembrance not merely rooted in the present but in a timelessness to stand the test of other times.

There is no exaggeration or charity in inferring that the Hindutvavadi resistance to the so-called destruction of Ram Setu deserves more credit than has been given to it. This is, emphatically, not to celebrate the political success of the patronage by the Sangh Parivar to the almost global expanse of the 'Ram Setu Bachao Andolan'. Rather, it is to humbly acknowledge its recognition that the legend of Ram Setu was peevishly undermined in postcolonial India—whereas it had no dearth of validators until about the 1940s. The above censoring occurred in public memory despite successive colonial plans for dredging in and around the structure that failed stupendously.

The Hindutvavadi ideology, which is now a majoritarian force, deems it more convenient to mask or overlook the great intellectual compassion, curiosity, and even reverence with which innumerable British observers approached the bridge of Lord Ram, often in opposition to the larger colonial regime. That led to even British public institutions internalizing Ram Setu's sacred legends in publicity campaigns for the Pamban Bridge. Hindutva, however, is not the only problem. The erasure of that historical phase is not only due to anticolonial nationalism but also because of the Indian secularist disregard for deviations from the narratives that many postcolonial Indian historians channelled in the ill-informed hope of serving national interests. Losing kinship with the ecumenical minds of the past cannot augur well for Ram Setu or the perennial heritage it belongs to.

Meanwhile, the former Congress-led United Progressive Alliance that is repeatedly criticized for the controversial affidavit

in the Supreme Court—allegedly denying Lord Ram's existence—
has clearly overstayed its sentence. It has had to shoulder blame
for an epistemic flaw that was structural and widespread—the
siloization of the physical from the metaphysical, the practical
from the poetical, the scientific from the spiritual. If Hindutva,
purged of its insecurities and fear of the other, can be revived
as a redeeming and redeemable force, so is the rational ideology
of the Congress. The problem is that spiritual and rational
discourses have been divided into ideological camps especially
at a time when they should be the concerns of all stakeholders.

The legend of Ram Setu and the *Ramayan* legacy cannot
be downplayed. That is what this book has single-mindedly
argued for. However, like the ruling regime of 2007, this author
too, after nearly seven rigorous years of archival research and
meditation, has found no evidence for archaeology to be used as
a scientific means of either validating or invalidating the legend
of Ram Setu. Meanwhile, the secular resistance to the 'Ram
Setu Bachao Andolan' needs to recall that several illustrious
members of various communist parties of India were known
to be enthusiastic pupils, if not avowedly passionate scholars,
of the Upanishads and other specimens of India's Vedantic and
Puranic literatures. Such old-guards would perhaps have sooner
acknowledged that it is fallacious to deny the existence of the
subject of the legend of Ram Setu—for even phenomenological
existence is existential after all.

ABOVE DOGMAS AND DOCTRINES

Nevertheless, when the legend of Ram Setu resurfaces in public
parlance, it should be the task of India's civil society to call out
the silencing of discourses of environmental justice; the cultural
rights, psychogeography and livelihoods of Tamil fishermen; and
the Palk Bay fisheries conflict with Katchatheevu as its nucleus.
These silenced entities are what bleakly typify the knowledge

economy of the twenty-first century, wherein the sensational, emotional, dramatic and intellectually crude ride roughshod over the sophisticated, nuanced, prosaic and humanely rich aspects of public participation in democracy.

In a world increasingly divided into polarizing opinions and algebraic narratives—where the promises of nuance, sensitivity, transformation and redemption become convenient scapegoats—the legend of Ram Setu underpins the dream of resurrecting subtle matters or what the great Indic wisdom traditions recognized as *sukshmata*. Bridges of the gods unfold in uncertainties of time and space, and manifest values of unmanifest spirits. As universally agreed, Lord Ram was not a vindictive and dogmatic incarnation of the divine ready to execute one if his name was not accorded absolute primacy. Rather, he valued being experienced in spirit—unlike, for instance, the powers that punished King Solomon for his supposed practice of idolatry. Just like science, especially good science, no good religion can claim to have a monopoly over every form of knowledge and moral code.

It may also be inferred that the judicial system of India is not the best authority to adjudicate on the metaphysics and subtle realities that govern the historicity, geology and phenomenology of the tombolo called Ram Setu. What the courts, however, may offer us is arbitration in cognitive justice—intellectual equity across knowledge systems—that could unite diverse structures of wisdom to honour Ram Setu's centrality in Indian life and global epistemologies. For its secrets lie in the sacred interplay of history, spirituality and cosmic stardust, urging us to await their truths rather than instant answers.

More than ever before, the *Ramayan* invites serious introspection, with its titular deity being the embodiment of qualities transcending scientific, historical and religious materialism. To poets, Ram Setu is one of the oldest monuments erected for love. To celebrated Indian atheists, even to those who were not born in Hindu households, the story of Ram continues to inspire universal values and inform India's cultural evolution. This points to the need for an experiential revolution geared towards memorializing Ram Setu as a modern-day symbol of the unity of knowledge and cathartic contemplation, not cultural, religious, or materialistic triumphalism.

Religious and scientific fanatics miss the realization that Ram Setu intermeshes material, biological and metaphysical dimensions. Much like what Canadian psychologist Jordan Peterson sees in the meme of the metaphorical dragon of ancient fables, the meme of the ancient bridge is embedded in the collective psyche of innumerable Indians. It is felt as inseparable from their biology and phenomenology and cannot be explained through a materialism that ignores the metaphysical. Hence, the tombolo deserves recognition not merely as a geological or historical site but also as a monument to the human imagination that has kept alive the threshold to the divine.

Producing knowledge on Ram Setu that is coloured by majoritarian moods yoked to ideological conformity is the worst treatment we could accord with the *Ramayan* legacy. To see Ram Setu as a veritable monument built by verifiable historical protagonists—who can go back in time to alter received versions of history retrospectively—could well be a triumph of faith and spiritual prowess. It may even be an imperative, and legitimate, step in the reimagination of one's cultural identity and integrity. But for that to be an official governmental stance, especially without professional contributions from historians, geologists, environmentalists and fishermen's groups who opposed the Sethu Canal, is bound to do more damage than good.

ON PLURALIZING STAKEHOLDERS

How Ram Setu's fabulous mainstays came to be brought and secured on its shivering sands—if not for *Ramayan*'s vanar sena or a primordial human civilization—will stay shrouded in secrets as long as the 'bridge' is besieged by coralline brine from the Gulf of Mannar and Palk Bay. However, the legend obliges historians of South Asia to enshrine the principle of freedom of enchantment and to redefine the spiritual in terms of the environment. The false binarization between secular designs of maritime progress and religious ideals of cultural heritagization and is highly limiting and shaky. Both Indic and colonial knowledge systems reveal an unbroken convention of holy excursions to Ram Setu since at least AD 1000, if not earlier. It is also equally true, though, that at average monthly wages ranging from ₹4,000 to ₹8,000,[414] Tamil fishers and seaweed collectors seek freedom on fiscal and not spiritual registers. And, if the nearly 4,500 marine plant and animal species of the underwater ecosystem had a voice in electoral matters, they would advocate for banning polymers, curbing invasive algae, regulating indiscriminate trawling, and addressing public negligence toward coral degradation and bleaching events in the Anthropocene era.

Ram Setu represents an intellectual enigma to revive the principle of the right to enchantment or freedom from disenchantment—whether this principle is seen in spiritual or scientific terms. But this needs to integrate themes of environmentalism, the Palk Bay fisheries crisis, the Law of the Sea, and the pervasive horrors of the Anthropocene. Also, the legend of Ram Setu cannot be deprived of its intellectual autonomy. It is high time that the 'bridge' had its own historicist reputation without being held hostage to the memories of Ayodhya's Ramjanmabhumi movement. For Ram Setu empowers us to ask if its saga is also that of the planet itself—an enchanting bionetwork that captivates geologists, historians, geographers, jurists, mythographers, secularists, nationalists and poets,

---

[414]Karnad, Gangal and Karanth, 'Perceptions Matter', pp. 222.

despite all that the human race has thrown at it.

Besides acknowledging that we have not been kind towards Ram Setu, it would also require the acknowledgement that its future should be enshrined with pluricultural, plurilingual and pluri-spiritual principles. This would recall chilling reminders of ethnic hostilities like what was seen recently in Gujarat's Gosabara wetlands. In May 2022, Allarakha Ismailbhai Thimmar, the leader of a fishing community from Gosabara, Porbandar (Mahatma Gandhi's hometown), pleaded before the Gujarat High Court for euthanasia, for himself and a 100 Muslim fisher families (about 600 people). The reason cited for this bizarre plea was the discrimination faced from authorities—known to largely comprise Hindu personnel.[415] Rameswaram's Muslim residents of less than five per cent and Christian populace of faintly over eight per cent mark a demography of immaculate nonresistance to any commemoration of Ram Setu on religio-cultural grounds. However, the social impact of enfolding Ram Setu's multicultural and multispecies legacies into a homogenous religious heritage needs to be gravely studied.

Furthermore, throughout Ram Setu's historiography, which, in the *Ramayan* legacy comes about only due to the need to rescue Sita, she is probably the sole female voice of continued importance in the epic's splendid chapter that is overly peopled by masculine protagonists—with the notable exceptions of prime ministers Indira Gandhi and Sirimavo Bandaranaike who oversaw Katchatheevu's transfer. So, while Ram Setu is heritagized in the name of Lord Ram and Sita, realistic means to remedy our fundamentally gendered attitudes in memorializing the human and non-human legacies of the structure demand exploration. The key is to foreground the female folks of Pamban's fisher families, who are easy preys of the Anthropocene, given their precarious professions of seaweed, algal and coral collection. In

---

[415]Khan, 'Gujarat Fisherfolk Leader Moves HC', 2022.

the age of the Gaia hypothesis—named 50 years ago after the eponymous Greek goddess, to suggest that the earth is a living and synergistic organism—the caution that hangs over Ram Setu is that 'a democracy that cannot' address the Anthropocene 'will have marked itself as inadequate to its most basic problems.'[416]

'AS WATER IS IN WATER'

The question is no more whether the Sethusamudram Sea is sacred or not. Rather, it is a problem of who possesses the privilege of sacralizing the ocean. In asking this bold question, *Ram Setu* asserts its independence from detractors of nationalism and rationalism. The time has come for clear-sighted dialogues rather than passionate polemics on Ram Setu. In its enchanting legacy lurks the secret to bilaterally foster Indo-Lankan collaborations on environmental conservation and awareness campaigns, and their shared interests in the civilizational parables that the two nations hope to bequeath their posterities.

Ultimately, it is to be stressed that what we think we know of Ram Setu is woefully inadequate before its immeasurable means to astonish us. Recent hydrological, meteorological and climatological evidence have staggeringly revealed traces of a monsoonal 'river in the sea' snuggling along India's eastern coastline, following a north-easterly course from the Indian Ocean to the Bay of Bengal. 'The occurrence of this river' near Ram Setu 'arises from the peculiar geography of the northern Indian Ocean that results in both a massive inflow of freshwater into the semi-enclosed northern Bay of Bengal and in strong coastally trapped currents along the eastern coast of India.'[417] The discovery points to deep spectral links along the Indian shoreline extending from the Indian Ocean to the Gulf of Mannar

---

[416]Purdy, *After Nature*, p. 267.

[417]Chaitanya, Lengaigne, Vialard, et al., 'Salinity Measurements', 2014.

to the Eastern Ghats, which drains into the Bay of Bengal. And this river-in-the-sea is our mystical metaphor—or a vehicle—to end our pilgrimage.

The Thai city of Ayutthaya—once the capital of the Siamese kingdom—shares more with the sacred city of Lord Ram's birth, Ayodhya, than its name. *Valmiki Ramayan*'s Thai adaptation, *Ramakien*, was authored over hundreds of years, since the tenth century or earlier. It also took inspiration from the Buddhist hagiography, *Hanuman Nataka* and *Vishnu Puran*. Nearly eight centuries of that sacred heritage were bludgeoned to bits during the Burmese siege at the time of the war of the second fall of Ayutthaya (1765–67). Afterwards, the epic was patiently rewritten under the patronage and guidance of King Rama I, the first sovereign of the Chakri dynasty of Siam. The sombreness of the circumstances in which the epic was reinscribed is writ large in its epilogue. It affirms that *Ramakien* was divined to be staged 'on celebrative occasions' to guard mortals from illusions by empowering them to stay 'mindful of impermanence'.[418] Turn to the frescos of Wat Phra Kaew, Bangkok's Temple of the Emerald Buddha, and you will find an illustration of the episode of Lord Ram's legions crossing Ram Setu depicted not as a causeway of human design but the spine of Nala, or Hanuman, or a hominid being, lying supine to form a sentient animistic bridge.

As we gaze into the painting and lose ourselves in the finery that decks the Setu, faith and reason transmute their supposed animosity into a partnership within the human quest for meaning and the desire to communicate across millennia. Ram Setu pulsates in the pale light—as though it were of the sunset's stretched out thin fingers caressing the Sethusamudram Sea. And the bridge overlooks the ripples in our unconscious, beckoning it to cross the threshold of its shores and emerge transformed.

---

[418]Reynolds, 'Ramayana, Rama Jataka, and Ramakien', pp. 56–57.

That which is today our Ram Setu was once and may well again become a bridge known by the name of another god. If we go deeper into its past, persuaded by our curiosities for dark palaeontological times, all its forms will seem dislimned, and made 'indistinct, as water is in water'.[419] And in epoch after epoch, the bridge of the gods and we shall sink or swim together.

Fig. 30: Painting at Wat Phra Kaew or the Temple of the Emerald Buddha, Bangkok, depicting characters or scenes from *Ramakien*, possibly Hanuman (or Nala) whose back is shown in the form of a living animistic conduit (Photograph by Iudexvivorum)

---

[419]Shakespeare, *Antony and Cleopatra*, p. 106.

ACKNOWLEDGEMENTS

The inception of the Indian version of this work, now titled *Ram Setu*, owes itself to the spirit of a great mind, the late Bibek Debroy. The book cannot afford to forego dedicating itself to his memory.

The origins of the research behind this book are greatly owed to the generous inspiration and care offered by the eminent scholars and intellectuals May Joseph and Philip Hayward, and were later supported by Adam Grydehøj, Godfrey Baldacchino, Jonathan Pugh, and several others, including the brilliant editorial staff of the journals *Shima* and *Island Studies Journal*. These and a thriving community of intellectuals known as 'island studies' have been great boons.

I am deeply thankful to C. Raj Kumar, R. Sudarshan, Sridhar Patnaik, S.G. Sreejith, Dipika Jain, the Office of the Dean of Research at the Jindal Global Law School, and other colleagues at O.P. Jindal Global University, including Denys P. Leighton and Mosarrap H. Khan. My sincere gratitude is also due to the economist Rathin Roy; the historian William Gould and the School of History at the University of Leeds; the anthropologist Edward Simpson and the South Asia Institute at the School of Oriental and African Studies, University of London; the National Archives; the scholar Parul Singh and BITS Pilani K.K. Birla (Goa); the distinguished historian and scholar Lakshmi Subramanian for her critical scholarly support; the noted geologist C.P. Rajendran for guidance on earth science; the illustrious scholar Nikhilesh Dholakia for continuous encouragement; and eminent journalists Adrija Roychowdhury (and *The Indian Express*), Jiby Kattakayam (and *MoneyControl*), Nitin Thakur (and AajTak Radio), Uddalak Mukherjee (and *The Telegraph*), and Harshita Mishra (and *NDTV*) for their empathetic and critical engagements with my research. Sincere thanks are also owed to Raj Kapil, Daniel Edwin Jayadas, Dr Xavier L. and Vijayashankar S.

I am grateful to professors Saugata Bhaduri, Dhananjay Singh, G.J.V. Prasad and Makarand Paranjape for their support. Many others, including Subhash Kak, Malashri Lal, Meenakshi Mund, Gina Heathcote, Papiya Mazumdar, Daniel Stein (also for his photographs), Sudip Patra, Jibunnessa Abdullah, Richard Alford, Paul Vinay Kumar, Chandra Sekhar, Amit Ranjan, Somjyoti Mridha, Debmalya Biswas, Mahua Sen, Satya Banerjee and Nikhil Kumar, have lent their scholarly and genial thoughts on a long journey—a journey also enriched by the kind and supportive staffs at the Central Archaeological Library (New Delhi), the National Library of India (Kolkata), the Library of the West Bengal Secretariat (Kolkata), the Central Secretariat Library (New Delhi), and the British Library (London). I am also grateful to Simon Bates, Emily Briggs and Lakshita Joshi of Routledge (United Kingdom).

The benevolent and philosophical support by well-known editor Yamini Chowdhury, of Rupa Publications, is indescribable. Her support bonds this story in a special character of gratitude. Besides, without the assiduous support of the team at Rupa, constituted by Rohan Datta, Shakya Bose, Padma Pegu and Amrita Chakravorty, this book would be surely incomplete.

Finally, my family, comprising my parents, Bishakha and Asit Chatterji, is to be sincerely credited and thanked for granting its memories and love to my many intellectual moods that have piloted this slow voyage to Ram Setu and the exploration of its multifaceted legacies.

BIBLIOGRAPHY

'Parliamentary Elections 2019: D.M.K. Manifesto', Chennai: DMK, 2019.

'Rennell, James', *The Penny Cyclopaedia of the Society for the Diffusion of Useful Knowledge, Vol. 19*, London: Charles Knight, 1841, p. 389.

'United Nations Convention on the Law of the Sea', New York: United Nations, 1995.

Abdul Kalam, A.P.J., 'Bridging the Hearts: Address at the Inauguration of the Amrita Setu, Kollam', *Dr. A.P.J. Abdul Kalam*, 2006, https://tinyurl.com/2d5c87w4, Accessed on 20 June 2022.

Abeyagoonasekera, A., 'Sethusamudram to samudra manthan: Containing Chinese influence in Sri Lanka', *Observer Research Foundation*, 28 July 2020, https://tinyurl.com/39tbpc4c. Accessed on 20 October 2021.

Abeyagoonasekera, A., *Sri Lanka at Crossroads: Geopolitical Challenges and National Interests*. Singapore: World Scientific, 2019.

Abram, D., N. Edwards and M. Ford, *The Rough Guide to South India*. New York and London: Rough Guides, 2007.

Adams, M. (2015). 'Indo-Lanka Fishery Issues: Traditional and Human Security Implications', *Proceedings of 8th International Research Conference, KDU*, Colombo: General Sir John Kotelawala Defence University, November 2015, pp. 65–70.

Agnihotri, A., 'Madhya Pradesh Towns Where Ravana is Worshipped, His Death is Mourned', *The Times of India*, 6 October 2016.

Aikin, Arthur (ed.), 'Percival's Account of Ceylon', *The Annual Review and History of Literature for 1803, Vol. II*, London: Longman and Rees, 1804

Aiyangar, K.S., *South India and Her Muhammadan Invaders*. London and Calcutta: Oxford University Press, 1921.

Aiyar, S.S.A., '150-year dream for 150-year-old ships', *The Times of India*, 23 September 2007.

Alberuni, *Alberuni's India (about A.D. 1030), Vol. I*, Edward C. Sachau (trans.), London: Kegan Paul, Trench, Trubner and Co., 1910.

Anand, R.P., 'The Kutch Award', *India Quarterly*, Vol. 24, No. 3, 1968, pp. 183–212.

Andersen, W.K., 'India in 1994: Economics to the Fore', *Asian Survey*, Vol. 35, No. 2, 1995, pp. 127–139.

Anthon, C., *A Classical Dictionary*, New York: Harper and Brothers, 1841.

Arthur, R., T.J. Done, H. Marsh and V.J. Harriott, 'Benthic recovery four years after an El Niño-induced coral mass mortality in the Lakshadweep atolls', *Current Science*, Vol. 89, No. 4, pp. 694–699.

Arulananthan, A., V. Herath, S. Kuganathan, A. Upasanta and A. Harishchandra, 'The Status of the Coral Reefs of the Jaffna Peninsula (Northern Sri Lanka), with 36 Coral Species New to Sri Lanka Confirmed by DNA Bar-Coding', *Oceans*, Vol. 2, 2021 pp. 509–529.

Bahuguna, A., S. Nayak and B. Deshmukh, 'IRS views the Adam's bridge (bridging India and Sri Lanka)', *Journal of the Indian Society of Remote Sensing*, Vol. 31, 2003, pp. 237–239.

Bajpai, L.M., *India, Sri Lanka, and the SAARC Region: History, Popular Culture and Heritage*. New Delhi: Routledge, 2020.

Bak, R.P. and E.H. Meesters, 'Population structure as a response of coral communities to global change', *American Zoologist*, Vol. 39, No. 1, 1999, pp. 56–65.

Balachandran, P.K., 'Lankans filled with misgivings about Fernandes' dream project', *Weekend Express*, 31 March 1999.

Balachandran, P.K., 'SL Concerns Over Proposed Sethusamudram Ship Canal Project', *Daily Mirror*, 24 January 2023.

Balachandran, S. and V. Kannan, 'Gulf of Mannar Marine National Park', *Important Bird and Biodiversity Areas in India: Priority Sites for Conservation*, A.R. Rahmani, M.Z. Islam and R.M. Kasambe (eds.) Bombay: Bombay Natural History Society, 2016, pp. 1682–1685.

Balachandran, S., 'Shore birds of the marine national park in the Gulf of Mannar, Tamil Nadu', *Journal of the Bombay Natural History Society*, Vol. 92, 1995, pp. 303–313.

Balagangadhara, S.N., *"The Heathen in his Blindness...": Asia, the West and the Dynamic of Religion*, Leiden and New York: Brill, 1994.

Balfour, E. (ed.), *Cyclopædia of India and of Eastern and Southern Asia, Vol. 4*. Madras: Scottish and Lawrence Presses, 1873.

Banerjee, P., *Politics of Time: "Primitives" and History-writing in a Colonial Society*, New Delhi and London: Oxford University Press, 2006.

Bardi, A.S., 'God or Geology? The Genesis of Ram's Bridge', *Sapiens*, 20 June 2017. https://tinyurl.com/3x33jbwt. Accessed on 20 June 2022.

Bavinck, M. and D. Johnson, 'Handling the legacy of the blue revolution in India- social justice and small-scale fisheries in a negative growth scenario', *American Fisheries Society Symposium*, Vol. 49, No. 1, 2008, pp. 585–599.

Bavinck, M., 'Marine Resource Management: Conflict and Regulation in the Fisheries of the Coromandel Coast', New Delhi: Sage Publications, 2001.

Baxter, S., *A History of the World in 500 Railway Journeys*, London: Quarto, 2017.

Bayly, C.A., 'The pre-history of "Communalism"? Religious conflict in India 1700–1800', *Modern Asian Studies*, Vol. 19, No. 2, 1985, pp. 177–203.

BBC, 'Gods row minister offers to quit', 15 September 2007, https://tinyurl.com/3k395dfj. Accessed on 20 August 2022.

BBC, 'Hindu groups oppose canal project', 12 September 2007, https://tinyurl.com/4c8mw66s. Accessed on 20 August 2022.

BBC, 'India PM Modi lays foundation for Ayodhya Ram temple amid Covid surge', 5 August 2020, https://tinyurl.com/4dtn4fvx. Accessed on 20 June 2022.

BBC, 'Report on Hindu god Ram withdrawn', 14 September 2007, https://tinyurl.com/4ysbyr34. Accessed on 20 August 2022.

Begum, F., 'Growing Mutuality in India-Sri Lanka Relations', *India Quarterly*, Vol. 61, No. 4, 2005, pp. 169–185.

Berlin, D.L., 'India in the Indian Ocean', *Naval War College Review* (Affiliated to the American Department of the Navy), Vol. 59, No. 2, 2006 pp. 58–89.

Beveridge, H., *A Comprehensive History of India, Division VII*, London: Blackie and Son, 1861.

Bhaduri, S., *Polycoloniality: European Transactions with Bengal from the 13th to the 19th Century*, New Delhi: Bloomsbury, 2021.

Bharati, S., *Essays and Other Prose Fragments*. Madras: Bharati Prachur Alayam, 1937.

Bharatiya Janata Party, 'Resolution on Ram Setu', 22 September 2007, https://tinyurl.com/4zf463ku. Accessed on 20 August 2022.

Bhattacharya, S., 'Eyeing China, DMK MP Writes to PM Modi Demanding Revival of Sethu Samudram Project', *Republic World*, 10 July 2020, https://tinyurl.com/yj4utwfd. Accessed on 20 August 2022.

Bhattacharyya, P., *Ideals of Indian Womanhood*, Calcutta: Goldquin and Co., 1921.

Blau, R., 'What is the opium of the people?', *1843 Magazine, The Economist*, 5 January 2015, https://tinyurl.com/6vwtuxpv. Accessed on 12 May 2020.

Blavatsky, H.P., *The Secret Doctrine*, London: The Theosophical Publishing Company, 1888.

Boer, R., 'Toward a Materialist Theology, or, Why Atheists (and Marxists) Should Write Theology', *Reasonable Perspectives on Religion*, Richard Curtis (ed.), Plymouth: Lexington Books, 2010, pp. 175–202.

Borde, R., 'Did the Subaltern Speak?', *Voices from the Periphery: Subalternity and Empowerment in India*, Marine Carin and Lidia Guzin (eds.), London: Routledge, 2012.

Bradshaw, M., G.W. White, J.P. Dymond and E. Chacko, *World Regional Geography*, New York: McGraw Hill, 2007.

Brice, A., *A Universal Geographical Dictionary; or, Grand Gazetteer, Vol. 1*. London: Robinson, Johnston, Davey, Law, et al., 1759.

Bristow, R.C., et al., 'Correspondence on the Physical Features of Adam's Bridge and the Currents Across it, Considered as Affecting the Proposed Construction of a Railway Connecting India with Ceylon', *Minutes of the Proceedings of the Institution of Civil Engineers*, Vol. 203, 1917, pp. 303–332.

Bröker, K.C.A. and A. Ilangakoon, 'Occurrence and conservation needs of cetaceans in and around the Bar Reef Marine Sanctuary, Sri Lanka', *Oryx*, Vol. 42, No. 2, 2008, pp. 286–291.

Brookes, R., *The General Gazetteer: Or, Compendious Geographical Dictionary*, London: J. Newbery, 1762.

Buckley, M., *An Indian Odyssey*, London: Vintage, 2009.

Bunyard, P. and K. Vyas, 'A Bridge too Far', *Ecologist*, Vol. 38, No. 9, November 2008, pp. 12.

222 RAM SETU

Campbell, J., *Excursions, Adventures, and Field-sports in Ceylon: Its Commercial and Military Importance, and Numerous Advantages to the British Emigrant, Vol. 1*, London: T. and W. Boone, 1843.

Capper, J., 'Outline of the Commercial Statistics of Ceylon', *Journal of the Statistical Society of London, Vol. 2*, London: Charles Knight and Co., 1839, pp. 424–433.

Cathcart, R.B., 'Sethusamudram ship channel macroproject: Anti-tsunami and storm surge textile arrestors protecting Palk Bay (India and Sri Lanka)', *Current Science*, 2006, pp. 1474–1476.

Cathcart, R.B., 'Tapping earth's upper-mantle methane gas resource at a nuclear drilling initiative area, Palk Bay, India/Sri Lanka', *Current Science*, Vol. 92, No. 6, 2007, pp. 729–732.

Cave, H.W., *Golden Tips: A Description of Ceylon and Its Great Tea Industry*. London and New York: Cassell, 1905.

Central Marine Fisheries Research Institute, 'Marine Fisheries Information Service', *Indian Council of Agricultural Research*, Vol. 30, 1981, p. 19.

Central Marine Fisheries Research Institute, *Marine Fisheries Census 2010, Tamil Nadu*, New Delhi: Department of Animal Husbandry Dairying and Fisheries, 2010.

Ceylon Chamber of Commerce, 'Proposed Canal Through the Island of Rameswaram', *Annual Report and Accounts*, Colombo, 1905, pp. 50–57.

Chaitanya, A.V.S., M. Lengaigne, J. Vialard, V.V. Gopalakrishna, F. Durand, Kranthikumar and M. Ravichandran, 'Salinity measurements collected by fishermen reveal a "river in the sea" flowing along the eastern coast of India', *Bulletin of the American Meteorological Society*, Vol. 95, No. 12, 2014, pp. 1897–1908.

Chaitanya, S.V.K., 'Gulf of Mannar's Vaan Island: Turning over a new reef', *The New Indian Express*, 14 February 2021, https://tinyurl.com/4smryzex. Accessed on 10 February 2022.

Chakrabarty, D., *The Climate of History in a Planetary Age*, Chicago: University of Chicago Press, 2021.

Chandramohan, P., B.K. Jena and V.S. Kumar, 'Littoral drift sources and sinks along the Indian coast', *Current Science*, Vol. 81, No. 3, pp. 292–296.

Chansoria, M., *China, Japan, and Senkaku Islands: Conflict in the East China Sea Amid an American Shadow*, London and New York: Routledge, 2018.

Chatterjee, A.K. *The Purveyors of Destiny: A Cultural Biography of the Indian Railways*, New Delhi & London: Bloomsbury, 2017.

Chatterjee, A.K., 'Do You Believe in Ram Setu? Adam's Bridge, Epistemic Plurality and Colonial Legacy', *Island Studies Journal*, Early access, 2022, pp. 1–25.

Chatterjee, A.K., 'Lord Ram's Own Sethu: Adam's Bridge Envisaged as an Aquapelago', *Shima*, Vol. 16, No. 1, 2022, pp. 94–114.

Chatterjee, A.K., *Adam's Bridge: Sacrality, Performance, and Heritage of an Oceanic Marvel*, London and New York: Routledge, 2024.

Chatterjee, A.K., *Indians in London: From the Birth of the East India Company to Independent India*. New Delhi and London: Bloomsbury, 2021.

Chennai: Directorate of Fisheries, 'A Census of Tamil Nadu Marine Fishermen', Government of Tamil Nadu, 1986.

Choudhary, A., *Vajpayee: The Ascent of the Hindu Right, 1924–1977*. New Delhi: Picador, 2023.

Clark, A., *Peeps at Many Lands: Ceylon*, London: Adam and Charles Black, 1910.

Colebrooke, W.M.G., 'Account of the Pearl Fisheries of the North-West Coast of the Island of Ceylon. By Captain James Steuart, Master Attendant at Colombo. Communicated by Lieut. Colonel William M.G. Colebrooke, of the Royal Artillery', *Transactions of the Royal Asiatic Society*, Vol. 3, 1833, pp. 453–462.

Colombo: High Commission of India, 'Operational details of USD 1 billion credit line: Press Release', 7 May 2022.

Communalism Watch, 'Condemn Killings! Condemn Communalisation of Sethusamudram Project!', 23 September 2007. https://tinyurl.com/2s3pmahk. Accessed on 20 April 2020.

Concrete and Constructional Engineering, 'Reinforced Concrete Causeway', Vol. 11, No. 147, 1916.

Coomaraswamy, A.K., *Myths of the Hindus and Buddhists*. London: George G. Harrap & Co., 1913.

Cope, C., *History of the East Indies*, London: M. Cooper, 1754.

CSIR, 'Sethusamudram Ship Canal Project', *CSIR News*, Vol. 48, No. 3, 15 February 1998, pp. 50–51.

Curzon, L., *Subjects of the Day*, Desmond M. Chapman-Huston (ed.), London: George Allen and Unwin, 1915.

Cust, R.N., *Linguistic and Oriental Essays*. London: Trubner and Co., 1880.

D'Anville, J.B.B., *A Geographical Illustration of the Map of India*, William Herbert (trans.) London: Henry Gregory, 1759.

Das, N.C., *Note on the Ancient Geography of India*, Darjeeling: Bengal Secretariat Press, 1896.

Davy, J., *An Account of the Interior of Ceylon, and of Its Inhabitants*, London: Longman, Hurst, Rees, Orme, and Browne, 1821.

De Butts, A., *Rambles in Ceylon*, London: W.H. Allen, 1841.

De Queyroz, F., *The Temporal and Spiritual Conquest of Ceylon*, S.G. Perera (trans.), Colombo: A.C. Richards, 1930.

De Silva, S., 'Sharing maritime boundary with India: Sri Lankan experience', Paper presented at the Working Group meeting of the Regional Network for Strategic Studies Centers (RNSSC) on WMD and Border Security Issues held from 12–15 October 2008 in Istanbul, Turkey. Washington DC, USA: US Defence University.

De Varthema, L., *The Travels of Ludovico Di Varthema in Egypt: Syria, Arabia Deserta and Arabia Felix, in Persia, India, and Ethiopia. AD 1503 to 1508*, J.W. Jones (trans.), London: The Hakluyt Society, 1863.

Devi, S., *Indian Nature Myths*, London: Macmillan and Co., 1919.

Director, 'Hon'ble Chief Minister of Tamil Nadu to Shri Narendra Modi, Hon'ble Prime Minister of India, New Delhi', Information and Public Relations Department, Chennai, 2 July 2014.

Director, 'Press Release No. 351: Text of the D.O. letter dt. 2.7.2014 addressed by Selvi J Jayalalithaa, Hon'ble Chief Minister of Tamil Nadu to Shri Narendra Modi, Hon'ble Prime Minister of India, New Delhi', Information and Public Relations, Chennai.

Divan, S. and A. Rosencranz, *Environmental Law and Policy in India: Cases and Materials*, Oxford: Oxford University Press, 2022.

DoD, 'Preliminary Assessment of Impact of Tsunami in Selected Coastal Areas of India', Chennai: Department of Ocean Development, Integrated Coastal and Marine Area Management Project Directorate, 2005.

Duarte, C. M., 'The future of seagrass meadows', *Environmental Conservation*, Vol. 29, No. 2, 2002, pp. 192–206.

Dunn, D., 'Did the Trojan War actually happen?', *BBC*, 9 January 2020, https://tinyurl.com/3xd6rvun. Accessed on 20 June 2022.

Eastern Economist, Vol. 76, No. 7, 13 February 1981.

Eck, Diana L., *India: A Sacred Geography*, New York: Harmony Books, 2012.

Economic and Political Weekly, 'Sethusamudram: Approval Without Debate', Vol. 40, No. 22/23, 28 May–10 June 2005, p. 2212.

Edward, J.K.P., P. Jamila, G. Mathews and D. Wilhelmsson, 'Status of corals of the Tuticorin coast, Gulf of Mannar, Southeast coast of India', *Coral Reef Degradation in the Indian Ocean (CORDIO)–Status Report*, 2005, pp. 119–127.

Encyclopaedia Britannica, Edinburgh: Andrew Bell and Colin MacFarquhar, 1768.

Engineer, A.A., 'Communalism and Communal Violence, 1996', *Economic and Political Weekly*, Vol. 32, No. 7, 1997, pp. 323–326.

Engineering News, 'An Ocean Viaduct in India with a rolling Lift Draw Span', Vol. 71, No. 19, 7 May 1914, pp. 997–1001.

Enriquez, C.M., *Ceylon Past and Present*, London: Hurst and Blackett, 1927.

Esslemont, G., R.A. Russell and W.A. Maher, 'Coral record of harbour dredging: Townsville, Australia', *Journal of Marine Systems*, Vol. 52, No. 1–4, 2004, pp. 51–64.

Estimates Committee: 1968–69, 'Sethusamudram Canal Project', Fourth Lok Sabha, Seventy-Third Second Report: Ministry of Shipping and Transport (Coastal Shipping). New Delhi: Lok Sabha Secretariat, 1969.

Estimates Committee: 1981–82: Seventh Lok Sabha, Thirty Second Report: Ministry of Shipping and Transport (Shipping—Major Ports), New Delhi: Lok Sabha Secretariat, 27 April 1982.

Everett-Heath, J., *The Concise Dictionary of World Place-Names*, New York: Oxford University Press, 2005.

Express News Service, 'Where is proof Ram built bridge, asks Karunanidhi', *The Indian Express*, 16 September 2007.

Fabricius, K.E., 'Effects of terrestrial runoff on the ecology of corals and coral reefs: review and synthesis' *Marine Pollution Bulletin*, Vol. 50, No. 2, 2005, pp. 125–146.

Field, A., 'The Legend of Adam's Bridge', *The American Antiquarian and Oriental Journal*, Vol. 25, 1903, pp. 39–40.

Filho, G.M.A., J.C. Creed, L.R. Andrade and W.C. Pfeiffer, 'Metal accumulation by *Halodule wrightii* populations', *Aquatic Botany*, Vol. 80, 2004, pp. 241–251.

Flood, V.S., J.M. Pitt and S.R. Smith, 'Historical and ecological analysis of coral communities in Castle Harbour (Bermuda) after more than a century of environmental perturbation', *Marine Pollution Bulletin*, Vol. 51, No. 5–7, 2005, pp. 545–557.

Flueckiger, J.B., 'Standing in Cement: Possibilities Created by Ravan on the Chhattisgarhi Plains', *South Asian History and Culture*, Vol. 8, No. 4, 2017, pp. 461–477.

Forbes, J., *Eleven Years in Ceylon, Vol. 1*, London: Richard Bentley, 1841.

Fraser, W.K. and Tytler, 'Report of the information reproduced from the Imperial Records Department', File number 327-G/29, Proposed Delimitation of the Gulf of Manaar and Palk Strait with a View to Safeguard the Marine Fisheries off the Madras Coast, Question of Ownership of the Island of Kachitivu, 1929, Foreign and Political Department, General Branch, Government of India, National Archives of India, 1922.

Fullarton, A., *A Gazetteer of the World: Or, Dictionary of Geographical Knowledge, compiled from the Most Recent Authorities, and Forming a Complete Body of Modern Geography, Vol. 5*. Edinburgh & London: A. Fullarton, 1856.

Fullerton, H., 'Report dated 5 December 1822, from H. Fullerton, Esquire, Civil Engineer, Southern Division, Trichinopoly District to Inspector of Civil Estimates', File F/4/1250, IOC, 1822.

Gaan, N., *Environmental Security: Concept and Dimensions*, New Delhi: Kalpaz, 2004.

Gacia, E. and C.M. Duarte, 'Sediment Retention by a Mediterranean Posidonia oceanica Meadow: The Balance between Deposition and Resuspension', *Estuarine, Coastal and Shelf Science*, Vol. 52, No. 4, 2001, pp. 505–514.

Gacia, E., H. Kennedy, C.M. Duarte, J. Terrados, N. Marbà, S. Papadimitriou and M. Fortes, 'Light-dependence of the metabolic balance of a highly productive Philippine seagrass community', *Journal of Experimental Marine Biology and Ecology*, Vol. 316, No. 1, 2005, pp. 55–67.

George, L., *Mother Earth, Sister Seed: Travels through India's Farmlands*. New Delhi: Penguin, 2016.

Gibson, C.C., *In Eastern Wonderlands*, Boston: Little, Brown and Co., 1906.

Gilmour, J., 'Experimental investigation into the effects of suspended sediment on fertilisation, larval survival, and settlement in a scleractinian coral', *Marine Biology*, Vol. 135, 1999, pp. 451–462.

Global Environment Facility, 'Conservation and Sustainable Use of the Gulf of Mannar Biosphere Reserve's Coastal Biodiversity', *Washington: Project Document*, GEF Project ID 634, GEF Secretariat, 1999.

Gohain, M.P., 'Is Ram Sethu a natural shoal? ICHR to delve under the sea', *The Times of India*, 25 March 2017, https://tinyurl.com/m54r5wu3. Accessed on 20 April 2020.

Gold, C., *Oriental Drawings*, London: Nicoll, 1806.

Goldman, R.P. and S.J.S. Goldman (trans. and annotated), *The Ramayana of*

Valmiki: An Epic of Ancient India, Vol. V: Sundarakanda, Princeton and Oxford: Princeton University Press, 2007.

Goldman, R.P., S.J.S Goldman, Barend A. van Nooten (trans. and annotated), *The Ramayana of Valmiki: An Epic of Ancient India, Vol. VI: Yuddhakanda*, Princeton and Oxford: Princeton University Press, 2009.

Gómez-Barris, M. and M. Joseph, 'Introduction: Coloniality and Islands', *Shima*, Vol. 13, No. 2, 2019, pp. 1–10.

Gopal, S., 'Introduction', *Anatomy of a Confrontation: Ayodhya and the Rise of Communal Politics in India*, Sarvepalli Gopal (ed.), London and New Jersey: Zed Books, 1993, pp. 11–21.

Gorresio, G., 'Ramayana: An Indian Epic', *The Calcutta Review*, Vol. 23, No. 45, 1854, pp. 162–216.

Gould, W., 'Congress Radicals and Hindu Militancy: Sampurnanand and Purushottam Das Tandon in the Politics of the United Provinces, 1930–1947', *Modern Asian Studies*, Vol. 36, No. 3, 2002, pp. 619–655.

Gould, W., 'Reviews: Politics after Television: Hindu Nationalism and the Reshaping of the Public in India. By Arvind Rajagopal. Cambridge: Cambridge University Press, 2001. Pp. viii, 393', *Modern Asian Studies*, Vol. 36, No. 2, 2002, pp. 491–511.

Gould, W., *Hindu Nationalism and the Language of Politics in Late Colonial India*, Cambridge and New York: Cambridge University Press, 2005.

Gould, W., *Religion and Conflict in Modern South Asia*, New York: Cambridge University Press, 2012.

Government of India, 'The Places of Worship (Special Provisions) Act, 1991', New Delhi: Universal Law Publishing, 2011.

Government of India, *Report of the Committee on Transport Policy and Coordination*, New Delhi, 1966.

Government of Tamil Nadu, 'Tamil Nadu Marine Fishing Regulation Act', 1983.

Graham, M., *Letters on India*, London: Longman, Hurst, Rees, Orme and Brown, 1814.

Grant, J., *Cassell's Illustrated History of India*, London and New York: Cassell, Petter, Galpin, 1880.

Griffith, R.T.H. (trans.), *The Ramayan of Valmíki: Translated into English Verse, Vol. 5*, London: Trubner & Co; Benares: E.J. Lazarus & Co., 1870.

Growse, F.S., *The Ramayana of Tulsidas*, Allahabad: North-Western Provinces and Oudh Government Press, 1883.

Guha-Thakurta, T., *Monuments, Objects, Histories*, New York: Columbia University Press, 2004.

Gunasekara, S.N., 'Security Dimensions of Sethu Samudram Ship Canal Project and United Nations Convention on the Law of Sea: India–Sri Lanka Context', *Journal of South Asian Studies*, Vol. 4, No. 1, 2016, pp. 19–26.

Gunasekara, S.N., 'State responsibility over Sethu Samudram Ship Canal Project: Indo-Sri Lanka Context', *Proceedings of the Annual Research Symposium*, Faculty of Graduate Studies, University of Kelaniya, 2012, p. 62.

Gundevia, Y.D., 'A Note on the Need for an Intensive Development of our South-East Coast Areas', 1959, *Selected Works of Jawaharlal Nehru, Vol. 48*, Madhavan K. Palat (ed.), New Delhi: Jawaharlal Nehru Memorial Fund, 2013, pp. 582–586.

Gupta, A., 'P. Chidambaram: His Third Budget and the United Progressive', *Business Today*, 17 July 2004.

Gupta, A., 'The Palk Straits Canal', *Business Today*, 1 August 2005.

Gupta, C. and M. Sharma, *Contested Coastlines: Fisherfolk, Nations and Borders in South Asia*. New Delhi and Abingdon: Routledge, 2007.

Gupta, M.N., *The Gospel of Sri Ramakrishna*, Swami Nikhilananda (trans.), Calcutta: Ramakrishna-Vivekananda Centre, 1977.

Guthrie, W., *An Improved System of Modern Geography*, Dublin: John Chambers, 1789.

Hamilton, A., *A New Account of the East Indies*, Edinburgh: John Mofman, 1727.

Haraway, D., 'Situated Knowledges: The Science Question in Feminism and the Privilege of Partial Perspective', *Women, Science, and Technology: A Reader in Feminist Science Studies*, Mary Wyer, Mary Barbercheck, Donna Cookmeyer, Hatice Ozturk and Marta Wayne (eds.). New York and Oxon: Routledge, 2014, pp. 455–472.

Hazra, I., 'Ram Setu: Good politics, bad economics', *Hindustan Times*, 22 September 2007.

Heeren, A.H.L., *The Historical Works of Arnold H.L. Heeren, Vol. 2*, London: Henry G. Bohn, 1846.

Hegadekatti, K., 'An Indo-Lanka tunnel to integrate island to BIMSTEC', *Fortune India*, 12 August 2022, https://tinyurl.com/2ba52c47. Accessed on 20 August 2022.

Hegel, G.W.F., *Philosophy of History*, J. Sibree (trans.), New York: American Home Library, 1837 [1905].

Heisenberg, W., *Physics and Philosophy; The Revolution in Modern Science*, New York: Harper and Row, 1958.

Hemminga, M. and C.M. Duarte, *Seagrass Ecology*, Cambridge: Cambridge University Press, 2000.

Henry, J.W., *Ravana's Kingdom: The Ramayana and Sri Lankan History from Below*, New York: Oxford University Press, 2022.

Herdman, W.A., 'The Pearl Fisheries of Ceylon', *Nature*, Vol. 67, No. 1748, 1903, pp. 620–622.

High Commission of Sri Lanka in India, 'India-Sri Lanka Joint Working Group on Fisheries: Statement by the Ministry of Foreign Affairs', Government of Sri Lanka, 31 January 2006, https://tinyurl.com/3v9atv2c. Accessed on 20 August 2022.

High Court of Judicature at Madras, *O. Fernandes vs Tamil Nadu Pollution Control Board*, WP No. 33528, 2004.

Hindu Human Rights, 'Rama Sethu: Burning our Bridges with the Sacred Environment', 8 February 2007, https://tinyurl.com/tw3swend. Accessed on 20 August 2021.

Hindu Janajagruti Samiti: For the Establishment of Hindu Rashtra, 'Save Shri Ram Setu Campaign', https://tinyurl.com/4w2aakjp. Accessed on 20 August 2022.

Hindu Janajagruti Samiti: For the Establishment of Hindu Rashtra, 'Shankaracharyas unite to save Lord Rama's bridge!', 23 February 2007, https://tinyurl.com/3nu62xre. Accessed on 20 August 2022.

Hindu Janajagruti Samiti: For the Establishment of Hindu Rashtra, 'VHP warns against destroying Ram Sethu', 11 March 2008, https://tinyurl.com/unk7prma. Accessed on 20 August 2022.

Hindustan Times, 'Hanuman heads for Palk Strait', 31 January 2007.

Hindustan Times, 'The Protest over Ram Setu', 20 November 2007.

Hiranandani, G.M., *Transition to Eminence: The Indian Navy 1976–1990*, New Delhi: Ministry of Defence (Indian Navy), 2005.

Hornell, J., 'Historical Survey of the Pearl Fisheries off the Madura Coast', *Madras Fisheries Bulletin*, Vol. 16, 1922, Madras: Government Press.

Hornell, J., 'Indian Varieties and Races of Turbinella', *Memoirs of the Zoological Survey of India*, Vol. 6, No. 2, 1916, 109–122.

House of Commons, *Report from the Select Committee on Steam Communication with India*, London, 1837.

Howard, E., *Travels Through Asia, Africa, and America*. London: M. Cooper, 1755.

Hughes, T.P. and J.E. Tanner, 'Recruitment failure, life histories, and long-term decline of Caribbean corals', *Ecology*, Vol. 81, No. 8, 2000, pp. 2250–2263.

IANS, 'Ram Setu "man-made," says Govt publication', *Hindustan Times*, 8 December 2007.

Illustrated Guide to the South Indian Railway, Madras: Hoe and Co., 1926.

India Environment Portal: Knowledge for Change, 'Sethusamudram ship canal project', https://tinyurl.com/2j9u4bew. Accessed on 20 August 2022.

India's Parliament: Selections from the Proceedings of the Fifth Session of the Second Legislative Assembly, 1926, 'Resolution Re Retention in its Present Site of Rameswaram Station on the South Indian Railway', Calcutta: Director, Bureau of Public Information, pp. 82–93.

Indian & Foreign Review, 'Indo-Sri Lanka Boundary in Palk Bay Defined', Vol. 11, No. 19, 1974, pp. 5–6.

Indian & Foreign Review, Vol. 11, No. 19, 15 July 1974, p. 24.

Indian Engineering, 'Communication Between India and Ceylon', Vol. 31, No. 10, 8 March 1902, p. 147.

International Commerce, 'India', Vol. 70, No. 25, 22 June 1964, p. 27.

Iyengar, P.T.S., *History of Tamils from the Earliest times to 600 A.D.*, Madras: C. Coomarasawmy Naidu & Sons, 1929.

Iyengar, T.R.S and K.S. Pillai, *Tamil Nadu*. Chennai: International Institute of Tamil Studies, 1927.

Iyer, R.R., *Towards Water Wisdom: Limits, Justice, Harmony*. New Delhi and London: Sage, 2007.

Iyer, T.P., *Ramayana and Lanka*, Bangalore: The Bangalore Press, 1940.

Jagtap, T.G., D.S. Komarpant and R.S. Rodrigues, 'Status of a seagrass ecosystem:

an ecologically sensitive wetland habitat from India', *Wetlands*, Vol. 23, No. 1, 2003, pp. 161–170.

Jain, S., P.K. Agarwal and V.P. Singh, *Hydrology and Water Resources of India*, Dordrecht: Springer, 2007.

James, P.S.B.R., 'Notes on the biology and fishery of the butterfly ray, Gymnura poecilura (Shaw) from the Palk Bay and Gulf of Mannar', *Indian Journal of Fisheries*, Vol. 13, No. 1 and 2, 1966, pp. 150–157.

Janardhan, A., 'Explained: An island marooned', *The Indian Express*, 12 December 2014.

Jaoul, N. 'Casting the "Sweepers": Local Politics of Sanskritization, Caste and Labour', *Cultural Entrenchment of Hindutva*, Daniela Berti, Nicolas Jaoul and Pralay Kanungo (eds.), New Delhi: Routledge, 2011, pp. 273–305.

Jarus, O. 'Ancient Troy: The city and the legend', *Live Science*, 8 February 2022. https://tinyurl.com/www358dj. Accessed on 20 August 2022.

Jayasinghe, W.T., *Kachchativu and the Maritime Boundary of Sri Lanka*, Pannipitiya: Stamford Lake Publication, 2003.

Jayasundere, C. and D. De Silva, '"Sethusamudram Ship Canal Project Where does the law stand?" How should Sri Lanka react?', *Proceedings in law, 9th International Research Conference-KDU*, Sri Lanka, 2004.

Jayawardena, D., 'Present status of the Sethusamudram Project', *Sunday Times*, 11 July 2010.

Jedidiah, M., *The American Universal Geography*, Boston: Young and Etheridge, 1793.

Jeyanthi, N., 'Cyclone Disaster Management', National Interactive Workshop held at Tamil Nadu Agricultural University, 25–26 February 2002.

Jeyaraman, B., *Periyar: A Political Biography of EV Ramaswamy*, New Delhi: Rupa Publications, 2013.

John, J., 'Sethusamudram Canal: An Expensive Voyage?', *Economic and Political Weekly*, Vol. 42, No. 29, 21 July 2007, pp. 2993–2996.

Johnston, A., 'A Letter to the Secretary Relating to the Preceding Inscription', *Transactions of the Royal Asiatic Society of Great Britain and Ireland*, Vol. 1, 1827, pp. 1537–548.

Jones, W., 'A Discourse on the Institution of a Society (Address to the Asiatic Society of Bengal in 1784)', *The Collected Works of Sir William Jones*, Jogendranath Ghose (ed.), Calcutta: Trubner and Co., 1827, pp. 1–5.

Jones, W., 'Dissertation on the Gods of Greece, Italy and India', *The American Museum or Universal Magazine*, Vol. 12, Philadelphia: M. Carey, December 1792, pp. 313–334.

Joseph, A., 'Investigating Seafloors and Oceans: From Mud Volcanoes to Giant Squid', Amsterdam and Oxford: Elsevier, 2017.

Joseph, M., *Sea Log: Indian Ocean to New York*. London and New York: Routledge, 2019.

Joshi, U., 'Assessing Indian-Sri Lankan ties in choppy waters: The fisherman issue vis-à-vis international law', *The Leaflet*, 23 December 2022, https://tinyurl.com/3yvx5tje, Accessed on 28 December 2022.

Journal of the Royal Society of Arts, 'Railway Connection Between India and Ceylon', Vol. 62, No. 3206, 1 May 1914, p. 525.

Kadhirvel, S., *A History of the Maravas, 1700–1802*, Madurai: Madurai Publishing House, 1977.

Kannan, R., *Anna: The Life and Times of CN Annadurai*, New Delhi: Penguin, 2010.

Karnad, D., M. Gangal and K.K. Karanth, 'Perceptions matter: how fishermen's perceptions affect trends of sustainability in Indian fisheries', *Oryx*, Vol. 48, No. 2, 2014, pp. 218–227.

Karunanidhi, M., 'Foreword', *Tamil Nadu District Gazetteers*, Ramanathapuram, Madras: Government of Tamil Nadu, 1972, pp. i–ii.

Kearney, R.N., 'Language and the rise of Tamil separatism in Sri Lanka', *Asian Survey*, Vol. 18, 1978, pp. 521–534.

Khan, S., 'Gujarat fisherfolk leader moves HC for euthanasia, alleges "discrimination, negligence"', *The Times of India*, 5 May 2022.

Kipling, R., *Departmental Ditties and Other Verses*, Calcutta: Thacker, Spink & Co., 1890.

Knox, T.W., *The Boy Travellers in the Far East, Part 3*, New York: Harper and Brothers, 1880.

KRISHNA's FOOD & travel, 'Ramakrishna is God. We don't admit it. Srila Prabhupada. Morning walk on May 17, 1973 in Los Angeles', *YouTube*, 22 April 2022, https://tinyurl.com/4xx232wu. Accessed on 20 December 2024.

Krishnan, M, 'A bridge that Lord Ram built—myth or reality?', *Deutsche Welle*, 14 December 2017, https://tinyurl.com/yccdhja5. Accessed on 20 April 2020.

Kumar, A., 'Photos no proof of Ram Setu: NASA', *Hindustan Times*, 14 September 2007.

Kumar, P.G., 'Ram Sethu: Stuck between politics, faith and bad economics', *Firstpost*, 29 March 2012, https://tinyurl.com/y95d54a4. Accessed on 20 June 2021.

Kumar, Virendra, *Committees and Commissions in India: 1947–1973*, Concept Publishing Company, New Delhi, 1988.

Kumaraguru, A.K., K. Jayakumar, J.J. Wilson and C.M. Ramakritinan, 'Impact of the tsunami of 26 December 2004 on the coral reef environment of Gulf of Mannar and Palk Bay in the southeast coast of India', *Current Science*, Vol. 89, No. 10, 2005, pp. 1729–1741.

Kurien, J., 'Entry of big business into fishing, its impact on fish economy', *Economic and Political Weekly*, Vol. 13, No. 36, 1978, pp. 1557–1565.

L&T-Ramboll, 'Detailed Project Report and Evaluation of EIA Study for Sethusamudram Ship Channel Project', Larson & Toubro–Ramboll Consulting Engineers Limited, 2005.

Lambert, Claude-Francois, *A Collection of Curious Observations: Asia, Africa and America, Vol. 1*, John Dunn (trans.), London: Dunn, 1750.

Lambo, A.L. and R.F.G. Ormond, 'Continued post-bleaching decline and changed benthic community of a Kenyan coral reef', *Marine Pollution Bulletin*, Vol. 52, No. 12, 2006, pp. 1617–1624.

Latour, B., *Facing Gaia: Eight Lectures on the New Climatic Regime*, Cambridge and Medford: Polity Press, 2017.

Library of Universal Knowledge, New York: American Book Exchange, 1881.

Lockman, J., *Travels of the Jesuits into Various Parts of the World*. London: John Noon, 1743.

Lok Sabha Secretariat, *Index to Lok Sabha Debates Fifth Series, February 18 to May 10, 1974*, New Delhi, 1974.

Lok Sabha Secretariat, *Lok Sabha Debates*, New Delhi, 14 April 1956

Lok Sabha Secretariat, *Lok Sabha Debates*, New Delhi, 14 March 1983.

Lok Sabha Secretariat, *Lok Sabha Debates*, New Delhi, 21 July 1971.

Lok Sabha Secretariat, *Lok Sabha Debates*, New Delhi, 21 March 1966.

Lok Sabha Secretariat, *Lok Sabha Debates*, New Delhi, 22 February 1956.

Lok Sabha Secretariat, *Lok Sabha Debates*, New Delhi, 22 November 1967.

Lok Sabha Secretariat, *Lok Sabha Debates*, New Delhi, 23 July 1974.

Lok Sabha Secretariat, *Lok Sabha Debates*, New Delhi, 27 November 1972.

Lok Sabha Secretariat, *Lok Sabha Debates*, New Delhi, 27 September 1958.

Lok Sabha Secretariat, *Lok Sabha Debates*, New Delhi, 5 May 1992.

Lok Sabha Secretariat, *Lok Sabha Debates*, New Delhi, 8 February–10 May 1974.

Lok Sabha Secretariat, *Lok Sabha Debates*, New Delhi, 8 June 1971.

Lok Sabha, 'Kachchatheevu Island', Unstarred Question No. 2538, answered on 4 December, Ministry of External Affairs, Government of India, 2019.

Lok Sabha, 'Katchatheevu Island: Sir Creek Issue', Unstarred Question No. 1824, Ministry of External Affairs, Government of India, 2019.

Lomas, J., 'On the Origin of Adam's Bridge', *Spolia Zeylanica*, Ceylon: George J.A. Skeen, 1905, pp. 202–204.

Los Angeles Times, 'A Long Bridge', 26 June 1915.

Lourey, M.J., D.A. Ryan and I.R. Miller, 'Rates of decline and recovery of coral cover on reefs impacted by, recovering from and unaffected by crown-of-thorns starfish Acanthaster planci: a regional perspective of the Great Barrier Reef', *Marine Ecology Progress Series*, Vol. 196, 2000, pp. 179–186.

Luthra, G., 'The new US Indo-Pacific Strategy: Balancing continuity with new and evolving environment', *Observer Research Foundation*, 15 March 2022, https://tinyurl.com/3hnkr7wx. Accessed on 20 December 2022.

MacKay, W., *Dictionary of the Religious Ceremonies of the Eastern Nations*, Calcutta: William MacKay, 1787.

Mackenzie, C., 'Remarks on Some Antiquities: On the West and South Coasts of Ceylon', *Asiatic Researches, Vol. 6.*, London: Sewell, Cornhill, Vernor and Good, et al., 1801, pp. 425–454.

Mahadevan, S. and K.N. Nayar, 'Distribution of coral reefs in the Gulf of Mannar and Palk Bay and their exploitation and utilization', *Indian Journal of Fisheries*, Vol. 19, No. 1 and 2, 1972, pp. 181–190.

MahaKrishnan, 'Ram Setu not National Heritage Monument- Dravidian Historical Research Centre's President', *Hindu Post*, 14 February 2022, https://tinyurl.com/wkat3yk9. Accessed: 20/06/2021.

Mahapatra, D., 'SC: Is Sethu a place of worship?', *The Times of India*, 16 April 2008.

Malham, J., *The Naval Gazetteer*, London: Allen and West, 1795.

Mani, V.S., 'India's Maritime Zones and International Law: A Preliminary Inquiry', *Journal of the Indian Law Institute*, Vol. 21, No. 3, 1979, pp. 336–381.

Manoharan, N. and M. Deshpande, 'Fishing in the troubled waters: Fishermen issue in India-Sri Lanka relations', *India Quarterly*, Vol. 74, No. 1, 2018. pp. 73–91.

Manoharan, N., *Policy Studies 28: Counterterrorism Legislation in Sri Lanka*, East-West Center Washington, 2006.

Marbà, N. and C.M. Duarte, 'Coupling of seagrass (Cymodocea nodosa) patch dynamics to subaqueous dune migration', *Journal of Ecology*, Vol. 83, 1995, pp. 381–389.

Martin, B., *Physico-geology: or, A new system of philosophical geography*. London: W. Owen, 1769.

Martin, R.M., *History of the British Colonies, Vol. 1*. London: Cochrane and M'Crone, 1834.

Martin, R.M., *The British Colonial Library, Vol. 10*. London: Whittaker and Co., 1837.

Marx, K., 'Contribution to the Critique of Hegel's Philosophy of Law: Introduction', *Marx and Engels Collected Works, Vol. 3*, Moscow: Progress Publishers, 1844 [1975].

Marx, K., 'The British Rule in India', *New York Daily Tribune*, 25 June 1853. From *Marxists Internet Archive*, February 2005, https://tinyurl.com/hbwnnvdt. Accessed on 12 August 2018.

Maurice, T. 'Dissertation I: The Geographical Divisions of India', *Indian Antiquities, Vol. 1*. London: W. Richardson, 1793.

Maurice, T., *The History of Hindostan; Its Arts, and Its Sciences*, London: Galabin and Gardiner, 1798.

Maurya, K.P., 'Need to ensure safety of sacred Ram Setu between India and Sri Lanka', Sixteenth Lok Sabha, Parliament of India, 2 December 2015, https://tinyurl.com/32h6kapv. Accessed on 20 June 2021.

McCloskey, J., S.S. Nalbant and S. Steacy, 'Earthquake risk from co-seismic stress', *Nature*, Vol. 434, No. 7031, 2005, pp. 291–291.

Memoirs of the Geological Survey of India, 'The Sub-recent Marine Beds', Vol. 20, No. 1, London: Trubner & Co., 1883, pp. 55–74.

Mendis, C., 'Sovereignty vs. trans-boundary environmental harm: The evolving International law obligations and the Sethusamuduram Ship Channel Project', United Nations/Nippon Foundation Fellow Paper, 2006.

Menon, N., 'Ram Setu: The Ecological Argument Against the Sethusamudram Project', *Kafila*, 26 February 2013, https://tinyurl.com/2buuc7zm. Accessed on 6 April 2020.

Mill, J., *The History of British India, Vol. 1*, London: Baldwin, Cradock and Joy, 1817.

Ministry of External Affairs, 'Agreement Between the Government of India and the Government of the Republic of Sri Lanka on the Maritime Boundary in the Gulf of Manaar and the Bay of Bengal, New Delhi, 23 March 1976', *India,*

Bilateral Treaties and Agreements: 1976–1977, New Delhi: Policy Planning and Research Division, Government of India, 1994, pp. 30–33.

Ministry of External Affairs, 'Exchange of letters constituting an Agreement Between the Government of India and the Government of Sri Lanka on the Wadge Bank Fisheries. New Delhi, 23 March 1976', *India, Bilateral Treaties and Agreements: 1976-1977*, New Delhi: Policy Planning and Research Division, Government of India, 1994, pp. 39–44.

Ministry of Shipping, 'Sethusamudram Project: Press Release', Release ID: 5277, 2 December 2004.

Ministry of Shipping, Road Transport and Highways (Department of Shipping), 'Notification: January 3, 2006', Ports Wing. *The Gazette of India, Extraordinary*, 3 January 2006. Ref. G.S.R. 3(E)., pp. 8–12.

Ministry of Transport, 'Resolution: Transport Wing, November 1, 1955', *The Gazette of India*, 12 November 1955, Ref. No. 9-PII (23)/55, p. 307.

Mint, 'Project a recipe for disaster, scientists say', 12 September 2007. https://tinyurl.com/bdepnp8j. Accessed on 20 August 2022.

Modi, Narendra, 'Dr. Kalam inspired the youth of India: PM Modi (text of the PM's speech at the public meeting at Rameswaram, Tamil Nadu)', *Narendra Modi*, 27 July 2017, https://tinyurl.com/dvezy6ks, Accessed on 20 August 2022.

MoEF, 'Letter No. J-16011/6/99-IA-III, Sethusamudram Shipping Channel Project by M/s Tuticorin Port Trust, Tuticorin, Tamil Nadu—Environmental Clearance', New Delhi: Ministry of Environment and Forests, 31 March 2005.

Moll, H., *Atlas Geographus: Asia*. London: John Nutt, 1712.

Monteith, W., 'Account of the Operations for Widening the Channel of the Pamban Passage', *The Madras Journal of Literature and Science*, Vol. 6, No. 16, 1837, pp. 111–142.

Moor, E. and W.O. Simpson, 'The Hindu Pantheon: A New Edition with Additional Plates', Madras: J. Higginbotham, 1864.

Moore, J.H., *A New and Complete Collection of Voyages and Travels*, London: Alexander Hogg, 1778.

Moorthy, N.S., 'Fishing issue: "Externalising" the "internal waters"?', *Observer Research Foundation*, 10 December 2013, https://tinyurl.com/3khdhd66. Accessed on 20 December 2022.

Moorthy, N.S., 'Working the Federal Polity, the Tamil Nadu Experience', *Observer Research Foundation*, 8 December 2004. https://tinyurl.com/59vx5zr8. Accessed on 20 December 2022.

Mudaliar, A.R, et al., 'Report of The Sethusamudram Project Committee', New Delhi: Government of India Press, 1957.

Muhammad, B., 'Sri Lanka: The Axis Mundi and the Cradle of Mankind', Berkeley: Berkeley Institute for Islamic Studies, 2018.

Murali, R.M., 'Applications of Remote Sensing and Geographic Information System (GIS) in Archaeology', *Recent Researches on Indus Civilization and Maritime Archaeology in India*, A.S. Gaur and A.S. Sundaresh (eds.), New Delhi: Agam Kala Prakashan, 2005, pp. 219–223.

Nagar, S., 'Sri Ranganatha Ramayaṇa: Rendering into English from Telugu', New Delhi: B.R. Publication, 2001.

Nagi, S., 'Nervous Govt now chants "Ram naam"', *Hindustan Times*, 23 September 2007.

Nalapat, M.D., 'Stop Delegitimizing the Vedic Age in India', *Sunday Guardian Live*, 3 February 2019, https://tinyurl.com/32j64zy7. Accessed on 20 February 2021.

Nandy, A. 'An Anti-Secularist Manifesto', *Gandhi's Significance for Today*, J. Hick and L.C. Hempel (eds.), London: Palgrave Macmillan, 1989, pp. 244–264.

Nandy, A., 'Nationalism, genuine and spurious: mourning two early post-nationalist strains', *Economic and Political Weekly*, Vol. 41, No. 32, 2006, pp. 3500–3504.

Nandy, A., 'The Intimate Enemy: Loss and Recovery of Self Under Colonialism', *Exiled at Home*, New Delhi: Oxford University Press, 2005.

Nandy, A., 'The twilight of certitudes: Secularism, Hindu nationalism, and other masks of deculturation', *Alternatives*, Vol. 22, No. 2, 1997, pp. 157–176.

Nanjappa, V., 'What ASI has to say about Ram Sethu', *Rediff News*, 17 September 2007, https://tinyurl.com/3ckkzhap. Accessed on 6 April 2020.

Narain, P., 'Adam's Bridge issue: now, NASA says it made no official statement', *Live Mint*, 14 September 2007, https://tinyurl.com/5n8tsn9v. Accessed on 20 August 2022.

Narain, P., 'Informal Hindu alliance starts fussing over Sethusamudram', *Mint*, 10 July 2008.

Narain, P., 'Silence, controversy shroud Sethu project', *Live Mint*, 24 September 2007, https://tinyurl.com/3re6njbb. Accessed on 20 August 2022.

Narain, P., 'Will the Sethu channel be a security risk?', *Live Mint*, 13 March 2008. https://tinyurl.com/5n8ps7mh. Accessed on 20 August 2022.

Narain, Priyanka P., 'Ram Setu project faces cash crunch', *Hindustan Times*, Mumbai, 27 September 2007.

Narayani, P.A., 'Lockdown improved coastal ecosystems of Gulf of Mannar, says study', *The Hindu*, 4 June 2020.

Natarajan, R., 'The Suez of Asia: Sethu Samudram Project', *Akashvani*, Vol. 32, No. 28, 28 May–3 June 1967, pp. 1–3.

Nath, A., 'Tamil Nadu govt calls for retrieval of Kachchativu island to end detention of Indian fishermen by Sri Lanka', *India Today*, 13 April 2022.

Neelakandan, A., *Hindutva: Origin, Evolution and Future*, New Delhi: Kali, 2022.

NEERI, 'Technical Feasibility and Economic Analysis of Proposed Sethusamudram Channel', Nagpur: National Environmental Engineering Research Institute, 2004.

Nehru, J., 'To Y.D. Gundevia: Migration to Ceylon', *Selected Works of Jawaharlal Nehru, Vol. 48*, Madhavan K. Palat (ed.), New Delhi: Jawaharlal Nehru Memorial Fund, 2013, p. 291.

Neocleous, M., *Imagining the State*, Maidenhead and Philadelphia: Open University Press, 2003.

Nolan, E., 'Troy: Fall of a City: Was Helen of Troy real? Is she based on a real person?', *Express*, 18 February 2018. https://tinyurl.com/3wmrmwc8. Accessed on 20 August 2022.

Nutt, J., *Atlas Geographus: Or, A Compleat System of Geography, Ancient and Modern,* Vol. 1, London: John Nutt, Benjamin Barker and Charles King, 1712.

O'Neill, R. and D.N. Schwartz, 'The Indian Ocean as a "Zone of Peace"', *Indian Ocean Power Rivalry,* T.T. Poulouse (ed.), New Delhi: Young Asia Publications, 1974, pp. 177–89.

Oberst, R.C., 'Federalism and Ethnic Conflict in Sri Lanka', *Publius: The Journal of Federalism,* Vol. 18, No. 3, 1988, pp. 175–194.

Obeyesekere, D., *Outlines of Ceylon History,* Colombo and London: The Times of Ceylon, 1911.

Organiser: Voice of the Nation, 'Protect Shri Ram Setu, demand Hindu leaders', 8 October 2007. https://tinyurl.com/4duc2df5. Accessed on 20 August 2022.

Orme, R., *A History of the Military Transactions of the British Nation in Indostan,* Vol. 1. London: John Nourse, 1763.

Pai, N., 'Non-State Threats to India's Maritime Security: Sailing Deeper into the Era of Violent Peace', *The Rise of the Indian Navy: Internal Vulnerabilities, External Challenges,* Harsh V. Pant (ed.), Abingdon and New York: Routledge, pp. 157–178.

Pande, I., *Medicine, Race and Liberalism in British Bengal: Symptoms of Empire.* London and New York: Routledge, 2009.

Pandolfi, J.M., R.H. Bradbury, E. Sala, T.P. Hughes, K.A. Bjorndal, R.G. Cooke and J.B. Jackson, 'Global trajectories of the long-term decline of coral reef ecosystems', *Science,* Vol. 301, No. 5635, 2003, pp. 955–958.

Paranjape, M., 'The Third Eye and Two Ways of (Un)knowing: Gnosis, Alternative Modernities, and Postcolonial Futures', *Postcolonial Philosophy of Religion,* P. Bilimoria and A.B. Irvine (eds.), Dordrecht: Springer, 2009, pp. 55–67.

Pargiter, F.E., 'The Geography of Rama's Exile', *The Journal of the Royal Asiatic Society.* London: Royal Asiatic Society, 1894, pp. 231–264.

Parker, H., *Ancient Ceylon,* London: Luzac and Co., 1909.

Parkin, B., 'Historian Romila Thapar: "There's always been this feeling in India that Russia is misunderstood"', *Financial Times,* 22 April 2022.

Parliament Digital Library, 'Shri Vijay Kumar Malhotra called the attention of the Ministry of Shipping, Road Transport and Highways', Fourteenth Lok Sabha, Parliament of India, 16 May 2007, https://tinyurl.com/btencfjk. Accessed on 20 June 2021.

Pasricha, A., 'India Feels the Squeeze in Indian Ocean with Chinese Projects in Neighborhood', *Voice of America,* 16 September 2021, https://tinyurl.com/5dbepcyd. Accessed on 20 December 2022.

Patterson, J., K.I. Jeyasanta, R.L. Laju, A.M. Booth, N. Sathish and J.P. Edward, 'Microplastic in the coral reef environments of the Gulf of Mannar, India-Characteristics, distributions, sources and ecological risks', *Environmental Pollution,* Vol. 298, 2022, p. 118848.

Patterson, J., M. Venkatesh, G. Mathews, et al., 'A field guide to stony corals (Scleractinia) of Tuticorin in Gulf of Mannar, Southeast India', *SDMRI Special Research Publication,* No. 4, 2004, p. 80.

Paul, P.L., *The Early History of Bengal, Vol. 1*, Calcutta: The Indian Research Institute, 1939.

Peebles, P., *Historical Dictionary of Sri Lanka*, Lanham and Plymouth: Rowman & Littlefield., 2015.

Pennant, T., *The View of Hindoostan*, London: Henry Hugh, 1798.

Peralta, G., J.L. Pérez-Lloréns, I. Hernández and Vergara, 'Effects of light availability on growth, architecture, and nutrient content of the seagrass *Zostera noltii* Hornem', *Journal of Experimental Marine Biology and Ecology*, Vol. 269, No. 1, 2002, pp. 9–26.

Percival, R., *An Account of the Island of Ceylon: Containing Its History, Geography, Natural History, with the Manners and Customs of Its Various Inhabitants*, London: C. & R. Baldwin, 1803.

Phadnis, U., 'Kachcha Thivu: Background and Issues', *Economic and Political Weekly*, Vol. 3, No. 20, 1968, pp. 783–788.

Philipp, E. and K. Fabricius, 'Photophysiological stress in scleractinian corals in response to short-term sedimentation', *Journal of Experimental Marine Biology and Ecology*, Vol. 287, No. 1, 2003, pp. 57–78.

PIB, 'Press Release: Fish Production and Consumption', 8 January 2019, https://tinyurl.com/2p8yv2w6. Accessed on 20 August 2022.

PIB, 'Press Release: The Fifth Meeting of the India-Sri Lanka Joint Working Group on Fisheries', 25 March 2022, https://tinyurl.com/4jyevdyx. Accessed on 20 August 2022.

PIB, 'Press Release: The Fourth Meeting of the India-Sri Lanka Joint Working Group on Fisheries', 30 December 2020, https://tinyurl.com/2v55db6p. Accessed on 20 August 2022.

PIB, 'Security of Fishermen: Statement by the Ministry of Defence', Government of India, 11 March 2013, https://tinyurl.com/2z63b6me. Accessed on 20 August 2022.

Pieris, P.E., 'Coins of Ceylon', *The Numismatist*, Vol. 18, No. 9, 1905, pp. 263–265.

Pillai, C.S.G., 'Recent corals from the south-east coast of India', *Recent Advances in Marine Biology*, New Delhi: Today and Tomorrow Printers and Publishers, 1986, pp. 107–201.

Pillai, N.V., *Setu and Rameswaram*, Rameswaram: V. Narayanan, 1929.

Pogson, W.R., *A History of the Boondelas*, Calcutta: Asiatic Lithographic Company, 1828.

Prabakaran, K. and K. Anbarasu, 'Coastal Geomorphology and Evolution of Rameswaram Island, Tamil Nadu, India', *Research Journal of Earth Sciences*, Vol. 2, No. 2, 2010, pp. 30–35.

Prasad, N., 'IRCTC Ram Sethu Express tour package: Explore Tamil Nadu heritage, covering 18 temples; journey details here', *Financial Express*, 22 February 2019.

Prasada, L., 'Indian poaching in Lanka's waters: Going round in circles for 5 decades', *The Sunday Times*, 14 November 2021. https://tinyurl.com/ywjxn2u8. Accessed on 20 August 2022.

Pratt, M.L., *People and Places: Here and There, Vol. 2: India*, Boston and New

York: Educational Publishing Company, 1892.

Pridham, C., *An Historical, Political, and Statistical Account of Ceylon and Its Dependencies, Vol. 2*, London: T. and W. Boone, 1849.

PTI, 'Ambika offers to resign on Setu case', *The Economic Times*, 15 September 2007.

PTI, 'Chinese-built Hambantota Port to be fully functional by next year', *Business Standard*, 12 July 2020.

PTI, 'ICHR not to conduct study whether Ram Setu man made, natural: Head', *Outlook*, 8 April 2018.

PTI, 'Karnataka Government Committed Towards Dignified Life for SCs And STs: CM', *Outlook*, 9 October 2022.

PTI, 'Ram Setu may leave Babri-like scar', *Hindustan Times*, 9 May 2008.

PTI, 'Shipping project: Nitin Gadkari allays fear about demolishing Ram Sethu', *The Indian Express*, 4 November 2014.

Purdy, J., *After Nature: A Politics for the Anthropocene*, Harvard: Harvard University Press, 2015.

Puthucherril, T.G., 'A Case Study of India's Policy and Legal Regimes on Ocean Governance', *Routledge Handbook of National and Regional Ocean Policies*, Biliana Cicin-Sain, David L. VanderZwaag, and Miriam C. Balgos (eds.), London and New York: Routledge, 2015, 462-492.

Qureshi, S., 'A Dussehra Without Burning Ravana: This Brahmin Community in Agra Wants an End to Practice', *India Today*, 12 October 2016.

Raghavan, V.R., 'Internal Conflicts: Strategic Overview', *Internal Conflicts: Military Perspectives*, Raghavan (ed.), New Delhi: Vij Books, 2012, pp. 15–176.

Raj, K.D., G. Mathews and J.P. Edward, 'Vaan Island of Gulf of Mannar, Southeast coast of India-on the verge of submergence', *Indian Journal of Geo-Marine Sciences*, Vol. 44, No. 6, 2015, pp. 892–895.

Rajamanickam, G.V. and V.J. Loveson, 'Results of Radiocarbon Dating from Some Beach Terraces Around Rameswaram Island, Tamil Nadu', *Sea Level Variation and Its Impact on Coastal Environment*, Rajamanickam (ed.), Tanjavur: Tamil University, 1990, pp. 389–395.

Rajamanickam, V.G., 'Sethusamudram Canal: The Life of Tamil Nadu', *Abstracts of the proceedings of the National Seminar on Ecological Balance and Sethusamudram Canal*, 1–3 October 2004, Alagappa University, Thondi Campus, pp. 29–30.

Rajamanickam, V.G., 'Sethusamudram: Can it remain safe and stable in its present form?' *Sethusamudram.in*, 12 August 2005, https://tinyurl.com/mtzyntkh. Accessed: 15/03/2018.

Rajappa, S., 'Why this double standard?', *The Weekend Leader*, Vol. 4, No. 36, 6 September 2013.

Rajarajan, R.K.K., 'Reflections on Rama Setu in South Asian Tradition', *The Quarterly Journal of the Mythic Society*, Vol. 105, No. 3, 2014, pp. 1–14.

Rajasingham, K.T., 'A Canal ... and an island ...!', *Weekend Express*, 17 January 1999.

Rajendran, C.P. 'A Post-Truth Take on the Ram Setu', *The Wire*, 6 January 2018, https://tinyurl.com/48uhfupa. Accessed on 6 April 2020.

Rajendran, C.P. 'Sethusamudram shipping canal project and the eternal silence of the Indian earth scientists', *Current Science*, Vol. 89, No. 2, July 2005, pp. 246–247.

Rajendran, C.P., 'Assessing the Stability of the Sethusamudram Shipping Canal', *Journal of the Geological Society India*, Vol. 66, No. 3, 2005, pp. 367–370.

Raju, A.S., 'Sethusamudram Ship Canal Project: Environmental Issues', *Disaster Management and Sustainable Development: Emerging Issues and Concerns*, Rajesh Anand, Narayan Chandra Jana and Sudhir Kumar Singh (eds.), New Delhi: Pentagon Press, 2009, pp. 78–87.

Raju, A.S., 'The (In)Security of Fishermen in South Asia', *Fisheries Exploitation in the Indian Ocean: Threats and Opportunities*, Dennis Rumley, Sanjay Chaturvedi and Vijay Sakhuja (eds.), Singapore: Institute of Southeast Asian Studies, 2009, pp. 163–176.

Rajya Sabha, 'Attack on Indian Fishermen: Q. No. 1970', Ministry of External Affairs, Government of India, 6 August 2015.

Rajya Sabha, 'Indo-Sri Lanka Joint Working Group on Fisheries', Unstarred Question No. 965, answered on 24 November, Ministry of External Affairs, Government of India, 2016.

Rajya Sabha, 'Release of Fishermen in Custody of Sri Lanka: Q. No. 1619', Ministry of External Affairs, Government of India, 28 December 2018.

Ramachandran, R., 'Myth vs Science', *Frontline*, 22 September 2007, https://tinyurl.com/52hfn7x2. Accessed on 6 April 2020.

Ramakrishna and Alfred, J.R.B., *Faunal Resources in India*, Kolkata: Zoological Survey of India, 2007.

Raman, R.A., 'Ram Setu 18,400 years Old: Study', *Deccan Chronicle*, 31 January 2018.

Ramanujan, A.K., 'Three Hundred Ramayanas', *Many Ramayanas: The Diversity of a Narrative Tradition in South Asia*, Paula Richman (ed.), New Delhi: Oxford University Press, 1992, pp. 22–49.

Ramasamy, S.M., D. Ramesh, M.A. Paul, S. Kusumgar, M.A. Yadava, A.R. Nair, U.K. Sinha and T.B. Joseph, 'Rapid Land Building Activity along Vedaranniyam Coast and its Possible Implications', *Current Science*, Vol. 75, No. 9, 1998, pp. 884–86.

Ramaswami, A., *Tamil Nadu District Gazetteers: Ramanathapuram*, Madras: Government of Tamil Nadu, 1972.

Ramaswamy, S., 'Catastrophic cartographies: Mapping the lost continent of Lemuria', *Representations*, 67, 92-129.

Ramaswamy, S., *Passions of the Tongue: Language devotion in Tamil India, 1891–1970*, Berkeley and Los Angeles: University of California Press, 1997.

Ramesh, R., 'Is the Sethusamudram Shipping Canal Project Technically Feasible?', *Economic and Political Weekly*, Vol. 40, No. 4, 22–28 January 2005, pp. 271–275.

Ramesh, R., 'Sethusamudram Ship Canal Project: Further Inputs', Unpublished.

Ramesh, R., 'Seven scientific inconsistencies in the Sethusamudram Shipping Canal', *Asian Times*, 20 June 2005.

Ramesh, R., 'Will to Disaster: Post-Tsunami Technical Feasibility of Sethusamudram Project', *Economic and Political Weekly*, Vol. 40, No. 26, 25 June–1 July 2005, pp. 2648–2653.

Ramesh, R., *Sethusamudram Shipping Canal Project and the unconsidered high-risk factors: Can it withstand them?*, Coimbatore, Tamil Nadu: Doctors for Safer Environment, 2004.

Rao, R.R., M.S. Girishkumar, M. Ravichandran, V.V. Gopalakrishna and P. Thadathil, 'Do cold, low salinity waters pass through the Indo-Sri Lanka Channel during winter?', *International Journal of Remote Sensing*, Vol. 32, No. 22, 2006, pp. 7383-7398.

Rasanayagam, M.C., *Ancient Jaffna*, London: Everymans Publishers, 1926.

Reclus, E., *The Earth and Its Inhabitants: The Universal Geography, Vol. VIII: India and Indo-China*, London: J.S. Virtue, 1876–94.

Reclus, E., *The Earth: A Descriptive History of the Phenomena of the Life of the Globe*, London: J.S. Virtue, 1886.

Rennell, J. 'An Account of the Ganges and Burrampooter Rivers', *Philosophical Transactions of the Royal Society of London*, Vol. 71, No. 1, London: Davis and Elmsly, 1781, pp. 87–114.

Rennell, J., *Memoir of a Map of Hindoostan; Or, The Mogul Empire*, London: M. Brown, 1783.

Rennell, R., 'Major James Rennell', *The Geographical Journal*, Vol. 75, No. 4, 1930, 289–299.

Reynolds, F.E., 'Ramayana, Rama Jataka, and Ramakien: A Comparative Study of Hindu and Buddhist Traditions', *Many Ramayanas: The Diversity of a Narrative Tradition in South Asia*, Paula Richman (ed.), Berkeley: University of California Press, 1991, pp. 48–59.

Riegl, B. and G.M. Branch, 'Effects of sediment on the energy budgets of four scleractinian (Bourne 1900) and five alcyonacean (Lamouroux 1816) corals', *Journal of Experimental Marine Biology and Ecology*, Vol. 186, No. 2, 1995, pp. 259–275.

Rishi, N., 'Sethusamudram project cost rises by Rs 4500 cr', *DNA India*, 16 March 2018, https://tinyurl.com/d2wzjpw6, Accessed on 20 August 2022.

Robinson, J., *Modern History, for the Use of Schools*, London: Richard Phillips, 1807.

Rodriguez, S., 'Review of the environmental impacts of the Sethusamudram ship canal project (SSCP)', *Indian Ocean Turtle Newsletter*, Vol. 6, 2007, pp. 16–20.

Rodriguez, S., J. John, R. Arthur, K. Shanker, A. Sridhar, 'Review of Environmental and Economic Aspects of the Sethusamudram Ship Canal Project (SSCP)', Bangalore: Ashoka Trust for Research in Ecology and the Environment, 2007.

Roy, A., 'Authors of Hindu epics Valmiki and Veda Vyas were Dalits, says Rajnath', *The Times of India*, 21 January 2019.

Roy, A., *Planning in India: Achievements and Problems*, Calcutta: National Publishers, 1965.

Sacratees, J. and R. Karthigarani, *Environment Impact Assessment*, New Delhi: A.P.H. Publishing, 2008.

Sagan, C., Ann Druyan, Steven Soter (writers), Adrian Malone, David Kennard and Rob McCain (directors) 'The Edge of Forever (Episode 10)', *Cosmos: A Personal Voyage* (documentary), United States: PBS, 30 November 1980.

Sanford, D.T., 'Ramayana Portraits—The Nageshvara Temple at Kumbakonam', *Marg*, Vol. 45, No. 3, 1994, pp. 43–60.

Sanil Kumar, V., N.M. Anand and R. Gowthaman, 'Variations in Nearshore Processes along Nagapattinam Coast, India', *Current Science*, Vol. 82, No. 11, 2002, pp. 1381–89.

Sankalia, H.D., *Ramayana: Myth or Reality?*, New Delhi: People's Publishing House, 1973.

Santoshi, N., 'In MP's Ravan Village, the Demon King is a Revered Deity', *Hindustan Times*, 15 October 2013.

Sarma, R.K., 'What is this Sethusamudram Project?', *The Economic Times*, 5 July 2005.

Schultz, Kai., 'In India, a Ghost Town and Mythological Bridge', *The New York Times*, 3 October 2017.

Schwartzberg, Joseph E. (ed.), 'From the Vedic through the Classical Age [Plate III A. 1(b)]', *A Historical Atlas of South Asia*, Chicago: University of Chicago Press, 1978 pp. 13.

Science Channel, 'Could this be the Legendary "Magic Bridge" Connecting India and Sri Lanka?', 10 January 2018, https://tinyurl.com/ms62reh8. Accessed on 20 June 2021.

Scientific American Supplement, 'By Rail to Ceylon', Vol. 82, No. 2124, 16 September 1916, p. 183.

Scott, J.B., *Spiritual Despots*, Chicago and London: University of Chicago Press, 2016.

Selvam, V., L. Gnanappazham, M. Navamuniyammal, K.K. Ravichandran and V.M. Karunagaran, *Atlas of mangrove wetlands of India, Part 1 - Tamil Nadu*. Chennai: M.S. Swaminathan Research Foundation, 2002.

Sen Gupta, A., 'Sethusamudram Project And BJP's Pseudo Science', *Delhi Science Forum*, 30 September 2007. https://tinyurl.com/y7s3a3jb. Accessed: 06/04/2020.

Sen, S. and M. Joseph (eds.), *Terra Aqua: The Amphibious Lifeworlds of Coastal and Maritime South Asia*, London and New York: Routledge.

Sen, S.N., *Ancient Indian History and Civilization*, New Delhi: New Age International, 1988.

Seralathan, P., 'Disposal of dredge spoil from Sethusamudram Ship Channel Project', *Current Science*, Vol. 90, No. 2, 2006, pp. 146–147.

Sethusamudram Corporation, Limited. 'Project Status—Dredging Details', 2011, https://tinyurl.com/2tytxuar. Accessed on 22 October 2011.

Shakespeare, W., *Antony and Cleopatra*, London: John Cawthorn, 1809.

Shankar, S., *Flesh and Fish Blood: Postcolonialism, Translation, and the Vernacular (Vol. 11)*, University of California Press.

Sharda, R., *RSS 360°: Demystifying Rashtriya Swayamsevak Sangh*, New Delhi: Bloomsbury, 2018.

Sharma, R., *Sonia versus Vajpayee: 14th Lok Sabha Elections*, New Delhi: Deep and Deep, 2004.

Sharma, T., 'In affidavit to SC, UPA rules on Ram: no proof', *The Indian Express*, 13 September 2007.

Shastri, H.P. (trans.), *The Ramayana of Valmiki*, London: Shanti Sadan, 1952.

Shekhar, K.S., 'Affidavit on Ram Setu in Supreme Court: Modi sarkar fulfils 2014 manifesto promise', *India Today*, 16 March 2018.

Shekhar, R. and A. Prakhar, 'The Indo-Lankan Fishing Water Conflict Vis-à-vis United Nations Convention of the Law of the Seas', Centre for Maritime Law (National Law University Odisha, Cuttack), 24 June 2020.

Sheppard, C. and S.M. Wells, *Coral Reefs of the World, Vol. 1*, Nairobi: United Nations Environment Programme; Gland: IUCN Conservation Monitoring Centre, 1988.

Sheppard, J.K., I.R. Lawler and H. Marsh, 'Seagrass as pasture for seacows', *Estuarine, Coastal and Shelf Science*, Vol. 71, No. 1–2, pp. 117–132.

Shivakumar, C., 'Is the Sethusamudram project being laid to rest by litigations?', *The New Indian Express*, 29 December 2020.

Shrinivasrao, Bhavanrao, *The Picture Ramayana*, Bombay: The British India Press, 1916.

Siluvaithasan, Augustine S. and Kristian Stokke, 'Fisheries under fire', *Norsk Geografisk Tidsskrift—Norwegian Journal of Geography*, Vol. 60, No. 3, 2006, pp. 240–248.

Sim, M., 'Report on the Straits Which Separate the Ramnad Province in the Peninsula of India from the Island of Ceylon', *The Journal of the Royal Geographical Society of London*, Vol. 4, 1834, pp. 7–25.

Singh, M. (2007). *Selected Speeches, Vol. 3*. New Delhi: Ministry of Information and Broadcasting.

Singh, R.P.B., 'Rāma's route after banishment', *Journal of Scientific Research*, Vol. 41, No. B, 1991, pp. 39–46.

Singh, S., 'India-Sri Lanka Agreement: A Victory of Mature Statesmanship', *Indian and Foreign Review*, Vol. 11, No. 21, 1974, pp. 6-7.

Sinha, Y., 'Budget Speech: February 29, 2000', *The Gazette of India, Extraordinary*, Ministry of Finance (Department of Economic Affairs) Notification, Part I-Section 1, Ref. 15(8)-B(D)/99, 2 March 2000, pp. 35–73.

Sirimal, G.A.D., 'Indian EAM's Visit to SL', *Daily Mirror*, 24 January 2023.

Sivarajah, P., 'Gulf of Mannar isle splits in two, may sink', *The Times of India*, 9 June 2013.

Sivaram, D., 'Geo-Strategic Implications of Sethusamudram', *Daily Mirror* (Sri Lanka), 6 October 2004.

Skeen, W.L.H., *Adam's Peak*, Colombo: W.L.H. Skeen, 1870.

Speir, C., *Life in Ancient India*, London: Smith, Elder, and Co., 1856.

Srinivas, S., 'The Palk Bay Dispute', *Social Political and Research Foundation*, Vol. 11, No. 9, 2021, pp. 1–8.

Srinivasan, M., 'Sri Lanka concerned at Sethu project impact', *The Hindu*, 26 November 2013, https://tinyurl.com/3293t6hj, Accessed on 20 August 2022.

Srinivasan, S. 'Ramayana Bronzes and Sculptures from the Cola to Vijayanagara Times', *The Multivalence of an Epic*, Parul Pandya Dhar (ed.), Manipal: Manipal

University Press, 2021, pp. 103–122.

Stanley, O.D., 'Ecological Balance of Sethusamudram Canal, India', *Journal of Coastal Development*, Vol. 8, No. 1, 2004, pp. 1–10.

Stephen, J., *Fishing for space*. Doctoral dissertation, Universiteit van Amsterdam, 2015.

Steuart, J., *A letter on steam navigation from the Red Sea to Madras and Bengal*, Colombo, 1837.

Steuart, J., *Notes On Ceylon And Its Affairs*, London: Steuart, 1862.

Stevens, W., 'An Account of a Voyage to Examine the Arches of Adam's Bridge', *A Collection of Plans of Ports in the East Indies*, Alexander Dalrymple (ed.), London: George Bigg, 1787, pp. 65–68.

Stevenson, R.E and N. Ruth, *An Index of Ocean Features Photographed from Gemini Spacecraft*, Texas: Department of Interior Bureau of Commercial Fisheries, National Aeronautics and Space Administration, Earth Resources Survey Program, 1968.

Subramaniam, V., 'The Making of Atal Bihari Vajpayee', The Hindu Centre for Politics and Public Policy, 22 August 2018.

Subramanian, T.S., 'Fishermen's protest', *Frontline*, 9 September 2005.

Subramanian, T.S., 'In rough waters', *Frontline*, 14 January 2005.

Subramanian, T.S., 'Tamil Nadu', *Frontline*, Vol. 16, No. 19, 10 September 1999, pp. 120–122.

Suckling, H.J., *Ceylon: A General Description of the Island and Its Inhabitants*, London: Chapman & Hall, 1876.

Sullivan, R.E., *Macaulay*, Cambridge and London: Harvard University Press, 2009.

Sunil, K.P., 'Theatre of the Absurd', *The Illustrated Weekly of India*, Vol. 111, No. 35–43, September to October 1990, pp. 37–38.

Supreme Court of India, 'Berubari Union and... v. Unknown', AIR 1960 SC 845, 1960 3 SCR 250, 1960.

Suryanarayan, V., *Conflict Over Fisheries in the Palk Bay Region*, New Delhi: Lancer Publishers, 2005.

Susskind, L.E., *Environmental Diplomacy*, New York and Oxford: Oxford University Press, 1994.

Swamy, S., *Rama Setu*, New Delhi: Har Anand, 2008.

Tagore, R., *Nationalism*. San Francisco: Book Club of California, 1917.

Taneja, N. and S. Bimal, 'India-Sri Lanka Trade Relations', *The Diplomatist*, 3 March 2020. https://tinyurl.com/uv7cac36. Accessed: 20/12/2022.

Tawney, C.H., *The Ocean of Story, Vol. 2*, N.M. Penzer (ed.), London: Chas. J. Sawyer, 1924.

Taylor, A.D., *The West Coast of Hindustan Pilot*, London: The Hydrographic Office of the Admiralty, 1898.

Taylor, W.C., *Oriental Historical Manuscripts, in the Tamil Language, Vol. 2*, Madras: Charles Josiah Taylor, 1835.

Temple, R., *India in 1880*. London: John Murray, 1880.

Tennant, J.E., *Ceylon: An Account of the Island—Physical, Historical, Topographical,*

Vol. 1, London: Longman, Green, Longman, and Roberts, 1860.

Thapar, R., 'Fallacies of Hindutva Historiography', *Economic and Political Weekly*, Vol. 50, No. 1, 2015, pp. 68–69.

Thapar, R., 'Where fusion cannot work—faith and history', *The Hindu*, 28 September 2007.

Tharoor, S., 'Nehru's Relevance in India Today', *The Massachusetts Review*, Vol. 58, No. 2, 2017, No. 228–236.

Tharoor, S., *The Hindu Way: An Introduction to Hinduism*, New Delhi: Aleph, 2019.

Tharoor, S., *Why I am a Hindu*, New Delhi: Aleph, 2018.

The Asiatic Journal and Monthly Register, Vol. 40, April 1843.

The Bombay Guardian, Vol. 32, No. 51. Saturday, 18 December 1886.

The British Critic, 'The View of Hindoostan', No. 12, August, 1798, pp. 141–149.

The Calcutta Review, 'Archaeology in India', Vol. 120, No. 239, 1905, pp. 39–53.

The Engineer, 'The Scherzer Rolling Lift Bridge Over the Pamban Channel', No. 117, 7 August 1914, p. 150.

The Gazette of India, 'Ports', No. 40, 2 October 1965, p. 827.

The Hindu, 'Abandon Sethusamudram project: workers' forum', 6 November 2014.

The Hindu, 'Demands made in memorandum submitted by Tamil Nadu Chief Minister M.K. Stalin to Prime Minister Narendra Modi', 18 June 2021.

The Hindu, 'Fishermen up in arms against promises of AIADMK, DMK', 27 March 2021.

The Hindu, 'Jayalalithaa calls Sethusamudram project useless; slams DMK', 29 March 2014.

The Hindu, 'Namboodiripad Holds Press Conference in Trivandrum', 5 January 1989.

The Hindu, 'New Pamban bridge to come up in two years', 2 March 2019.

The Hindu, 'New Pamban bridge work picks up momentum, expected to be over by March 2023', 4 December 2022.

The Hindu, 'Rail traffic on old Pamban bridge permanently stopped', 3 February 2023.

The Hindu, 'Ram Sethu was built by Indian engineers, says HRD Minister', 28 August 2019.

The Hindu, 'Ram Setu not an ancient monument, former V-C tells SC', 11 February 2021.

The Hindu, 'Secularism is not opposed to religion: Romila Thapar', 28 December 2016.

The Hindu, 'Tamil Nadu Assembly Elections | Fishermen up in arms against promises of AIADMK, DMK', 27 March 2021.

The Hindu, 'Valmiki's Divine Vision', 3 April 2017.

The Hindu, 'Very Low Frequency Radio Transmitter Planned', 20 January 1984.

The Hindu, 'When the big dams came up', 20 March 2015.

The Indian Express, 'As more Indian fishermen are detained by Sri Lanka, hard questions need to be asked in the Palk Strait', 23 December 2021.

The Indian Express, 'Bhakra Dam, Not Nehru Dam', 18 November 1955.

The Indian Express, 'Indo-Ceylon Official Conferences: Revival Likely', 18 November 1955.

The Indian Express, 'Nehru Opens Work on Bhakra Dam', 18 November 1955.

The Journal of the Ceylon Branch of the Royal Asiatic Society of Great Britain and Ireland, 'Review: Ceylon, Past and Present', Vol. 30, No. 80, 1927, pp. 467–469.

The London and China Telegraph, 'The Paumben Channel', Vol. 15, No. 510, 9 June 1873, p. 376.

The London Literary Gazette, 'Steam Navigation to India', No. 702, 3 July 1830, pp. 433–434.

The Modern Part of an Universal History, Vol. 6, London: Richardson, Osborne, Hitch, Longman, et al.

The New Indian Express, 'Broken spud a nightmare for fishermen', 16 May 2012, https://tinyurl.com/mv8yunzf. Accessed on 20 August 2022.

The New Statesman, 'Indian Railways', 17 April 1915.

The New York Times, 'An Indo-Ceylon Railway', 5 February 1911.

The Railway Review, 'Bridges', Vol. 36, No. 21, 23 May 1896, pp. 293–294.

The Strand Magazine, 'Idols', July–December 1896, pp. 513–519.

The Sunday Times, 'New Avatar Looms Over Rama's Bridge', 19 October 2014, https://tinyurl.com/3tu9rwpn. Accessed on 20 June 2020.

The Times of India, 'SC Tells Govt: Don't Damage Ram Sethu', 1 September 2007.

The Transactions of the Bombay Geographical Society (1836–1838), 'Survey of the Gulf of Mannar', Bombay: American Mission Press, 1844, pp. 379–380.

The White House, 'Fact Sheet: Indo-Pacific Strategy of the United States', 11 February 2022, https://tinyurl.com/mryjjv5m. Accessed on 20 December 2022.

Thirumalaiselvan, S., M. Rajkumar, R. Vinothkumar, L. Remya and S.M. Batcha, 'Seagrass, seaweed, and mangrove ecosystem of Gulf of Mannar and Palk Bay region', *Course Manual on Marine Fisheries and Mariculture*, Mandapam Regional Centre of ICAR-CMFRI, Marine Fisheries Po, 2020, pp. 129–141.

Thurston, E., *Madras Government Bulletin: Pearl and Chank Fisheries of the Gulf of Manaar*, Madras: Superintendent Government Press, 1894.

Thurston, E., *Notes on the Pearl and Chank Fisheries*, Madras: Superintendent Government Press, 1890.

Thurston, E., *The Madras Presidency: With Mysore, Coorg and the Associated States*, Cambridge: Cambridge University Press, 1913.

Time, 'Crisis over 160 Acres', 15 March 1968, pp. 24–27.

Times Now, 'Sri Lankan court asks 13 Indian fishermen to pay Rs 1 crore each for bail, OPS seeks help from EAM Jaishankar', 13 April 2022.

TimesNowNews.com, '"I don't need credit, Lord Ram does": Why is PM Modi not declaring Ram Setu a national monument, asks Swamy', 22 October 2020 https://tinyurl.com/586cykuk. Accessed on 15 September 2021.

TNN, 'In sasural Mandsaur, demon king gives "permission" to be slain', *The Times of India*, 8 October 2019.

TNN, 'Massive rally against Ram Sethu project', *The Economic Times*, 31 December 2007.

TNN, 'Scholars divided on Setu issue', *The Times of India*, 18 September 2007.

Tomascik, T., R. Van Woesik and A.J. Mah, 'Rapid coral colonization of a recent lava flow following a volcanic eruption, Banda Islands, Indonesia', *Coral Reefs*, Vol. 15, No. 3, 1996, pp. 169–175.

Trautmann, T.R., *Aryans and British India*, California: University of California Press, 1997.

Turner, H.G., 'Railway Connection between India and Ceylon', *Journal of the Royal Society of Arts*, Vol. 62, No. 3207, 1914, p. 561.

Ullekh, N.P., *The Untold Vajpayee*, New Delhi: Random House India, 2018.

UNDP, 'Conservation and Sustainable Use of the Gulf of Mannar Biosphere Reserve's Coastal Biodiversity', United Nations Development Programme, https://tinyurl.com/2s39kxb9. Accessed on 20 August 2022.

United Nations, 'Agreement between Sri Lanka and India on the Boundary in Historic Waters between the two Countries and Related Matters 26 and 28 June 1974', Ratified at Colombo and New Delhi.

United Nations, 'Pacific Settlement of Disputes (Chapter VI of UN Charter)', United Nations: Security Council, 2021, https://tinyurl.com/mrx3pb45. Accessed on 20 December 2022.

United Nations, 'Rio Declaration on Environment and Development', *Report of the United Nations Conference on Environment and Development, Rio de Janeiro, 3–14 June 1992, Vol. I*, United Nations, General Assembly, 1992.

United Nations, *Vienna Convention on the Law of Treaties, 1969*, 1980.

Upadhyay, K., 'Mocktale: Kejriwal alleges huge corruption in construction of Ram Setu, shares proof', *The Times of India*, 6 May 2016.

Urwick, W., *Indian pictures, drawn with pen and pencil*, London: The Religious Tract Society, 1881.

Vajpayee, A.B., *Selected Speeches, Vol. 3*. New Delhi: Ministry of Information and Broadcasting, 2002.

Varghese, R.A., 'Archaeology for the courtroom', *Journal of Social Archaeology*, Vol. 24, No. 2, 2023, pp. 1–21.

Varma, P.K., 'Ramcharitmanas: Mantri's remark reeks of ignorance', *Deccan Chronicle*, 22 January 2023.

Vasan, R.S., 'Maritime Counter-Terrorism: An Indian Perspective', *Maritime Counter-terrorism: A Pan-Asian Perspective*, Swati Parashar (ed.), New Delhi: Pearson Longman, 2008, pp. 53–64.

Venkataraman, K. and A.R.B. Sinha, 'Coral Reefs', *Ecosystems of India*, J.R.B. Alfred, A.K. Das and A.K. Sanyal (eds.), Kolkata, Zoological Survey of India, 2001, pp. 261–290.

Venkatesan, J., 'Parts of ASI Affidavit to Be Withdrawn', *The Hindu*, 14 September 2007.

Venkatesan, V., 'Sethusamudram case in the Supreme Court: Soli Sorabjee's submission', *Law and Other Things*, 6 May 2008, https://tinyurl.com/bdhhbu9e, Accessed on 6 April 2020.

Victor, A.C.C., 'Sethusamudram ship canal project in the Gulf of Mannar Marine

Biosphere Reserve', *Souvenir 2000*, Mandapam: Central Marine Fisheries Research Institute, 2000, pp. 25–27.

Vidyaranya, M., *Sankara-Dig-Vijaya: The Traditional Life of Sri Sankaracharya*, Swami Tapasyananda (trans.), Chennai: Sri Ramakrishna Math, 1996.

Vijay, T. (2007). 'Why the Ram Setu must not be destroyed', *Rediff News*, 25 April 2007, https://tinyurl.com/47upz3nd. Accessed: 20/06/2021.

Vincent, S., 'Palk Bay fishing problem requires Indo-Sri Lankan joint-governance', *Maritime Affairs: Journal of the National Maritime Foundation of India*, Vol. 16, No. 2, 2020, pp. 71–88.

Vincent, W., *The Commerce and Navigation of the Ancients in the Indian Ocean*, *Vol. 2*. London: T. Cadell and W. Davies, 1807.

Vivekanandan, V., 'Crossing Maritime Borders', *Forging Unity: Coastal Communities and the Indian Ocean's Future: Conference Proceedings*, Chennai: International Collective in Support of Fishworkers, International Ocean Institute, 2001, pp. 76–89.

Vombatkere, S.G., 'Letter to President, PM, Sonia Gandhi on Ram Setu and Sethusamudram Project', *Mainstream*, Vol. 45, No. 40, 26 September 2007. https://www.mainstreamweekly.net/article334.html. Accessed: 20/4/2020.

Wait, W.E., 'The Distribution of Birds in Ceylon and its Relation to Recent Geological Changes in the Island', *Spolia Zeylanica*, Vol. 10, No. 36, 1919, pp. 1–32.

Walther, J., 'Report of a Journey Through India', R. Bruce Foote (trans.), *Records of the Geological Survey of India, Vol. 23*, London: Kegan Paul, Trench & Trubner & Co., 1890, pp. 110–119.

Ward, W., *History, Literature and Religion of the Hindoos, Vol. 1*, London: Black, Parbury and Allen, 1817.

Waring, F.J. 'On the Physical Features of "Adam's Bridge" and the Currents Across it', *Minutes of the Proceedings of the Institution of Civil Engineers*, Vol. 203, 1917, pp. 284–295.

Warrier, S., 'Which Tamils are they talking about?', *Rediff News*, 19 July 2005, https://tinyurl.com/2nx4yvfw, Accessed on 20 December 2022.

Watts, A., 'Democracy in the Kingdom of Heaven', audio transcript from *Behind the Image*, Alan Watts Organization, 31 October 2022, https://tinyurl.com/mry43dhv. Accessed: 10/12/2022.

Waycott, M., B.J. Longstaff and J. Mellors, 'Seagrass population dynamics and water quality in the Great Barrier Reef region', *Marine Pollution Bulletin*, Vol. 51, No. 1–4, 2005, pp. 343–350.

Wear, D.J., M.J. Sullivan, A.D. Moore and D.F. Millie, 'Effects of water-column enrichment on the production dynamics of three seagrass species and their epiphytic algae', *Marine Ecology Progress Series*, Vol. 179, 1999, pp. 201-213.

Weber, M., C. Lott and K.E. Fabricius, 'Sedimentation stress in a scleractinian coral', *Journal of Experimental Marine Biology and Ecology*, Vol. 336, No. 1, 2006, pp. 18–32.

Weerakoon, D., S.D.A Goonatilake, T. Wijewickrama, A. Rajasuriya, N. Perera,

T.P. Kumara, G. De Silva, S. Miththapala, A. Mallawatantri, 'Conservation and Sustainable Use of Biodiversity in the Islands and Lagoons of Northern Sri Lanka', Grand, Switzerland: IUCN, International Union for Conservation of Nature, 2020.

Weeratunge, N., C. Béné, R. Siriwardane, A. Charles, D. Johnson, E.H. Allison and M.C. Badjeck, 'Small-scale fisheries through the wellbeing lens', *Fish and Fisheries*, Vol. 15, No. 2, 2014, pp. 255–279.

Wheeler, J.T. (1867). *History of India, Vol. 2*. London: N. Trubner and Co.

Wilkins, C. (1792). 'A Royal Grant of Land: Translated from the Original Sanscrit in 1781', *Dissertations and Miscellaneous Pieces Relating to the History and Antiquities, the Arts, Sciences, and Literature of Asia, Vol. 2*, Charles Wilkins, William Jones, et al., (eds.), London: Nicol, Walter, and Sewell, pp. 255–265.

Williams, M., *Indian Epic Poetry*. London: Williams and Norgate, 1863.

Wink, A., 'From the Mediterranean to the Indian Ocean', *Comparative Studies in Society and History*, Vol. 44, No. 3, 2002, pp. 416–445.

Winterbottom, A., 'Producing and using the historical relation of Ceylon: Robert Knox, the East India Company and the Royal Society', *The British Journal for the History of Science*, Vol. 42, No. 4, 2009, pp. 515–538.

Withanage, H., 'Sethusamudram: Who stand for Sri Lankan interests?', *Sethusamudram*, 1 February 2008, http://hwithanage-sethusamudram.blogspot.com/, Accessed on 20 April 2020.

Wright, T. (ed.), *Travels of Marco Polo*, London: George Bell and Sons, 1880.

Yechury, S., 'Faith accompli', *Hindustan Times*, 12 June 2007.

Yogasundram, N., *A Comprehensive History of Sri Lanka*. Colombo: Vjitha Yapa, 2008.

Yule, H. and A.C. Burnell, *Hobson-Jobson*, (William Crooke ed.), London: John Murray, 1903.

Zadoo, V., 'Big vessels may have to skip Lanka canal', *Business Standard*, 6 February 2013.

Zimmerman, R.C., 'Light and photosynthesis in seagrass meadows', *Seagrasses*, A.W.D. Larkum, R.J. Orth, and C.M. Duarte (eds.), Dordrecht: Springer, 2006, pp. 303–321.

INDEX

Adam's Bridge, xvii, xx, xxi, 2, 5, 15, 19, 24-29, 42, 43, 45, 46, 50, 52, 53, 54, 57, 58, 61, 71, 72, 73, 76, 78, 88, 89, 100, 106, 110, 124, 135, 150, 153, 155, 170, 180, 188, 221, 222, 224, 231, 234, 242, 246

AIADMK, 109, 133, 135, 176, 196, 243

Ancient Monuments and Archaeological Sites and Remains Act, 14

Archaeological Survey of India, 148, 150, 153, 155, 168, 171

Bandaranaike, Sirimavo, 186, 191, 196, 213

British East India Company, 13, 49, 56, 61, 188

Dhanushkodi, 2, 4, 5, 14, 15, 17, 22, 28, 31, 32, 33, 34, 35, 64, 66, 71, 78, 79, 82, 83, 87, 92, 101, 107, 114, 138, 139, 175, 185

Dravidian Historical Research Centre, 170, 177, 231

Dutch East India Company, 42, 188

Environment Impact Assessment, 133, 136, 239

Gandhi, Indira, 108, 186, 193, 213

Gandhi, M.K., 86

Geological Survey of India, 21, 22, 68, 69, 147, 150, 158, 162, 232, 246

Gorresio, Gaspare, 25, 76, 226

Griffith, Ralph T.H., 24, 25, 67, 68, 71, 226

Gulf of Mannar, 29, 35, 36, 62, 97, 103, 111, 115, 117, 118, 119, 120, 124, 128, 129, 130, 136, 138, 148, 165, 186, 199, 203, 212, 214, 220, 222, 224, 225, 229, 230, 231, 234, 235, 237, 241, 244, 245

Gulf of Mannar Biosphere Reserve, 118, 165, 225, 245

Hindu nationalism, 94, 173, 234

Hindutvavadi, 14, 15, 32, 34, 112, 114, 148, 154, 163, 181, 208

Hornell, James, 27, 29, 84, 228

Indian Council of Historical Research, 171

Indo-Lankan International Maritime Boundary Line, 187

Iyengar, P.T. Srinivas, 89, 90, 91, 93, 228

Jayalalithaa, J., 135, 168, 177, 195, 196, 224, 243

Jones, William, 4, 37, 53, 229, 247

Kalam, A.P.J. Abdul, 5, 7, 17, 150, 151, 152, 173, 184, 219, 233

Karunanidhi, M., 108, 176

Krusadai, 118, 129

Kumaratunga, Chandrika, 198

Lankan civil war, 18, 34, 109, 110, 186, 194, 195

Law of the Sea, 197, 199, 200, 212, 219

Liberation Tigers of Tamil Eelam (LTTE), 111, 194, 195, 200

Macaulay's Minute, 58

Macaulay, Thomas Babington, 25

Macdonell, A.A., 22

Martin, Robert Montgomery, 24

Marx, Karl, 12

Maurice, Thomas, 53, 73

Mill, James, 25, 57, 72, 180

Modi, Narendra, 10, 145, 168, 170, 173, 185, 195, 202, 220, 221, 223, 224, 233, 241, 243, 244

Mudaliar Committee, 98, 99, 100, 101

National Aeronautics and Space Administration (NASA), 109, 114, 147, 150, 230, 234

Palk Bay, 29, 97, 103, 113, 117, 119, 120, 123, 124, 126, 136, 138, 140, 141, 142, 143, 144, 145, 148, 149, 164, 166, 186, 188, 195, 203, 204, 209, 212, 222, 228, 229, 230, 231, 241, 242, 244, 246

Palk Strait, 3, 15, 19, 20, 33, 63, 67, 70, 76, 107, 108, 122, 124, 134, 150, 161, 162, 163, 170, 172, 189, 196, 197, 199, 225, 228, 243

Pamban bridge, 175, 243

Pamban Railway Bridge, 86

Pillai, N. Vanamamalai, 91

Project Rameswaram, 147

Rajapaksa, Mahinda, 145, 184, 198

Ramanathapuram, 26, 104, 106, 118, 132, 133, 137, 138, 188, 190, 230, 238

Ramcharitmanas, 7, 11, 154, 245

Ram Setu Bachao Andolan, 150, 152, 156, 158, 168, 170, 177, 203, 208, 209

Rennell, James, xxi, 14, 37, 39,

40, 41, 42, 49, 55, 59, 64, 71,
77, 100, 219, 239
Rio de Janeiro declaration, 200

Sangh Parivar, 111, 112, 114,
117, 150, 169, 208
Sethu Project, 97, 98, 100, 101,
103, 104, 105, 106, 108, 109,
113, 114, 120, 125, 132, 133,
134, 137, 140, 161, 163, 164,
167, 177, 179, 180, 193, 200,
201, 202
Sethusamudram Canal Project,
97, 101, 117, 168, 224
Sethusamudram Corporation,
135, 136, 163, 164, 240
Sethusamudram Project
Committee, 97
Sethusamudram Shipping Canal
Project, 13, 17, 122, 123, 124,
199, 238, 239
Setubandh, 86
Shastri, Lal Bahadur, 191
Singh, Manmohan, 137, 198
Stalin, M.K., 195, 243

The Places of Worship (Special
Provisions) Act, 1991, 146,
226
Tuticorin, 46, 47, 77, 83, 97, 98,
101, 102, 117, 118, 120, 128,
129, 130, 132, 133, 134, 137,
138, 164, 167, 179, 199, 224,
233, 235
Tuticorin Port Trust, 101, 133,
179, 233

United Nations Convention on
the Law of the Sea, 197, 199,
219
United Nations Development
Programme, 118, 120, 245
United Nations Environment
Programme, 111, 116, 241
United Progressive Alliance,
149, 153, 154, 176, 179, 208
United Progressive Alliance
(UPA), 240

Vienna Convention, 195, 245

Walther, Johannes, 22, 44, 69,
178

www.ingramcontent.com/pod-product-compliance
Lightning Source LLC
Chambersburg PA
CBHW020441100426
42812CB00036B/3408/J